ALL TALK

In the series

Culture and the Moving Image,

edited by Robert Sklar

ALL TALK

The Talkshow in Media Culture

Wayne Munson

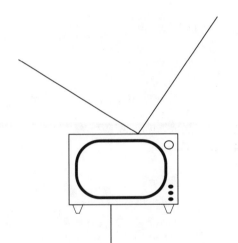

 TEMPLE UNIVERSITY PRESS
Philadelphia

Temple University Press, Philadelphia 19122
Copyright © 1993
by Temple University. All rights reserved
Published 1993
Printed in the United States of America

Library of Congress Cataloging-in-Publication Data
Munson, Wayne, 1951–
    All talk : the talkshow in media culture /
Wayne Munson.
        p.   cm. — (Culture and the moving image)
    Includes bibliographical references and index.
    ISBN 0-87722-995-3 (cl.)
    1. Talk shows.   2. Postmodernism.
I. Title.   II. Series.
PN1990.9.T34M86   1993
791.44'6—dc20
                                        92-9389

For Beatrice

Contents

Acknowledgments

I am very grateful for the help of New York University's Department of Cinema Studies—especially Robert Sklar, Robert Stam, William Boddy, Richard Allen, and William Simon—throughout the writing of the first stage of this manuscript. Robert Sklar, editor of the Culture and the Moving Image series of which this book is a part, deserves special thanks for his guidance and support.

I am thankful for the support of my colleagues at the Framingham and Fitchburg State Colleges. A course I had the pleasure of teaching at Framingham, Media and Interpersonal Communication, excited my thinking about talkshows. Jeff Baker, Thelma Berman, Barbara Bloom, Terry Thomas, Steve Rogers, and Betty Sullivan gave this project, and me, support at crucial points along the way.

Two other friends and colleagues, Derek TePaske and James Robison, were sources of stimulating discussion vital to the evolution of my ideas. They were always on the lookout for articles, interviews, and crucial bits of information that would be useful to my study. I am also indebted to my long friendship with Mark Moore and our countless discussions of the media.

My mother-in-law, Grace Manning, deserves my deepest affection and thanks for housing me during many of my teaching and writing years. Mark Gardiner, Katherine Feldman, James and Nancy Richards, Elizabeth Turner, Derek and Cecca TePaske, Nancy Fitts, Thelma and Leonard Berman, Mark and Nancy Moore, Kathleen Crowley, Jeffrey and Mary Ellen Baker, Donna and George Walcovy, Nancy and Jeffrey Featherstone, Kathleen Brennan, Frank Graeff, "Trip," and Cara all had the dubious distinction of putting me up on various occasions during the course of my work. I owe them each a Hilton.

Iona College Media Coordinator Gregory Harris, an ardent fan and irrepressible student of the talkshow, was an initial source of inspiration for this study. His unusual attention to talkshows made me look at them in a new light.

William Newman of the University of Connecticut was tremendously helpful in granting me the use of his office. Without his help, I would still be writing. He also took the time to review the manuscript and advise me on it.

I deeply appreciate the help of the staff at Temple University Press—especially Janet Francendese and Deborah Stuart—and the careful work of copy editor Patricia Sterling.

Finally, I thank my wife, Beatrice Manning, for her immeasurable support—emotional, intellectual, financial, and other kinds too numerous to mention—throughout every stage of this project. It would not have been possible without her.

ALL TALK

The Sense of the Talkshow

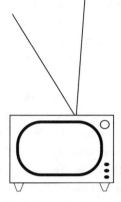

Radio talk host Barry Champlain, in the film *Talk Radio*, introduces his nightly show as "the last neighborhood in America." He sees himself, his listeners, and his callers as "stuck with each other" in an inescapable love-hate attraction he cannot explain except as "addictive." His assessment of the talkshow: "Marvelous technology at our disposal—instead of reaching up to new heights, we're going to see how far down we can go, how deep into the muck we can immerse ourselves." New York radio personality Steve Post once similarly characterized the call-in show as something that "should have, and could have, revolutionized the use of radio as a real medium of communication" instead of becoming just another "slick format."[1]

By contrast, Boston talk host and national talk radio organizer Jerry Williams trumpets the talkshow as "the last bastion of freedom of speech for plain, ordinary citizens."[2] As if to confirm this view, Mikhail Gorbachev and Boris Yeltsin took questions by satellite from American callers during a special ABC talkshow hosted by Peter Jennings two weeks after the failed August 1991 coup. Pat Buchanan's 1992 run for the Republican presidential nomination has demonstrated the power of his exposure on programs such as *Crossfire*. Politically, talkshows have been outposts for the disaffected since the 1960s. But the 1992 presidential campaign demonstrated their increasing importance to the political mainstream, especially as more and more Americans consider themselves disaffected with politics-as-usual. Even sources like the *Boston Globe*, an example of the mainstream journalism that talkshows are increasingly sidestepping in American political life, conceded that talkshows had become "the

1

most prominent mode of communication of this presidential campaign." [3]
Ross Perot, who initially proposed his candidacy February 20, 1992, on
CNN's *Larry King Live*, extended call-in participation beyond the talkshow with his grassroots approach and his 800 number—a tactic Jerry
Brown also used. In June 1992 Perot and Bill Clinton each answered host
and audience questions over the course of two hours on special editions
of *Today* and *CBS This Morning*, respectively. In a further extension
of mediated political participation, Perot proposed government through
electronic town hall, in which, as president, he would outline choices in
a televised address and then let citizens choose through interactive cable
or telephone voting. Just days after President George Bush scorned talkshows as erosive of the dignity of his office, handlers staged some of his
White House photo opportunities in the style of *Donahue*: the president
appeared shirt-sleeved, wireless microphone in hand, informally fielding
questions from the ordinary Americans seated around him. While Bush
continued his concession to the 1992 talkshow campaign by appearing
on Rush Limbaugh's radio talkshow (by then heard on five hundred stations nationwide) and on *Larry King Live*, Clinton played his saxophone
on *Arsenio*—and also appeared on *Larry King Live*. Indeed, the importance of King's show to the campaign brought him into the limelight
along with the very candidates he interviewed. By October 1992, *60 Minutes*, *The New York Times*, and *New York* magazine had all featured
him as a political "king maker" who, with his "softball" interviews, was
"emceeing the election."

Perot's status as political amateur—his down-home one-liners and
spontaneous, outsiderly roughness reminiscent of an angry radio talkshow caller—contrasted with the seeming slickness of the other candidates to suggest yet another dimension of the talkshow's political impact: media performance and its credibility. Add to this the Democrats'
use of soul-baring, "tell-all" "reintroduction" stories during their July
convention—Clinton's difficult childhood family life, the Gores' son's
near-fatal accident—and it seemed as if American politics was, in the
words of *Time*'s Charles Krauthammer, undergoing "full Oprahization."
While Krauthammer, among others, deplored the trend ("orgies of self-
revelation"), commentators such as Ellen Goodman liked it ("real-life
family portrait"). The centrality of the talkshow as a key political text

culminated in the second of the three televised presidential debates. On October 15 in Richmond, Virginia, ABC correspondent Carole Simpson was host-moderator for a debate-as-talkshow in which an audience of 209 undecided voters had the chance to question the candidates. The audience insisted that the candidates stick to the issues and avoid character attacks and negativity, and the candidates, apparently constrained by the format and its interactive proximity, did. In what proved to be a new record in debate viewership, about half of America's television households tuned in. After years of condemning media campaigns as overly manipulative, negative, and "soundbitten," pundits proclaimed the success of the talkshow as a new and improved political stage—more revealing and credible because it is somehow less susceptible to media "handling."[4]

All of this suggests a political terrain in which candidates now use talkshows for a fuller, cheaper, more direct link to the public—a way around the narrow filter of broadcast news and its ever-shrinking soundbites—after hearing that same public use talkshows to vent *its* anger at a political system seen as unresponsive, elitist, and gridlocked. Once a political "outsider," the talkshow has now moved "inside." Or is it both at once? Has the medium loosely known as the talkshow become another source of harmful effects for a degraded "public life" in which we "amuse ourselves to death"?[5] Or is it a harbinger of a new, revitalized public and political life in which the citizenry is finally "heard" through interactivity?

Such questions suggest the importance of the talkshow in contemporary American culture. Like the news, the talkshow has become an everyday political instrument as well as advice-giver, erzatz community, entertainer, and promoter. Extending the talk-of-the-town tradition that goes back to P. T. Barnum's promotional "humbugs,"[6] it has become powerful enough to determine whether or not a newly published book becomes a best seller.[7] Its range of topics defies classification: from the sensational and bizarre (teenage lesbian daughters and their mothers; *Playboy*'s first transsexual centerfold) to the conventional and the advisory (natural childbirth; preventing the spread of AIDS) to politics and world affairs. As of this writing, the radio format known as talk is booming; it claims 875 stations nationwide, up from 238 in 1987. *Talkers*, a newsletter for radio talk hosts, publishes a monthly, "Top Ten Talk Topics." Television talkshows have also enjoyed continuous growth since the 1980s. By 1992, the successful talkshow was the most "steadily" moneymaking type of program on television. Radio hybrids such as talk-and-oldies and talk/rock—the latter epitomized by shock radio "king" Howard Stern, whose New York–originated show spread to Los Angeles, Washington, D.C., Baltimore, and Philadelphia—have emerged as part of this talk explosion. Cable talk channel CNBC uses the slogan "information that hits home." The National Association of Radio Talk Show Hosts, whose first annual convention in 1989 drew only twenty-five hosts, welcomed nearly 250 to its 1992 meeting in Washington, D.C., and proved influential enough to get Vice-President Dan Quayle to give its keynote address and presidential candidate Bill Clinton to appear via satellite. The audience appetite for talkshows appears "bottomless."[8]

The talkshow is also a readily available barometer of public opinion, an imaginary and discursive space where topical issues "sizzle" and political "bashing" can happen in safe anonymity.[9] When Governor Lowell Weicker sought to sell his Connecticut income tax plan, he appeared on radio call-in shows—the very "place" where, in New Jersey and Massachusetts, tax *revolts* had reached critical mass. He was well aware that he was putting himself on the "firing line."[10] Just over a year later, as the 1992 presidential campaign-by-talkshow was heating up, Governor Weicker and Don Imus, the tough but funny morning talker on WFAN New York (an AM station with a signal most of Connecticut can pick up), swapped jobs for a day. If any medium encourages the blurring of borders and the swapping of roles, it is the talkshow.[11]

The negativity of talk radio was the particular finding of a 1990 report by the Center for Media and Public Affairs, conducted for the American Jewish Committee. A content analysis of black- and white-oriented call-in shows in New York, Philadelphia, and Chicago, it found talk radio "far more an expression of racial divisiveness than of ethnic affirmation" and unable to meet its "public responsibility to promote racial harmony in these troubled times."[12] Anti-tax and anti–big government revolts fed by talk radio have inspired the scaling-down of state services such as public education. Having assumed such responsibilities, the talkshow has become integral to American political life by covering not just *what* happens but *where* things happen. Consider another example: the allegation that a homosexual congressman from Massachusetts, Barney

Frank, paid a prostitute for sex and then hired him as his personal assistant became a compelling topic across a range of talkshows—*Meet the Press*, *The McLaughlin Group*, *Geraldo* (on which the alleged prostitute told the story as he perspired in tight close-up), and *Nightline* (on which the topic's media coverage itself become a topic).[13] The talkshow conflates the sensational, the advisory, and the political in a promiscuous, hall-of-mirrors inclusiveness.

All Talk grapples with the sense and nonsense of the talkshow. Phil Donahue says that his show "sandwich[es] the Persian Gulf in between the male strippers."[14] His choice of images poignantly expresses the inclusive, contingent, postmodern logic of the talkshow, making it a hybrid of provocative and incongruous linkages for the sake of ratings.

The talkshow swings between the global and the disposable. In the spirit of *glasnost,* the former Soviet government sponsored a television call-in show, *Ask the KGB*; the BBC World Service broadcasts the international call-in program *It's Your World*; the Voice of America offered a financial call-in show to Poland in the fall of 1989. But despite this pervasiveness of importance, the talkshow has been a throwaway form— videotapes of *The Alan Burke Show*, a confrontational "hot talk" syndication of the 1960s (Burke presaged the style of hosts like Morton Downey, Jr.), were erased for reuse.[15]

In the 1990s, audience participation extends beyond talk and game shows into news and prime-time entertainment. *America's Funniest Home Videos* uses viewer-submitted camcorder footage in a competition for "funniest" that borrows heavily from the game show. Cable systems in Montreal and Springfield, Massachusetts, offer a service whereby viewers can select among several camera angles when watching a football game or a concert. Home viewers in Sacramento can play along with *Jeopardy!* and *Wheel of Fortune* by computer. A Los Angeles company has developed *Sherlock Phones*, an interactive television program that lets viewers phone in their preferences for the plot twists of a whodunit.[16]

That love-hate attraction between talkshow and public, so vividly addressed in the film *Talk Radio*, acknowledges how audiences, media, texts, culture, and history intersect in a way that calls into question the borders between them. This book approaches talkshows as just such points of intersection. In his *Harmless Entertainment: Hollywood and the*

Ideology of Consensus, Richard Maltby sees the media-audience relationship as a contract in which a medium may govern the perceptions of its audience, but only with the "consent of the governed": that is, with "the active participation of that audience." [17] Any study of the talkshow must account for its inscription of "consent" as well as its "government" of perception. What James W. Carey said of the very first electronic medium, the telegraph, also applies to the interactive talkshow: it opens up "new ways of thinking about communication within both the formal practice of theory and the practical consciousness of everyday life." It also becomes "a thing to think with, an agency for the alteration of ideas." In so doing, it reproduces "the contradictions in our thought, action, and social relations." [18] My study of talkshows approaches them as things "to think with" and asks how they construct knowledge, reality, culture, politics, and the self.

The talkshow attains its importance in and as a nexus of all sorts of "talk"—journalism, fiction, criticism, politics, research, Hollywood films. Debates have raged around a number of talkshow issues: the "infotainment" and "trash TV" phenomena, "shock radio," the definition of "responsible" or "real" journalism, and the organizing of talk hosts ostensibly for political purposes. These issues mark a historical moment when generic hybridization and an undermining of forms—in Hal Foster's word, a postmodern "disentrenchment" [19]—prompt what I would call a condition of productive instability. Just as Barry Champlain is "stuck" with his audience and apparatus, Donahue's male strippers are stuck with—and next to—the Persian Gulf. The talkshow's more stable paradigms—host, guest, and caller; its unscripted dialogue—*and* such shifting elements as topics and guests, are "stuck with each other" to a point where any purity of knowledge or stability of form is disentrenched.

The name itself epitomizes its promiscuous inclusiveness. The term "talkshow" combines two communicative paradigms, and like the term itself, the "talk show" fuses and seems to reconcile two different, even contradictory, rhetorics. It links conversation, the interpersonal—the premodern oral tradition—with the mass-mediated spectacle born of modernity. It becomes, among other things, a recuperative practice reconciling technology and commodification with community, mass culture with the individual and the local, production with consumption. In so doing, the mythic American past of the participatory town meeting and the interpersonal "handshake" politics of speech and presence meet the imagined "present" of technological simulation, reproduction, and com-modification. The talkshow's rampant inclusions make it a postmodern phenomenon. I use "postmodernity" as a hermeneutic construct, rather than some objective reality, because it is especially productive for a media practice that itself constructs reality, subjectivity, and knowledge along postmodern lines.[20]

The talkshow "genre"—to the degree that it even *is* a single category—has come to assume many "messy," hybridized variations in the thousands of talkshows that air locally and nationally—even internationally—in any given week. News talk has been an established radio format since 1960, when KABC Los Angeles committed itself to a format that mixed call-ins and interviews with heavy doses of news.[21] Besides call-in or interview shows, or those that mix the two on current affairs topics, talk formats include psychological and other "service" or advice programs on topics as diverse as personal finance, household and auto repair, and sex. Of course, at the very beginnings of radio there was daytime homemaking talk, public affairs talk or forums, commentary on the news, religious talk, comedy talk, health talk; however, few early programs involved audience participation apart from letters read and responded to on the air.

Many of today's subject-defined programs are personality oriented. Dr. Ruth Westheimer's sex advice show, originally broadcast on WNYC-FM New York on Sunday nights, is as much about her unique voice and affect as they are about her obviously engaging topic. The same is often true of controversial talk—"hot" or "confrontalk." WABC New York's Bob Grant is an irascible master of the caller putdown ("you're a fake, a phony, and a fraud"). Confrontalk of a kind similar to *The Morton Downey, Jr., Show* of the late 1980s has been a syndicated tele-vision talk genre since the 1960s, when it was practiced by the likes of Alan Burke and Joe Pyne. "Insult humor" of a type popularized in the 1960s by Jack E. Leonard and Don Rickles seems to have been an influ-ence on, for example, the performance of syndicated conservative radio call-in host Rush Limbaugh, whose liberal bashing has a mock-pompous, satirical edge.

Sports talk is another type common to both television and radio. AM stations such as WFAN New York, initiating the all-sports radio format in 1987 (subsequent to cable television's ESPN, which began in 1980), have considerable talk and call-in programming as well as live coverage of games.

Radio's move to talk formats, beginning in the 1960s, was a consequence of radio's growth, audience fragmentation, and competition with television since the 1950s. Like top-40 programming, talk radio sought a specialized segment of a fragmented audience: top-40 focused on youth and young adults; talk and all-news targeted an older, underserved audience.

"News/talk magazine" is probably the best label to apply to television programs such as *Today*, *Good Morning America*, and Charles Kuralt's *Sunday Morning*. They combine rotations of live and reported news with service-oriented features such as consumer advice and film reviews, celebrity interviews, and worldwide, on-location production. *Meet the Press* and *Face the Nation* are typical of news interview programs. The 1989 debut of ABC's *Prime Time Live* represented a further hybridization of the news/talk magazine, the investigative documentary, and the live audience participation talkshow (which by now is minimal). Most episodes focus on a single topic. They bring together anchors, field reporters (via satellite), interviews, and taped "focus pieces" that journalistically establish the topics to be discussed. *Nightline* is similar but without the studio audience and the greater scope afforded by *Prime Time Live*'s sixty-minute length. The celebrity talk or "chat show"—sometimes called "talk/variety"—is the dominant late-night talk genre; its all too familiar hosts have included Johnny Carson, Arsenio Hall, Jay Leno, and David Letterman.

"Talk/service" is the name given to *Donahue*, *The Oprah Winfrey Show*, *Sally Jesse Raphael*, *Geraldo*, and similar shows because, when the form was first conceived more than twenty years ago, the goal was to give lively, useful information—centered on interpersonal and psychosocial matters—to women. More recently, however, these programs have been condemned as "bizarre talk." The "talk/variety" shows of Mike Douglas, Merv Griffin, and Dinah Shore were generally more popular through the 1960s and 1970s as light afternoon women's fare skewed toward older and less commercially desirable viewers. Their successors, the *Donahue*-inspired talk/service shows with a dynamic host roving through the audience, microphone in hand, sought a bigger set of consumers: young to middle-aged women.

In terms of distribution, talk/service programs and news magazine talkshows are commonplace across all available means—network, syndication, and local broadcast. Since the advent of satellite networking and 800 telephone numbers, national AM radio call-in shows and talk networks are flourishing. Among the first were NBC's Talknet and ABC's Talkradio Network, which have hundreds of affiliates nationwide. Smaller twenty-four-hour talk services include the American Radio Network, TalkAmerica, Ltd., which is a weekend service specializing in confrontalk, and the Business Radio Network, which is syndicated in Canada and the United States. Radio program "doctors" foresee the coming of the talk format to FM as the next development in participatory talk programming.[22] The November 1991 debut of National Public Radio's *Talk of the Nation* suggests this is already happening.

The Talkshow and the Postmodern

Cultural critic Lawrence Grossberg has argued that "postmodern practices point to the articulation of certain modernist practices and concepts into a popular sensibility."[23] The talkshow draws upon the broad historical ruptures in Western discourse. It relies on modernist postures— the host's ego, subjectivity, expressionism, and apparent autonomy and authenticity—while that host's and program's coherence is secondary to affect or attitude: that is, to the emotional investment in multiple meanings and lifestyles—a postmodern tendency. At the same time the talkshow's emphasis on ad-libbed interpersonal communication and its presentational, bodily immediacy lend a premodern dimension as well. The genre projects itself as uniquely "user friendly" and accessible, even as it operates within a media frame that is highly technological, corporate, and residually "mass" or one-way. The talkshow works by playing with the very range and contradictions it incorporates—"incorporation" implying both inclusion and economic appropriation.

Like tabloid news, talkshows seem to be perfect examples of what cultural theorist John Fiske, in his *Understanding Popular Culture*, calls "producerly texts"—commercial products that lend themselves to an audience's own production of popular culture by expropriating those very products in everyday use to defy the social norms so often contradicted by daily experience. Such products' excess, carnivalesque inversions, evasions, and links to oral culture allow this expropriation. While Fiske's appreciation of popular culture and how it works explains its value for active audiences, my study of talkshows focuses on how they fit into and help shape our broader cultural condition: that is, a condition shared by the media producers (the financial economy) as well as audiences (the cultural economy). I agree with Fiske, echoing de Certeau, that not only has the dominant commercial order "created, paradoxically, the means of its own subversion," but "its very existence now *depends* upon those fissures and weaknesses that make it so vulnerable to the incursions of the popular" (emphasis added).[24] With its audience participation, the talkshow seems tailor-made to exploit and intensify this productive dependency. Talkshows represent one of the financial economy's most efficient ways to *re*expropriate not only the everyday resistances and negotiations of popular culture but the dominant order as well. Moreover, the distinction between them has become especially blurred in the talkshow. Like Fredric Jameson's experience of the fragmentary postmodern space of Los Angeles' Bonaventure Hotel, talkshows confound our coordinates, the lines on our cognitive maps, our familiar distinctions and stabilities— yet all in a new kind of productivity.[25]

Along with other interactive media, the talkshow to a degree reverses the homogenizing technological trajectory of modernity that began with the spatial bias inscribed in print, literacy, and then mass communications, and that involved abstract coding systems enabling the separation of communication from transportation, of knowledge from knower and known object.[26] The talkshow reidentifies knowledge with knower through performance but does so in a residually modernist frame of spectacle and mass mediation. The talkshow uses the very contradictions it exposes, bringing together a constellation of voices. I use "constellation" as philosopher Richard J. Bernstein does: as the most appropriate way to describe how talkshows juxtapose rather than integrate multiple, heterogeneous, discontinuous elements. Rather than *reconcile,* talkshows (barely) *contain.* Postmodernity, like the talkshow, substitutes "both-and" for modernity's "either-or."[27]

My approach offers a corrective to the offhand disparagement that talkshows commonly endure. "High" critics or academicians and even "middle ground" media such as the news weeklies have condemned the talk phenomenon, calling it everything from "trash TV" to a deceptive, "para-social" pseudocompanion. While I hardly applaud every talkshow or talkshow practice, I *am* trying to appreciate the genre—how it works and what its cultural position is—in both symptomatic and explanatory terms. To consider its audience participation is especially crucial at a time when more and more interactive media are emerging.

The notion of audience participation in commercialized entertainment goes back at least to the nineteenth-century lyceum, the women's service magazine, and—in an integration of spectator into performance space—the turn-of-the-century amusement park, dance hall, and cabaret. Like those of the urban *flaneur,* such integrative performance practices embodied self-consciously *modern* forms of heterosocial mass culture—the gathering of diverse strangers in urban activities—which broke with the family-oriented homosociality of Victorian or immigrant morality. The working women and prosperous urbanites who practiced such forms of leisure approached them as *trans*gressive, *pro*gressive, and *ex*pressive gestures, mixing people of different backgrounds in a nocturnal pursuit of self-actualizing risk. While such participatory entertainment offered "social progress through self-fulfillment"—a modernist meaning that still resonates in the talkshow—and a search for authentic selfhood less constrained by "the weighty hand of civilization,"[28] the talkshow explodes the notion of any one authentic self or of any single developmental mode. It mixes cheap amusement with reformist highmindedness, celebrity with anonymity, fulfillment with its lack, progress with regression, promotional "humbug" with the seminar, the conventional with the exotic, expertise with the amateur, the clinical with the emotional.

In order to understand talkshows in postmodern terms, we must first understand the modern. In *The Discourse of Modernism*, Timothy Reiss cites Mircea Eliade in describing modernity's project as "an unprecedented effort to explain the world, so as to conquer and transform it." Reiss characterizes the medieval epistemology as one of "patterning" based in an episteme of "resemblance" that operated as "a discursive *exchange within* the world," whereas the modern episteme is "analytico-referential" and regards the "expression of knowledge as a reasoning *practice upon* the world." Premodern "patterning" makes no distinction between the word and any other natural sign, whereas modernity's discourse separates the name from the known and the enunciator, the world from discourse.[29]

Modernity not only recognizes the arbitrariness of the sign—especially that of language's abstract, referential, and differential system—but acknowledges this arbitrariness as "conceptually 'useful' ": the word no longer inheres in the thing.[30] This discursive shift has helped make possible a host of historical developments: the abstract reasoning of Newtonian physics; more readily "packaged" and transmissible knowledge; and the concept of a knowing, unitary self now separate from—but believing itself capable of possessing—the world as externalized object, and the truth as transcendental and total.

Like Galileo's telescope, the word in modernity interposes itself not only with what is implicitly believed to be a transparent accuracy but *analytically,* as a grasping medium between the conceptualizing mind and the world as knowable object. Rather than the world organizing human discourse as in the patterning model, modernity regards the construction of knowledge *through* speech and language as organizing the world.[31]

Accompanying modernity's epistemic break was the collapse of the premodern social order. Religious authority, says sociologist Barry Glassner, was replaced by a rationalized authority of "separate groups of professionals, each with special technical abilities," responsible for "separate spheres of activity."[32] The Enlightenment faith in social modernism as progress—the teleology of modernization—"would promote not only the control of natural forces," according to Jürgen Habermas, "but would also further understanding of the world and of the self, would promote moral progress, the justice of institutions, and even the happiness of human beings."[33] Postmodernity represents a crisis not only in modernism's epistemology but in its teleological social project and its technical divisions of world, self, and endeavor into separate spheres in which the professional-expert has authority and control.

There has been a great deal of unsettled theorizing about postmodernism and postmodernity. Where any agreement on definitions exists, it is on the notion that postmodernity—a broad cultural condition characterizing the West, particularly the United States, in the latter half of the twentieth century—entails a crisis in philosophy and representation affecting language, knowability, and technology. "Postmodernism," a term sometimes used interchangeably with "postmodernity," now more commonly describes recent artistic production that breaks significantly with modernist practices even as it appropriates and subverts them.[34]

As a self-conscious development in the arts, postmodernism celebrates commodity culture in ways its adversarial precursor, aesthetic modernism—based solidly in modernity's discourse of invention, control, and a unified, autonomous, and knowing self—did not. Matei Calinescu has aptly pointed out that there have been two modernisms. There is the social project of progress through either capitalism or the socialist state, technology, and reason (all bound up in the modernist discourse Reiss so aptly details). But there is also a primarily aesthetic, anti-commody, anti-mass, and adversarial modernism, a second version critical of the expansive, totalizing progressivism of the first.[35] To Jean-François Lyotard, the grand, legitimizing discourse of both notions of modernity has broken down, giving way to local, pragmatic, destabilizing, and self-interested "language games." Power is based in performativity (maximum performance, irrespective of any legitimizing metanarrative) rather than on an ideal truth or reason anterior to language.[36]

To Fredric Jameson's list of postmodern characteristics—pastiche, collage, perpetual present, schizophrenia (a result of shifting meaning and identity)—Dana Polan would add *incoherence,* "the literal sense of the inability or unwillingness of culture to cohere, to follow an evident logic": that is, to follow the "older logical models" (such as classical narrative) and the forms of interpretation used to explain them. The "strangeness" of postmodern culture may provide a pleasure in incongruity, but it offers no stable meaning and subject position. This is homologous with contemporary economic conditions that no longer necessarily have an interest in ideologically creating "a ready-and-waiting pool of interpellated subjects." Events seem to be governed by contingency rather than logic. A "certain non-sense" triumphs. In his analysis of a "Blondie" comic strip, Polan asserts the interpretive value in postmodern theory: it confronts and theorizes the "fundamental *weirdness* in contemporary mass culture."[37]

Lawrence Grossberg also notes this "non-sense" in American television—the "disturbing heterogeneity of its appeals," its "absurdist fragmented scenarios." In postmodernity, meaning is displaced by affect; the two were once intertwined but have, under conditions of postmodern simulacra, split apart. Without origins or stable meanings, there is no real source of "impassioned commitment." Postmodern media culture creates the condition of fandom, of affective investment in appropriated objects wherein the investment further empties them of meaning. Grossberg names "infotainment" as a new media consumable that "takes consumption out of the realm of mere comfort and competition (i.e., keeping up with the Joneses) and into the arena of the impossible construction of one's own difference. One consumes, in this new reality, as a way of designing the self." The objects of such investment constitute an "inauthentic authenticity" for the subject. He defines this condition as a "popular sensibility" wherein difference (identity) is constructed temporarily in affect (pose).[38] His very choice of terms expresses the postmodern play with contradiction and subversion of sense. The consumer-spectator-subject is—as this multiplicity of hyphens suggests—no longer a singular, unified construct. The postmodern subject plays multiple and simultaneous roles: for example, parent, spouse, consumer, corporate manager, biker. He or she, says Terry Eagleton, "is neither simply the self-regulating synthetic agent posited by classical humanist ideology nor merely a decentered network of desire" or "libidinal attachments." Instead, he or she has become "a contradictory amalgam of the two."[39]

What Grossberg calls "inauthentic authenticity," Ian Angus and Sut Jhally call "staged difference," involving images "consumed as simulations of social identities." This development results from what they see as the third stage of industrial culture—"information society," marked by the postmodern merger of culture and economy such that the homogenization accomplished in the second stage (mass culture and modernity) is torn asunder by a "politics of images; . . . sex, race, ethnicity are no longer suppressed." Instead, "they are simulated and floated as images in the social imagination. Social identities are constructed through the images on which the desire of audiences temporarily alights."[40] The simulated image becomes reality; the self, a screen on which images are projected.

The postmodern self is "an 'other' to be constantly searched for and authenticated." The two affirmations of modernity—the dominance of nature through knowledge (security, control, fixed meaning), and the creation of the free, equal, and knowing subject—have been short-circuited by the third-stage industrial production of simulated difference.

The hyperreal, that highly accomplished simulation of "reality," has, for Arthur Kroker and David Cook, "exploded the self over a technological field" and made the individual susceptible to attack through its *virtual products,* both individuals and images, in a steady stream of fashions."[41]

The talkshow has become the ideal vehicle for showcasing and even *becoming* that fashion stream. Its audience participation makes the stream uniquely accessible. Gender, race, ethnicity, lifestyle, handicap, personal problem, unique experience—such differences are no longer repressed in this "third stage." They become the talkshow's emphasis. Confronting boredom and channel clutter with constant, intensified novelty and "reality," talkshows offer a variety of Others to the fluid spectatorial self. The talkshow mingles the "professional" or "expert" with the "amateur," the guest or participant who appears by virtue of particular personal experience or simple audience membership. It shrewdly combines the folk and the popular with the mass, the immediate and interpersonal with the mediated, in a productive dialectic that both reflects and constructs an image economy's "voracious need for change and innovation" and for "continually changing the rules, and replacing the scenery," as Andrew Ross puts it.[42] This circularity and undecidability are as characteristic of the talkshow as the very name itself. Is it "talk" or "show"? Conversation or spectacle? Both? Neither? The talkshow has it both ways, offering "more" as well as "other" in its very everydayness.

Other Voices

What critics and researchers have said *about* talkshows has proved as important to defining them as what has been said *on* them. For example, the 1989 English translation of Jürgen Habermas's *Structural Transformation of the Public Sphere* has rekindled interest in the public sphere in ways suggesting its centrality to a contemporary culture where "critical publicity"—rational-critical debate focused on the common good—has been replaced by a "staged and manipulative publicity" stemming from the assertion of private interests.[43] A recent Habermas-inspired essay, "Chatter in the Age of Electronic Reproduction," situates the talkshow within the framework of a new public sphere in which politics emanates "from social, personal and environmental concerns, consolidated in the circulation of discursive practices rather than in formal organizations," thus allowing "an opening for the empowerment of an alternative discursive practice"—the emergence of a new political stage in an age of PACs and Beltway insularity. The essay's authors see the talkshow as a new, "electronically defined common place" where other "common senses" may develop.[44]

Over the years, however, most studies of talkshows have made them suspect. The first significant study—Donald Horton and R. Richard Wohl's 1956 "Mass Communication and Para-Social Interaction: Observations on Intimacy at a Distance"—accused television talkshows of fostering a dangerous "illusion of intimacy" for lonely spectators.[45] One of the latest studies—Alan Hirsch's 1991 *Talking Heads: Political Talkshows and Their Star Pundits*—charges most political talkshows with indulging in a "politics of kicks" which, since the 1960s, has corrupted public life and "undernourished" democracy by impoverishing political debate. Echoing media historian Neil Postman's blanket condemnation, Hirsch implicates the talkshow in a media culture in which we are "amusing ourselves to death."[46] Less extreme and more careful in its content analysis, Murray Burton Levin's *Talk Radio and the American Dream* (1987) deftly analyzes the rhetoric of Boston's *The Jerry Williams Show* during the late 1970s, noting call-in radio's "delegitimizing," even "subversive" effect. Its alienated, conservative, and largely working-class callers anticipated the age of Ronald Reagan. Levin also evaluates the form's use of "contrived authenticity" and the way it elevates "the trivial and trivializes the significant."[47] Yet another study, Donal Carbaugh's *Talking American: Cultural Discourses on "Donahue"* (1988) uses the talkshow as a database to demonstrate how American speech is characterized by discourses on the self and the act of speaking that privilege individuality and choice—"resistant personal orders"—over any sense of *social* order.[48] Sociologist Gaye Tuchman's 1974 "Assembling a Network Talk-show" goes behind the scenes and discovers how the highly reproductive, gatekeeping, and contingent aspects of the talkshow lower the uncertainty about broadcast success yet stifle cultural innovation.[49]

Approaching the talkshow as a nexus of cultural, political, and economic forces requires analysis not only of particular talkshows but of the talk *about* talkshows: press and audience reception, previous research, the broadcast industry's rhetoric and intentionality, and the intertexts of which the talkshow is so much a part. Because the talkshow and the talk around it are eminently *public,* performative constructs, my study draws for the most part on that very public record and performance. Because there are—and have been—so many talkshows, I navigate this immense thicket by centering on key talkshow meanings and practices as they inflect American media, culture, and politics.

One of the talkshow's most striking attributes is its depth of intertextuality. Although all communication is intertextual, no other form owes more of its fundamental substance to *other* media texts, thus making its closure—to the degree it *can* be "closed"—especially dependent on the spectator-participant's intertextual cognition. The guest may be the star of the latest hit film or recording, the author of a best-selling book, or a much-publicized political figure caught up in the issue of the moment. In almost all its varieties, the talkshow not only engages in but parasitically intensifies image production. If broadcasting is a "feminine" technology effacing "aura," as some have claimed,[50] then the talkshow has evolved into a particularly reproductive practice that warms up cultural leftovers in a version of the "trash aesthetic"—even an anti-aesthetic—that shares some of the attributes of camp.[51]

The postmodern market economy has found in the talkshow its ideal commodity *and* commodifier. As an imaginary, cyberspatial product promoting *other* products while also commodifying the spectator-consumer, the talkshow is highly plastic, thrives on change, and can package any timely topic into product, spectacle, and performance—all in very short order.[52] Like the news, it can achieve national or worldwide distribution quickly. Just as satellite communications have no respect for national, cultural, or geographic boundaries, so the talkshow brashly collapses a host of aesthetic and subject boundaries—"subject" meant in both senses of the term: as topic and as human individual. It represents a postmodern "both-and" aesthetic first articulated by architect Robert Venturi in 1966. By "having it both ways," it is as contradictory and chaotic as it is inclusive, as authentic as it is simulating.[53]

In *No Sense of Place,* Joshua Meyrowitz locates the impact of electronic media on social behavior in its "reorganization of social situations": it merges public spheres, exposes what were once behavioral "back regions" (as Erving Goffman defined them), and offers "a new social order" that undermines our sense of place.[54] Meyrowitz correctly notes that the collapse of "old" situational barriers has brought about the privatization of public life. But he makes the mistake of situating the media in a framework that privileges interpersonal communication— face-to-face, real-time exchange in a localized physical domain. What happens when the ever more interactive media have become so integrated into our daily experience that they form a continuum with the interpersonal?

It is my view that a medium like the talkshow creates not "placelessness" but a hyperlocal or cyberspatial "place." Old lines are being erased, but new ones are being drawn—new social and political connections, new "neighborhoods." The talkshow is not so much the *last* neighborhood in America—however apocalyptic some of the talk about it—as it is the newest and least understood.

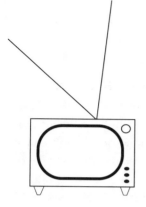

1

Turning to Talk: The Talkshow's Development

The talkshow, no less than any other programming format, adheres to the network rule of "safety first"; the result, according to Todd Gitlin, is recombination, "the triumph of the synthetic"—spinoffs, copies, a handful of thinly disguised yet repeated formulas. Recombination—low-risk, standardizing, and cost-efficient, innovating no more than necessary to be profitable—nevertheless requires a degree of novelty, a just-sufficient dose of the modernist, "make it new" sensibility that arose with Romanticism. For Gitlin, consumer society's genius is "its ability to convert the desire for change into a desire for novel goods."[1] The novel and the newspaper were Western capitalism's first "literary" creations and, along with accounting and advertising, among its first unique communicative forms. Their very names—"novel," "news"—indicate the market economy's desire for the new as well as for a predictive, quantifying knowledge that permits control of the transitory and the unstable—a knowledge necessary for timely and profitable action in ever-shifting markets.

As a recombinatory construct, the talkshow collects the old in new packages by appropriating both modernist and Romantic tendencies (adversarialism, self-assertion) through the host's ego; it has been called "a host-driven medium."[2] But it also includes premodern, commonfolk oral expression, the nostalgia of the town meeting and the "simple life," republican accessibility, and the element of chance. It is perhaps the media's most efficient recombinatory form, one that can manufacture narrative and spectacle out of anything almost immediately.[3] In so doing, it commodifies conversation and plunders the topical by indulging in a wildly intertextual "impurity"—an impurity endowing it with an elegantly productive instability. This chapter traces how such impurity has been produced and *productive* throughout the talkshow's development, especially in its audience participation.

Commodifying Knowledge

Audience participation in the media first became an identifiable practice with the birth of the eighteenth-century magazine, which followed the seventeenth-century emergence of the English coffeehouse as a salonlike setting for intellectual talk focusing on Enlightenment philosophy and the arts. The coffeehouse offered a kind of talk alternative to church, palace, court, or parliament. It was more than a coincidence that this extraparliamentary "talk space" of the rising, learned middle class led to the appearance of Richard Steele's *Tatler*, Steele and Addison's *Spectator*, and other periodicals with such names as *Town Talk*, *Tea Table*, and *Chit Chat*.

Coffeehouse conversation, like the magazines, was devoted to the philosophical and aesthetic issues of the day, but also to gossip, which these early magazines—among the first forms of mediated news—satirically picked up on. Although linked to coffeehouse intellectualism, they nonetheless ridiculed pretense and espoused simplicity of manner. At the same time, they were read and discussed *in* the coffeehouses. Their purpose was as much to influence public opinion as to provide a venue for essayists and poets.[4] The Enlightenment spectator could now become a participant in the public pursuit of rational, disinterested (in the sense of being outside of government) knowledge and self-expression, asserting a modernist autonomy, agency, and control in inquiry. Being a mere spectator implied an acceptance of someone else's authority in the use of reason or the acquisition of knowledge—a notion contrary to the tenets of the Enlightenment and modernity—whereas participation was discursively linked with autonomous or personal accomplishment and self-invention in the modernist break with the "immaturity" of the past.[5]

Audience participation found its way into textual production in a kind of feedback loop joined at the coffeehouse. Jürgen Habermas has noted that the magazines' dialogue form "attested to their proximity to the spoken word." He sees this circular coffeehouse-magazine practice as an early manifestation of the bourgeois public sphere whose intent was to promote "the self-enlightenment of individuals" at a time of "the emancipation of civic morality from moral theology and of practical wisdom from the philosophy of the scholars."[6] The coffeehouse and the magazines derived from it positioned the spectator as a participant capable of the self-pursuit of knowledge, at the same time making for themselves the necessary apparatus for that pursuit.

In the northeastern American colonies the coffeehouse became but one of several participatory talk practices that grew out of Enlightenment ideals; others included the philosophical society, the literary circle, and the lyceum. Each had some link with the emerging mass media: they drew topics from the headlines of newspapers, discussed books, or invited authors to speak. They echoed similar institutions that developed in seventeenth- and eighteenth-century Europe as a key part of what Habermas has called bourgeois "civil society," a public sphere in which the common good could be rationally debated by the new middle class, free from private (market) interests and prior to implementation by the state.[7] In the United States, such "talk spaces" joined the informal cracker-barrel, back-fence, and saloon traditions linking talk practices to agrarian economy, domesticity, and leisure.[8]

The lyceum movement, begun in 1826 by Josiah Holbrook in Millbury, Massachusetts, brought the impulses of the Jackson era (a reaction against the Federalist mistrust of the people as "the mob," seeing them instead as "the source of all wisdom" and distrusting "the experts")[9] together with the eighteenth-century privileging of science and rational inquiry. Originally, the lyceums were member-run, community-oriented associations of mutual instruction in "useful knowledge" through lectures, discussions, libraries, and scientific experimentation. But the lyceum was aimed at the young workingman, and its principal thrust was to be "moral and fraternal rather than intellectual."[10] The 1829 constitution of the Boston lyceum regarded the "dangerous" age for young men—beginning at seventeen—as a time during which their passions could be channeled into the lyceum's evening activities.

The lyceum avoided interfering in the workday, the rights of parents, and politics. Its discussions emphasized science, thus making it nonthreatening to existing social and economic arrangements. A Worcester County newspaper article applauded the Millbury lyceum as "a powerful influence in effecting a reformation in morals"; Holbrook sold his lyceum concept by extolling its good effects upon youth.[11] Curiously, as an institution that realized modernity's drive to inquiry, progress, and equality through the commoner's participation and control, it also exercised its own control strategy. A depoliticized forum would encourage the young workingman's moral self-improvement through what would come to be known as adult education. Despite the high-minded talk around the movement, which grew rapidly into a national phenomenon in the mid-1800s, the lyceum was also a commodity. Holbrook's motives in promoting the concept were at least partly financial; its national growth made him wealthy through published writings, tours, and the sale of scientific apparatus used by the lyceums.[12]

In the mid-1800s the movement grew more commodified and less participatory. An educational talk practice once based on local participation and control became a celebrity lecture circuit. A "star system" of well-paid speakers, including such figures as Charles Dickens and Ralph Waldo Emerson, took over. The concurrent growth of media (newspapers and magazines, the telegraph) and transportation (the railroads) made possible the national marketing and distribution of evening speakers as well as soap or cereal. Moreover, the speakers were frequently authors touring in part to promote the sale of their books. Large, profitable booker-promoter agencies—the American Literary Bureau, the Williams Lecture and Musical Bureau, the Redpath Lyceum Bureau—came to dominate and professionalize the lyceum circuit and, later, the chautauquas.[13]

The emergence of women's service magazines in the late nineteenth century also encouraged audience participation. Under the editorship of Edward Bok (1889–1919), the Ladies' Home Journal developed its female audience through contests, surveys offering prizes to respondents, and advice columns soliciting readers' letters—devices used to stimulate personal contact between magazine and audience. Editors often acted on reader advice, especially after the magazine established a reader-editor service in 1935. Bok deliberately undertook a content approach that would make the Ladies' Home Journal an "intimate and personal" service to women. Through the increasing use of experts, it gave advice on health, home, and child rearing. In addition, much like McClure's and other muckraking magazines of the era, it crusaded against abuses in the patent-medicine industry and would no longer accept its advertising. (The crusade, or at least the appearance of it, has also become an occasional part of the audience participation talkshow; *Donahue*'s championing of feminism is one example.) Other women's service magazines engaged—and engaged their readers—in similar campaigns. *Collier's* battled for the Pure Food and Drug Acts (which were finally enacted in 1906). The *Women's Home Companion* promoted packaged groceries. *Good Housekeeping* tested consumer items.[14]

Associated with these magazines' participatory impulse was their cultivation of *self*-culture tied to a discursive strand that has been called "republican" or "domestic simplicity."[15] The best possibility for social reform, in this view, lay in "enlightened self-improvement" such as could be accomplished by women through home-centered activities that stressed "the simple life." "Republican simplicity" involved common-folk *participation* in the building of the country. The *Ladies' Home Journal* provided "an uplifting practical guidebook for middle-class simplicity" perceived to be the foundation and strength of the republic.

Notions of common-folk participation had had a long-standing link not only with a vision of democracy but with the virtue of simplicity: that is, with being plain, ordinary, and frugal. As such long-held American virtues were being articulated in a mass medium based on the emergence of national advertisers, national brands, standardized and mass-produced consumer products, these concepts became commodified through reader participation. That the women's service magazine, widely considered the first mass circulation medium,[16] strategically attempted—with considerable success—to develop a "warm" and intimate rapport with female readers suggests an early mediated attempt at what the talkshow is so often accused of doing: simulating local, interpersonal communication as an antidote to national and corporate institutions. Yet in the same period the production of goods was increasingly taking place outside the home, where it could become mass production, an outgrowth of the rationality of industrial modernity and its need for markets. The local focus of production and consumption was gradually replaced by national products and distribution: chain stores and catalogue companies such as Sears, Roebuck; national producers such as Nabisco.

Consequently, audiences for such media magazines also became mass consumers in an "itinerant" marketplace. The disruptions of modernity, which took people from an ethic based on localism and self-sufficiency to one of spectatorship and consumption,[17] were eased by the magazines through the rear-view mirror of nostalgic participatory practices. Like those of the talkshow, these were inscribed within a commodified media frame necessitated by and for advertising; they were stitched together, against a historical-ethical backdrop of self-reliance, into an emerging image culture that restructured needs and desires to foster consumption. As modernity broke with the past, it also had to ease the transition for its now anonymous consuming subjects.[18]

The "domestic simplicity" theme is an early example of the nostalgia appeal still a part of the talkshow's "town meeting" aspect. The *Ladies' Home Journal*'s participatory approach was itself nostalgic in its effort to replicate the trusted, advice-giving neighbor or the local grocer who knew where everything in his store came from. Media use of participation tapped not only the democratic connotations of the town meeting, self-governance, and a shirt-sleeves ethic of action and trust but the virtuous "low culture" strains of revivalism and a Jacksonian "plain folks" social preference as well. An anti-intellectualist reaction against "high" cultural forms was also evident.[19] Still, such concepts redefined subjectivity and spectatorship as participatory through a largely ethical imperative: the subject had to produce as well as consume in the democratic self-creation of knowledge and culture. From the women's service magazine to the talk/service program, the continuation of "service" is significant—what was once an ethical imperative has become *aestheticized*.

The commercialization of leisure intensified by the lyceum and the women's service magazine continued with the urban development of saloons, dance halls, amusement parks, and cabarets. These coexisted with voluntary social forms such as the workingmen's club, the mutual benefit society, the local baseball team, and the street corner. Whether commercial or voluntary, working-class entertainment had previously been largely homosocial—segmented by gender, race, and class. For women, those homosocial forms were marked by domestic privacy and restraint. By the turn of the century, however, young workingwomen and prosperous urban couples were pioneering heterosocial and expressive—

publicly participatory—forms. Women, seeking the company of men in public leisure, became a market for the "cheap amusements" of the dance hall, amusement park, and nickelodeon, as Kathy Peiss demonstrates. They asserted a new, expressive, working-class public life—a "new mass audience"—that rejected the domesticity and gentility of middle-class mores associated with Victorianism, the Protestant ethic, or Old World immigrant culture.[20]

The young workingwoman's use of leisure time, particularly for the urban immigrant family, became a source of conflict between intergenerational or gendered notions of "control, resistance, acquiescence, and subterfuge."[21] For these women, an active, public use of leisure time—a time now segmented from labor just as public and private had also become increasingly separate spheres in their temporary emergence from domesticity—carried the connotations of modernist autonomy, self-discovery, and self-invention. Participation was valued as modern, standing in contrast to a passive, repressed, domestic subject position bound to an earlier era. An "emergent group of leisure entrepreneurs" responded to this youthful market and "ultimately popularized" heterosocial public entertainments. What began as a "trickle-up" participatory initiative on the part of a new set of subjects, working women, was quickly joined by the "trickle-down" influence of commodified mass culture playing to a recognized market.[22]

The development of the cabaret and the nightclub, particularly in New York in the early years of the century, furthered heterosocial and participatory leisure practices by extending them to the middle class and the well-to-do. As Lewis A. Erenberg characterizes it, the cabaret introduced the interactive space that put performer and spectator in intimate proximity. Cabaret acts commonly involved members of their audiences— those who took part were "sports," not "stuffed shirts"—although the spectator-participant maintained a degree of anonymity.[23]

The "lewdness" of the ragtime dance craze of the 1910s may have been seen as posing a moral threat, but the cabaret opened the door to greater expressiveness through the intimacy, spontaneity, and informality of its performance. This new theatrical form "symbolized broader changes in the culture," breaking down "the formal boundaries that had separated the entertainers from the respectable, men from women, and upper- from lower-class culture." The cabaret became "a new public environment for the exploration of alternatives to the private character of the nineteenth century," bringing "intimacy and expressiveness into everyday life."[24] Sociability and personal contact were other cabaret attractions. The intimate setting fostered the emergence of a new kind of performer, a friendly and personable entertainer: the star "personality" who embodied "a new myth of success" involving an "urban life of consumption and pleasure."[25]

Given its separate, nocturnal setting and regulated risk, its "institutionalized spontaneity" and "vicarious action,"[26] the cabaret was a public place where life could be "lived to the fullest" without jeopardizing one's work or day life ("private selves and class position") as it extended the private—leisure having once been domestic—into the public.[27] The generally affluent cabaret public "used money, technology, and artifice to create an environment for acting out" and for the "comfortable testing of new definitions of the self within the setting of upper class civilization" as well as within the "impersonality of the public realm."[28] The cabaret foreshadowed some of the characteristics of audience participation in broadcasting, particularly in the game and talk shows. Its modernist trajectory would become one voice in the talkshow's pastiche.

Electronic Talk

As a specifically defined genre, the talkshow dates from the dawn of radio broadcasting—a natural development, given that the microphone, a device designed principally for speech pickup, is the medium's key transducer. If a sense of messy liveness, spontaneity, and authenticity raised the credibility of radio news in the medium's early days, the talkshow also benefited.[29] A look at the network schedules for 1928–29, for example, shows twenty-one programs categorized as "talk": public affairs, religious, daytime homemakers', and miscellaneous talk. By 1947–48 the number is up to fifty-five. In the listings for either season, varieties of talkshow constitute a significant percentage of the full schedule—15 to 25 percent during radio's "golden age."[30]

Typical of hundreds of such shows were *Victor Lindlahr*, a health talk program that began on the Mutual network in 1936; the CBS advice show *The Voice of Experience*, with social worker Marion Sayle Taylor; the daytime beauty program *Nell Vinick*; and *The Back to God Hour*. Most of these programs were monologues—experts' talking *at* the audience—rather than dialogue or audience participation shows—but *The Voice of Experience*, running from 1933 until 1940, used a form of audience participation through listener contributions to the host's fund for the "less fortunate." The host worked with people, such as prostitutes, whose lives and experiences prefigure the sensationalized, difference-based subject matter of many talkshows today.[31]

These programs encompassed a wide array of subjects: news and current issues, religion, hobbies, the arts, celebrity gossip, and homemakers' interests; a complete "golden age" list would be pages long. On the basis of scope alone, what the term "talk show" meant, apart from a propagation of discursive knowledge, was indeed so diverse and unstable as to defy any singular definition other than "information" or "conversation" in the broadest sense. In economic terms, one or even a handful of on-air voices could offer efficient, cost-effective programming as a desirable vehicle for advertisers. But within the vast breadth of the label "talk," such programming would take directions determined by, and eventually determining, its cultural and historical situation.[32]

Audience participation was one such direction. The category emerged in conjunction with the interview and human interest categories. Shows with names such as *Reunion of the States*, *Pull Over Neighbor*, *Paging John Doe*, and *Meet Joe Public* were among those hosted by Art Baker, an interviewer who specialized in participatory programs through the 1930s and 1940s.[33] Spontaneous, unscripted daytime talk and variety programs, such as NBC's long-running *Breakfast Club* (1933–68), responded to listener requests by the 1930s.

Another early genre involving the audience was the game show. *The Answer Man*, a syndicated program that debuted in 1937 and survived for fifteen years, had listeners submit questions on any subject; the show received about 900,000 letters a year. Mutual's *Auction Gallery* had people from across the country bidding by mail against the on-air experts, but only after the bidding was opened to the studio audience during the live broadcast. *Information Please*, moderated by Clifton Fadiman, received thirty thousand letters a week from listeners hoping to win prizes by stumping a panel of experts. Jack Barry hosted *Juvenile Jury*, in which

children between five and twelve years old gave their views on their peers'
problems through unscripted, unrehearsed responses to selected letters.[34]
The Personal Column of the Air, a Proctor and Gamble show running
on both NBC networks (Red and Blue), lasted only a year (1936–37) but
invited listeners to send messages addressed to people they had lost track
of.[35] These programs aired five days a week, fifteen minutes a day. *Truth
or Consequences*, however, required an elaborate thirty-minute audience
warmup during which the announcer picked contestants from the studio
audience.

The amateur-variety category also had some of the attributes of the
game show: competition in performance and, of course, audience participation. *Arthur Godfrey's Talent Scouts* and *Major Bowes' Amateur Hour*
were among the most prominent. Godfrey, who came to network radio
with Walter Winchell's help, was noted for his ability to sound relaxed
and sincere and yet become emotional and even risqué. As a newscaster
for CBS, he wept while providing live coverage of Franklin D. Roosevelt's funeral—a reaction, unique among the funeral's broadcast reporters, that endeared him to many. The incident also showed how playing
with rules or boundaries can be especially productive for the talk host.
On a live broadcast of *Talent Scouts* during the 1950s, he fired the show's
singer, Julius LaRosa.[36] He was known for his risqué on-air handling
of sponsors but was popular enough to get away with it. While hosting a morning show for CBS, he pronounced the name Bayer Aspirin as
"bare ass prin," a transgression that greatly amused his listeners without
really undermining the sponsor. The liberties Godfrey took and their acceptance within *his* performance context mark the broadcast beginnings
of the effective popularization and commodification of transgression—a
tendency later evident from Henry Morgan to Jack Paar to Joe Pyne to
Phil Donahue, Morton Downey, Jr., David Letterman, and the radio call-
in hosts. When transgression is commodified, modern oppositionalism is
folded back into the very political economy it pretends to oppose.

The *Amateur Hour*, which began on radio in 1935 and continued as a
television program into the early 1960s—*Ted Mack's Original Amateur
Hour*—was an immediate hit at the time of its Depression debut. Many
would-be participants sacrificed everything for the chance to go east and
appear on the show. By its second year the program was getting ten thou-

sand applications a week, auditioning five to seven hundred hopefuls, and selecting only twenty. Many ended up on New York's relief rolls, including some of those fortunate enough to appear on the show only to be brutally "gonged off" by the Major or Mack; Bowes kept a body-guard in the event of trouble. The amateurs selected to go on the air were paid ten dollars and a before-air meal, during which time Mack got to know them well enough to ask pertinent questions on the air. A few stars emerged from the more than fifteen thousand who appeared; the most famous is Frank Sinatra. Listeners voted each week by phone or mail. When Bowes put together traveling companies in cities with CBS affiliates, local phone banks allowed the residents to register their votes.[37] The source of the program's popularity was twofold: surprise and pleasure in the occasional outstanding amateur (the audience surrogate/participant), and the comic pathos of the untalented who *thought* they could perform and did so ingenuously until gonged off.

The popular, long-running radio and television game show *Truth or Consequences*, which first aired August 17, 1940, exemplified the participatory program's nostalgia appeal in its sense of interpersonal communication, while also making comic use of its audience participants and their clumsy amateur performance—a kind of mediated "republican simplicity." Seven contestants, selected from the New York studio audience just before air time, would compete on the show; most would end up "paying the consequences" for having incorrectly answered a question. Listeners from around the country mailed in questions and suggested "consequences." Each time the host, Ralph Edwards, read one or the other, he gave the name and city of the audience contributor, who received five dollars for each question used and ten for each consequence. A correct answer was greeted by an organ's "chord of truth"; an incorrect answer got "Beulah the buzzer." Fifteen dollars went to a contestant who answered the question correctly; five dollars and five cakes of Ivory soap, the sponsor's (Colgate-Palmolive's) product, to each contestant who did not "tell the truth." However, the one who drew the loudest applause for payment of consequences—some ridiculous and incongruous act performed for the audience's pleasure—earned a "grand prize" of another fifteen dollars.

The show's format and introductory rituals were designed to encourage participation by making the audience feel "at home." The announcer, Mel Allen, introduced the show by reminding listeners that it derived from "the old parlor game of the same name" and would be "kind to everyone who plays it, like Ivory soap is to the hands of all who use it." He described the game as "the Ivory radio party" and, at the end, thanked the participants for being such "sports."

On one typical show, Edwards introduces and chats with the first contestant, Mr. Johnson, a bookkeeper. He fails to answer correctly a question submitted by a woman from Union City, New Jersey: between what two points was Paul Revere's ride? His consequence is to recite "Little Bo Peep" while eating an apple suspended from a string. Edwards describes the grotesque situation as listeners hear Mr. Johnson "acting out" his consequence to the laughter of the studio audience. The next contestant, an unmarried woman from Birmingham, must go into the studio audience with the "roving microphone," pick out a man, and propose to him. When she tells the man she has chosen that she is in New York to find a millionaire, he bluntly responds, "I'm not her type," and a spontaneous comic exchange ensues. The grand prize winner is a man from Weehawken whose consequence is to roll on the floor and amorously bark the song "Let Me Call You Sweetheart" to a live seal. The show produces its spectator-contestant as multivalent, an amalgam: a "real" person with a name and a job but also a comic role-player, consumer, *and* commodity.

Meanwhile, nonparticipatory educational radio talkshows were appearing. Some built important reputations. *The Town Crier*, hosted by Alexander Woollcott (who already had a large following as a writer, newspaper critic, and actor), premiered in 1929 with interviews, reviews of books and the arts, and discussion of issues of the day. A favorable Woollcott book review could mean spectacular sales. Perhaps the most powerful literary critic in the country, Woollcott endorsed James Hilton's *Goodbye Mr. Chips* and helped make it a tremendous success.[38]

The late 1930s saw the emergence of educational talkshows involving debate on current issues. *The People's Platform*, on CBS from 1938 to 1952, featured lively discussion by four guests and was moderated by the noted educator Lyman Bryson. The guests consisted of one "big name" individual, one expert on the subject at hand, a woman, and an "average" man (one wonders if the obligatory woman was also "average").

To engage the evening's topic, the four had dinner together before the broadcast. While they ate, the producer reportedly eavesdropped through a microphone hidden in the table's centerpiece.[39]

The People's Rally, which also debuted in 1938 but endured only one year, was a Mutual program combining debate on current issues with the quizzing of audience members. NBC's *America's Town Meeting* was broadcast live from New York's Town Hall. Premiering in 1935, the show featured lively arguments on current issues. Mutual's answer to this NBC show was *American Forum of the Air*. Both were sustaining programs until the late 1940s. While they involved audience participation, they were generally considered "public affairs talk" as opposed, obviously, to "comedy audience participation programs" such as *Truth or Consequences*, or to "comedy talk" such as *The Henry Morgan Program*, which involved a series of outrageous skits, including Morgan's send-ups of his own sponsors.

Audience questions and comments for the public affairs talkshows were spontaneous until America's involvement in World War II, when wartime conditions encouraged the reigning in of such unscripted forms as "man-in-the-street" interviews and request shows; censorship required that everything be written out in advance.[40] The talk or participation show's relation to the "outside world," a permeable one, posed a danger. Even after the war, that blurred border remained a threat. But by the 1960s, at a time of political polarization, change, and social confrontation, the broadcast industry was cultivating that threat as a productively transgressive way to attract audiences to an unpredictable and exciting program form.

Vox Pop, the "voice of the people," began in 1932 in Houston as a local "human interest" show and became one of the longest-running and most popular of the interview programs. It aired on NBC until 1938, then on CBS until 1946, and finally on ABC through 1947. Among the imitations it inspired were Mutual's *Inquiring Reporter* and NBC Blue's *Our Neighbors*. The show dealt in spontaneous man-in-the-street interviews involving political, personal, trick, or "nonsense" questions calculated to surprise the interviewee into an amusing response. Eventually, trick questions with prizes for correct guesses were added to the interviews. *Vox Pop*, along with the *Amateur Hour*, initiated the practice of broadcasting from different cities (a practice continued by *Donahue*, *Oprah*, and other nationally syndicated talkshows). *Vox Pop* even went to Mexico, Puerto Rico, Cuba, and the 1939 New York World's Fair.[41] Emerging with this attempt at a closeness to "the people"—a closeness paralleled by the spontaneous intimacy of the "average" audience participant's amplified voice—was the program's potential for sensation resulting from an unrehearsed intimacy. Then as now, the talkshow in its spontaneity, courted the risqué.

On the show's network debut, July 7, 1935, two "sidewalk reporters," Parks Johnson and Jerry Belcher, alternate in interviewing people on the street near New York City's Columbus Circle. The fast-talking interviewers dominate by interspersing an occasional personal question among nonsense queries in quick, gameshow manner: "To which side does a pig's tail curl?" "Do you use both sides of your mouth when you smile?" "Out of what kind of worrying do you get the most satisfaction?" Some "quiz" questions are topical: "Have you ever seen a 'yes' man?" is a political reference common during Franklin D. Roosevelt's administration. Next to Johnson's and Belcher's polished, fast-on-their-feet questions, the "average" interviewees are halting, comically awkward, or ingenuous. Contrast and incongruity are at the root of the humor; the common folk become the slick interviewers' foils. Arcane or absurd questions surprise the people, thus magnifying their performative awkwardness and prompting their honest, emotional reactions. Sometimes their laughter breaks the formal frame of the interview situation; more often, the interviewee plays along, heightening the listener's sense of the absurd.

The program's studio announcer, Ben Grover, initially sets the "street scene" by assuring listeners that what they are about to hear is unrehearsed. Street sounds form an audible background. The small crowd gathering around each interview become surrogates for the listener; they can often be heard laughing. The "people are funny" aspect of *Vox Pop* obscures the performative effort of the interviewers—their pace, timing, and verbal facility in response to the interviewee's spontaneous reply—to create a situation of pleasant unbalance. Maintaining that state of the unpredictable in a relaxed and friendly context is itself a delicate balance. The show's premise involves constructing a performance framework around an incongruity between interviewer (polished, rapid, controlled) and interviewee (rough, stumbling, spontaneous, but often surprising, fresh, and extemporaneously funny). The chaotic—the uncontrolled and unpredictable—is elicited and exploited but contained in and by the format's structure. At the end of the show, the studio announcer reframes the situation in a nonthreatening, user-friendly light, calling the show and its quizzing reporters "fun," "simple," yet "educational."

Like some modernist arts, *Vox Pop* used chance elements. But it integrated them into a polyvalent, interactive mass-cultural form that packaged indeterminacies and contingencies as comic incongruity and absurdity. Like the participants in *Truth or Consequences*, the subject-selves were represented as eclectic, multiple—capable of rapid and unpredictable shifts in role.

The interviewers seemed to aim for a cross section—men, women, and a child (a boy whose hero was Dizzy Dean) were interviewed. Afterward, each "guest" received three cakes of the sponsor's product: Fleischmann's Yeast, touted as beneficial to digestion and complexion. The interviewee, as audience surrogate, was thus also inscribed into the program's textual material not just as a kind of coproducer (by virtue of his or her on-mike presence) but as consumer as well. Like the yeast cakes, he or she was "packaged" and devoured by both text and institutional practice. The show's pseudodocumentary premise, so apt for the 1930s "discovery" of public opinion, barely masked its privatization through sponsorship. The audience-participant's subjectivity was multiplied to the program's and sponsor's advantage: he or she was "man-in-the-street" as well as consumer—and in-the-rough comedian.

Other shows categorized by the industry as "comedy audience participation" included *Art Linkletter's House Party* (which made the transition to television and involved a stream of common-folk guests, including children), *Rumpus Room* (involving children and hosted by Johnny Olson), Art Linkletter's *People are Funny*, and such game hybrids as *Beat the Clock* and *Honeymoon in New York*. The industry's linking of audience participation with comedy arose from the lightness and contrast such a program concept offered, in the unscripted ingenuousness of its nonprofessional, "average person" performers, next to the scripted formality of slicker program genres. Like the interviewees on *Vox Pop*, the "folk" in front of the microphone seemed clumsy and thus funny. Perhaps most exploitative of this was Allen Funt's *Candid Mike*, which started on ABC in 1947, continued on television as *Candid Camera*, and still returns as the occasional special. It relied on audience participation, but its voyeuristically observed participants were hardly willing ones as they stumbled into Funt's practical-joke setups.

The 1930s surge of programs based on audience participation coincided with the emergence of the concept of public opinion, which found its institutionalization in George Gallup's 1935 establishment of the American Institute for Public Opinion. The 1930s image of the "average American" became a significant discursive part of advertising and market research, consumerism, industrial development, and living standards. "The American Way of Life" was a theme of the 1939 World's Fair and its corporate exhibits.[42]

Related to this discourse was what historian Warren Susman sees as the beginning of an era of America's suspension "between two cultures —an older culture, often loosely termed Puritan-republican, producer-capitalist culture, and a newly emerging culture of abundance" based in consumerism.[43] The former was participatory in its emphasis on involvement in production; the latter threatened to supplant active participation with the passivity implied by the idea of "average" consumers who were part of a "mass" audience. Audience participation in the radio of the period inscribed a nostalgia for "the people" at a time when they were being more and more defined as "average" and "mass" to fit useful consumption profiles. The audience participation program represented a negotiation of these two cultures in a way consistent with what Habermas saw as the "fiction" of public opinion, which became a favorable object of the "staged and manipulative publicity" of private (market) interests supplanting the general-interest "critical publicity" that typified the eighteenth-century public sphere—a sphere that has since collapsed in part because of the manipulative nostalgia of private interests.[44]

Even as a part of the modernist project of technological development and economic expansion, radio in the United States could project an "illusion of intimacy" through the proximity of voice to microphone and the calculated use of performance affect.[45] Radio could seem personal and direct, premodern, prebroadcast; its apparent immediacy could efface its national, industrial, and technological aspects. It could appear to simulate of interpersonal communication: the closeness and timbre of the voice, the affect of the speaker, and apparent direct address. Personalities capable of tapping this potential—President Roosevelt was one; the 1930s political activist Father Coughlin another[46]—proved very effective radio communicators. Edward R. Murrow's ad-libbed, on-the-scene reporting, along with the occasional difficulties of shortwave overseas news relays, reinforced a documentary feel that offered connotations of authenticity and "simplicity," despite the medium's obvious status as discourse, performance, apparatus, and institution. Through Murrow's on-location reports or FDR's fireside chats, live radio could create a sense of "intimate participation" in the audience.[47] Boundary-blurring audience identification with the radio personality became possible.

Audience participation could work hand-in-hand with this simulation of intimacy to mask the medium's mass, industrial, consumption-focused design. Like the documentary, "average American," public opinion spirit of the 1930s, radio's use of audience participation and intimate-seeming conversation amplified that spirit, at the same time obscuring the industrial structure of centralized transmission and dispersed, domestic reception.[48]

"Want to Be Different?
Turn to Talk"

Audience participation and its link with the talkshow would continue after network radio's demise. The concept of locally oriented programming—principally dependent upon music recordings, the appeal of station personalities, local news, service, information, and local advertising (along with some barter syndication and national spot advertising)—took hold in the 1950s with Todd Storz's invention of the top-40 format.[49] As wild, freewheeling, and disk jockey–dominated as the format seemed, it came under the increasing control of the station's program director and his or her research-based decisions, which limited the playlist and defined clock-hours, day parts, jingles, promotions, and DJ personalities.[50] A practice of tight control underlying an "uncanned" on-air sound was thus established in the "new" local radio. Given this control—evident in formats tightened to reach a precise advertiser-desired segment of the market (in the case of top-40, youth and young adults)—the "old" networks began to supply specialized news and programming for the different station "sounds." [51] Such developments paved the way for the "narrowcasting" concept furthered since the 1960s by the proliferation of radio formats and cable television. The radio format—a carefully designed, narrowcast package—was and is a studied integration of programming and advertising tailored to a specific target audience.

Talk programming on post-network radio evolved its own format, but not before individual talk programs were broadcast on the music stations. The beginnings of interactive talk radio—the call-in show—are cloudy at best. In attempting to fathom these beginnings, it is important to see radio talk's intertextual, institutional, and spectatorial relationships with the other evolving formats, particularly the all-news and news/talk programs that emerged at roughly the same time. Its relationship to public controversy, its appearance of spontaneity, and its calculated blending of information and entertainment in a constant, productive defiance of notions of generic integrity all underlie its emergence.

As early as 1930, disk jockeys invited listeners to phone in comments, which they would then paraphrase on the air. [52] Barry Gray of WMCA New York, one of the longest talkshow practitioners and widely considered one of the best, claims to have invented the overnight call-in radio talkshow in 1945 when he was a DJ at WOR. [53] According to Gray, the whole concept developed accidentally when, bored with his show at about three o'clock one morning, he answered his phone and conversed *on the air* with the caller, who happened to be Woody Herman. As time went on, Gray's overnight show had more talk and less music. He began inviting celebrity guests for talk in the studio and continued to take calls.

The move away from an exclusive emphasis on *celebrity* guests was the result of a controversial incident at New York's Stork Club in which Gray and his program became embroiled. Apparently Josephine Baker went to the club once in the early 1950s as part of her campaign to integrate the nightclubs. She got in, but the owner refused to let her be waited on. After sitting there for forty-five minutes, she went to WMCA's studio to be a guest on Gray's talkshow and discuss the incident; the following evening she returned and brought her lawyer. This angered Walter Winchell and Ed Sullivan, both of whom were newspaper columnists as well as broadcasters who showcased celebrities; each saw celebrity talkshow appearances as competition. Winchell, an influential show business commentator whose attention could mean a great deal to the success of a performer, went so far as to ban from his column anyone who appeared on Gray's show. The subsequent drying-up of celebrity guests forced Gray to turn to more ordinary individuals such as "interesting cab drivers" and, significantly, politicians. Consequently, local overnight talk radio became—and has remained—"more political," a result that Gray thought made it "more interesting." He estimates having interviewed some 40,000 guests over a period of almost forty years. His explanation of talk radio's appeal: "People like to eavesdrop."[54] Broadcasters were beginning to perceive controversy and voyeurism as talkshow trademarks.

Call-in programming also developed out of the top-40 format. Request lines, initiated to encourage listener loyalty and generate data on music preferences, opened the way for the use of live or taped on-air requests. Most of these request "actualities" involved (and still involve) short bits of conversation. In the mid-1950s Todd Storz put a call-in show on WHB Kansas City, while Pittsburgh's KDKA had a late-evening program called *Party Line*.[55] The technique projected a station's desired audience into its programming—a key part of radio's economic reintegration into its locality with the decline of the networks. At the same time, the call-in request echoed a modernist participatory thrust permitting public expressiveness and self-assertion. These actualities eventually grew in length and in the late 1950s evolved into full-blown call-in shows on news or community subjects. These coincided with the emergence of the local community forum program featuring caller questions for local officials.[56] Clearly, as the call-in show gained a foothold it would maintain its political dimension. The mid-1960s would find 80 percent of stations, regardless of format, carrying some talk programming.[57]

Talk radio had emerged as a discrete format by October of 1961, when KABC Los Angeles converted completely to talk programming—a process begun over a year earlier. KMOX St. Louis and KVOR Colorado Springs made similar gradual conversions at about the same time. Of the three, KABC and KMOX (a CBS affiliate) were network owned and operated, pointing up what is still a significant institutional pattern: many of the continuous and successful talk radio stations have been network owned and operated, heavily involved also in news programming, and located in or near major urban areas. As a full-time format, talk radio requires a larger staff per program than does music; there are costly tele-phone charges involved in national and global interviewing; and news programming with strong coverage of the local beat—an element vital to the talk station for its supply of the in-demand talk topics—is also very labor-intensive and costly. Hence, network ownership underwrote a long period of station losses until ratings and billings rose to profitability.[58] The format's urban preference, a continuation of the participatory urban entertainment practices of cabaret or amusement park, stems from its need for an abundance of "hot" news issues, figures, experts, and guests, along with callers willing and able to engage in discussion. The contem-porary city offers a setting of exploitable instability through its constant stream of novelty, people, and events.

All-talk was not the only high-overhead, nonmusic AM format to appear in the 1960s. All-news radio was the other. Certain similarities between the two are striking, and their symbiotic relationship during this period was critical. The June 27, 1966, issue of the trade publica-tion *Broadcasting* contains in tandem special reports on the emergence of talk and news formats, both of which were "motivated by the urge to sound different" on the part of AM stations competing in urban mar-kets saturated with top-40 and threatened by the imminent growth and nonduplication of what had largely been sister FM stations. Like talk radio, all-news stations sought and got an older audience, although its composition was (and still apparently is) predominantly male and rela-tively affluent. All-news is also much more labor-intensive than music-format stations, especially automated ones relying on "beautiful music" or, today, twenty-four-hour satellite-fed syndications. The first five all-news stations in or serving the United States—Westinghouse's WINS New York and KYW Philadelphia; Arthur W. Arundel's WAVA Arling-ton, West Virginia; WNUS Chicago; and Gordon McClendon's XTRA Tijuana—each required a staff of thirty to fifty, about twenty of whom were on-air news personnel. Like talk radio, all-news stations regarded themselves as *services* to the listening community rather than *stations* in the traditional sense.

At that time, all-news and all-talk shared the distinction of being the only formats, with the exception of "beautiful music," that built their ratings and rate cards on "cumes"—cumulative listenership over a number of quarter-hour periods—rather than the single quarter-hour listening totals used to compare music stations. It seemed that the unpredictable and constant turnover of news stories offered a listener-appealing novelty in contrast to the repetition of the music stations' tight playlists. This turned out to be especially true in 1967 when WCBS-AM in New York, as the eighth all-news station, made what had been essentially a rotating-headlines format (as WINS still is today) more *feature*-oriented to hold listeners longer. Audience loyalty and the more "foreground" nature of news and talk programs' reception, as opposed to the distinctly "background" nature of music listening, increased the two new formats' appeal for advertisers, enabling them to charge more on average for an ad minute. Such was, and still is, the basis of their profitability.

There was one significant institutional difference, however, in the development of the news and talk formats: whereas the networks pioneered talk radio, the first all-news stations were introduced by individual owners. These included Gordon McClendon, who gave top-40 jingle-laden, constant-promotion sound and conceived the "beautiful music" format.[59] Talent costs best explain this difference. Popular talk hosts become distinctive, recognizable personalities—able to command higher salaries, thanks to the loyal followings they can build, than can interchangeable news readers. The higher costs of radio "stars" necessitates the financial capacity of a large, established network. Nevertheless, the distinction between the all-news and all-talk formats has become blurred in what is now called news/talk, which mixes substantial network and local news programming with an array of call-in shows that utilize news material. By the late 1980s, news was becoming a bigger part of the mix at such stations "because of a general trend in society toward a need to consume product in a more immediate fashion," as one news/talk station executive put it.[60] The satisfaction of a mobile society's desire for immediate information is the way news/talk practitioners have defined their "calling."[61]

Despite talk radio's expense, the risk proved worth it for a number of the AM stations that converted in the 1960s. Though the cost of conversion ran some stations' expenses up by 300 percent, their "desire to be different" led to ratings gains of 25 to 250 percent. Whichever sub-format talk stations subscribed to—*call-in* (mixing live or taped studio interview or informational programs with listeners' phone calls), *talk/ interview* (studio interviews, no call-ins), or *news/talk*—they all relied heavily on news. Each sought "to get the listener interested and involved" through the catalyst of the on-air personality, who could be "solicitous, insulting, soothing, serious, or flip" and whose subject matter could be "anything under the sun."[62] With "never to be boring" as their primary objective, hosts, unlike DJs, had to work very hard to be well informed and develop topics of maximum interest to a now "foreground" audience (many of the first talk hosts had originally been DJs accustomed to a "background" format). The image of the talkhost as shirt-sleeved worker has an institutional and historical basis in the labor-intensive demands of the form.

The host-personality could also add more authority to the advertising inserts by reading them him- or herself. A 1966 study commissioned by CBS-owned talk stations suggested that "a radio advertiser would be justified in spending up to twice as much, on a cost-per-thousand basis, for a talk station's audience as for a music audience."[63] This is usually still the case. Despite the fact that its predominantly male audience is considered harder to reach and thus is more expensive in cost-per-thousand terms, talk radio delivers a more desirable foreground audience, attracts older and more affluent adults, and stands out in large urban markets crowded with music formats. Further, it shows greater public service and community involvement (this was especially helpful before the 1981 radio deregulation and the 1987 repeal of the Fairness Doctrine's equal-time rule) and promotes loyalty (long listening periods).[64] Significantly, all-news radio shares each of these advantages.

The growing popularity of "audience-connected radio" in the 1960s was evident in CBS's claim that the seven radio stations it owned and operated, all using a talk format at the time, reported electronically recording well over a million attempted phone calls in a one-month period in 1966.[65] Station managers still saw the format as requiring large markets (at least 250,000 to 500,000 people) because of its expense and need for high advertising rates and enough stimulating issues, people, and resources to sustain interesting talk from day to day over a period of years.[66] Talk and all-news stations both took years to establish themselves in their markets and turn a profit. Once they did, however, their high degree of listener loyalty made them virtually impervious to the problems that periodically plague music stations: the ups and downs of the music industry and the fickleness of the music audience.[67]

A look at the practices of talk radio's first eighteen stations suggests the degree to which impact and controversy, along with news, information, and service, were their programming objectives. For management, the seemingly uncontrollable chance elements inherent in talk radio would also prove yet necessary and appealing part of the format. Boston's WEEI steered conversation toward the "gut" 1960s issues whenever possible: "money, taxes, religion, teenagers, politics, race troubles." Boston competitor WNAC put its controversial talk programs on later at night, gearing its daytime and early evening shows to "talk for fun": recipe call-ins, on-air classifieds, advice. Its late-night, controversy-centered call-in show, *Comment*, dealt with such issues of the day as LSD, the "God is Dead" movement, and draft-card burning. Similar shows on other stations had such names as *Opinion Please*, *This Is Los Angeles*, *Viewpoint*, *Feedback*, *Denver PM*, *Controversy*, *Mayor's Beef Session*, and *Anything Goes*.[68] WATV Birmingham claimed that its "no holds barred" afternoon call-in show was so stimulating and informative that it was monitored by the local newspapers and wire services "for the news it makes." Interview shows too began sensationalizing their talk with the help of their news departments. One Atlanta station pursued prostitutes and drug addicts and dealers in order to attract male audiences in the afternoon without losing its predominantly female audience (most daytime talk programming, of course, targeted women, as relatively few adult women were as yet working outside the home).[69]

Trade advertisements for talk radio stations used controversy as a dramatic appeal. KBON Omaha offered potential advertisers "provocative 'get together' radio" that generated listener attentiveness and knowledge: "KBON people *know* what's going on."[70] KABC promoted itself as provocative and exciting, characterizing its talk host Bob Grant as "the most controversial figure on nighttime radio"; Pamela Mason's conversation was "uninhibited," and sports talk host Jim Healy was sparking "excitement and controversy." At the same time, these personalities gave the advertiser a "far-reaching, money-moving voice."[71] The voice of the talk radio personality might be stimulating and attractive for the listener/consumer, but for the advertiser it was billed as penetrating and "money-moving." Talk radio's economic strategy was to exploit news-generated controversies and contemporary problems about which people were emotionally charged—and therefore vulnerable—so as to get their deeper attention and more effectively sell them something. Because the commercials often were (and still are) read by the host, their degree of program "interruption" was questionable, while credibility (salience) remained high.

Still, the upstart format was widely seen as dangerous and unusually demanding of the station's resources. The manager of WBBM Chicago envisioned Fairness Doctrine–based complaints arising from the perception that some shows were too one-sided. Extending the interrelationship of talk radio and news was the fact that the legal and regulatory issues facing the news/talk host—libel, accuracy, the Fairness Doctrine, Section 315 (equal time rule)—were similar to those facing the broadcast journalist. Moreover, the correlation detected in the mid-1970s between "slow news" periods and a decline in talk radio's ratings prompted a significant number of station managers to predict "a dismal outlook for the format," suggesting that talk stations needed to be aware of controversies "almost before they become news."[72] It also motivated talk radio to ignite some controversy of its own; given its financial dependence on sensation, there was strong incentive for the talkshow to make its own news, perhaps even to the point of fabrication—a charge occasionally leveled at the journalists as well (of course, the interview situation does manufacture news).

Talk radio's moment-to-moment unpredictability troubled the new format's managers in an industry that fears any absence of control. Yet it is those very elements of chance, fostered by call-in participation, that have given the format its uniqueness, surprise, drama, and appeal. The "alternative" FM radio that emerged in the 1960s—"alternative" in that it was noncommercial as well as experimental in its programming—productively engaged talk radio's chance, chaos, and participatory elements. Steve Post, former personality at New York's free-form WBAI and a pioneer in alternative radio, tells of how the station's late-night call-in show, *Radio Unnameable*, became a live information source—a "switchboard"—during the 1968 Columbia University unrest; those occupying buildings as well as observers called in. (Acting as crisis nerve centers is something both commercial and noncommercial talk stations now do, especially during such disasters as hurricanes.) Noncommercial radio could also be indulgent with "nut" callers, such as WBAI's "enema lady."[73]

From an institutional standpoint, however, the *commercial* talk radio formats seemed caught in a productive dilemma. WTAK Detroit's general manager confessed that he had "no illusions" about talk radio, calling it an "expensive, demanding, dangerous, and unpredictable" format requiring "a completely aware, intelligent, and articulate staff" and generating many on-air developments that "can cause ulcers." WNBC's general manager defined audience participation programming as a "sort of telephone Russian roulette" that takes considerable talent to play. The management of KABC and KNX in Los Angeles recognized that talk radio talent was hard to find because, in the words of KABC's general manager, it needs "somebody who knows a little bit about a lot of things." The head of WACE Springfield (Massachusetts) noted that his talk personalities were suffering from "incipient battle fatigue" due to so many on-air hours and the dearth of equally talented replacements.[74] But with the development of several talkshow formulas—the political gripe program, sports talk, a gamut of advice shows—along with the introduction of call screening procedures, delay systems, and computers, talk radio management would strive for and achieve greater control over its "Russian roulette" by the 1970s.

From television's *Candid Camera* and the talkshow to Marshall McLuhan's concept of electronic "retribalization," "*involvement* and *participation* became ever more urgent cultural imperatives" in the 1960s.[75] As Andrew Ross has shown, the decade's countercultural discourses demonized technology, including the mass media, and sought a return to premodern, oral styles and practices.[76] Yet those discourses were finally postmodern in that they incorporated modernist, transgressive strains as well as premodern orality in their confrontational and romantic politics: "modernism in the streets." The radio call-in show developed as part of a period that rediscovered what Morris Dickstein called "the joys and horrors of politics."[77] The audience participation talkshow, adapted from radio to television in 1967 by *Donahue*, related personalized knowledge and expression in a way that echoed the decade's "lust for deep experience" and emphasis on the *personal* element at work in a history now regarded as "lumbering" and "out-of-control," and in which the "fetish of objectivity" had collapsed.[78]

Like 1960s "new journalism," audience participation news/talk radio was a revolt against impersonal authority, the stodgy, and the forbidden; it also affirmed authentic selfhood—another key quest of the decade—over objectified knowledge in a social order in which "the arbitrary, the terrible, the irrational" had become routinized.[79] Like a Vonnegut novel, the talkshow was a "promiscuous mixture." The ideal of the melting pot had collapsed; differences would no longer be repressed.[80] A new Romanticism emerged that restored self, personality, and ego as conduits of knowledge. Much of this discourse was anti-machine. Broadcasting's exploitation of interactivity with the spectator was a way of appearing to mitigate its modernist "machineness" while at the same time *using* it in what Fredric Jameson has called the postmodern's "symbiotic or parasitical relationship" with the modern.[81] The call-in show could also mitigate the modernist "culture of expertise"[82] by allowing the host and audience participants to question a guest-expert. Participation in the broadcast apparatus appeared to allow "everyman" to take control of an out-of-control technosocial situation. Yet the broadcast industry was *itself* also getting control of the situation—even redefining it—by textualizing and commodifying listeners and spectators, their diversity, and even their resistance, through the talkshow. This happened just as mass cultural forms were appropriating aesthetic modernism.

Many talk radio stations were helped with their programming's voraciousness by the growth of syndication. *The Joe Pyne Show*, which originated as a local offering at KLAC Los Angeles in October 1965, featured the era's most flamboyant talk host and was syndicated to 165 other stations; Pyne eventually moved to television (1966–69) via KTTV Los Angeles. His formula consisted in inviting offbeat guests to appear, only to attack them and give his "beefing" studio audience the chance to do the same.[83] KABC syndicated Pamela Mason. WOR's *Jean Shepherd* show was syndicated, as was Barry Gray's. Other prominent talk syndications included *Joyce Brothers*, *William F. Buckley News and Comment*, and *Our Changing World with Earl Nightingale*. The rise of talk syndications also led to a renewed demand for syndicated programming in general, especially for dramas such as *The Shadow, The Green Hornet,* and *Gang-busters*—radio shows that had disappeared by the 1960s.[84] It seems ironic that the advent of talk radio initially made possible by the financial depth of the established networks and the conversion of the stations they owned and operated, also stimulated their competitors, the syndicators. By the 1980s the further expansion of broadcast talk would make syndicators even more powerful and encourage them to start their own networks— the Fox television network has thus far been the most successful.

All of this suggests that talk radio has been caught in a contradiction from the outset. On the one hand, its deliberately provocative, less inhibited, more spontaneous quality is, in the industry's perception, exactly what makes it uniquely attractive to adult audiences neglected by music formats. By stimulating a greater depth of listener involvement, talk radio's "foregroundness" has promised more advertiser effectiveness and thus justified higher rates. On the other hand, such a listener-attracting strategy is dangerous. Libel, Fairness Doctrine violations, monotony, boring or pathetic or "too old" callers, the shortage of hosts who can "make the mike catch fire,"[85] the heavy workload and expense—all these problems have threatened the format's economic viability.[86] Most of the threats stem essentially from a lack of control—far less a problem in other formats. To survive, talk radio had somehow to contain rather than eliminate its perilous unpredictability.

Unpredictability connotes a sense of credibility vital to the talkshow's effectiveness, but it also makes for a productive instability, a *use* of chaos, that lets talk radio stand out against the tight, predictable formulas of hit stations, romance novels, action-adventure films—the whole formulaic array of popular culture. Call-in talk radio (and its television offshoots) has become a paradigm for a commodified medium-spectator relationship that responds to postmodern conditions in which meaning constantly fluctuates. It reproduces the consumer culture's shifting array of goods and the lifestyle connotations necessary to their appeal. Its ever changing, "throwaway" form appealingly and effectively (re)produces information in bite-sized packages for the information-overloaded subject. That the call-in program erupted in the historical construct we now call the 1960s—a time of disruption and debates, wars of words and ideologies—seems fitting. The talkshow successfully commodified this disruption, turning controversy, politics, and "shocking" alternatives into consumables. Subjectivities also became consumable; the wildness of the decade could be appropriated. A 1960s guidebook issued by the Metromedia station group for its talk hosts warned "Remember please, we are broadcasters first and worldsavers second."[87]

The broadcasters' control techniques have represented the modernist urge for efficiency through clear definition, planning, and predictability of outcome in commodity production. But talk radio—produced also by the participating spectator who cannot be fully controlled—depends upon a measure of the uncontrollable to remain desirable to the spectator-participant. Having intentionally generated an instability, even danger, broadcasters have tried to control it only enough to maintain talk radio's cathexis, ratings, and reputation as marginal, déclassé, and thus more credible and accessible: to contain its contradictions without subverting the format's appeal. One problem with respect to caller unpredictability was that because talk radio attracted an older demographic, too many of the callers might be old, infirm, and sad-sounding to a point of causing more "attractive" younger adults (those with greater purchasing power) to tune out. To attract young male audiences, prized in the 1960s as a hard-to-reach segment with disposable income, the early news/talk stations added sports call-ins. Such callers also provided the station the "sound" advantage of being more energetic, upbeat, and less boring.[88]

To weed out off-subject, libelous, harassing, or repeat callers, "seamless" live editing techniques had to be used without diminishing talk radio's rough spontaneity and realism.[89] One result was the employment of a call screener (sometimes also called the operator or producer). Not all talk programs have screeners—Larry King still eschews them—but their use continues despite their added costs. Too many poorly selected calls, so the institutional logic goes, would cost the station even more dearly in the loss of the most desirable audiences. Caller demographics are particularly important to "shrink talk" shows; callers who reveal a great deal about themselves prove essential to the kind of audience such shows attract. Apparently, "shaky, elderly voices . . . repel more youthful listeners"; ABC's usually sympathetic psychologist Dr. Toni Grant confessed that "they're very hard to listen to" and keeping them off the air was "a reality of radio programming."[90]

Sometimes "too old" callers are simply told, "Sorry, your call doesn't fit the program"; one station even referred them to the local Medicare phone number.[91] More often, such callers are delayed or "dumped"—to use the industry's unceremonious word—through the screener's continuous "call-stacking," which means altering the lineup of calls, as they come in, in order of preference. Thus, screeners need not hang up on unwanted callers; they simply sink lower and lower in the stack.[92]

The screener's call-stacking is indicated on a computer visible to the host, who sees the caller's first name only (to provide anonymity and discourage impostors) and a summary of his or her comment. Additional control is provided by delay systems—originally using tape, now digital—that retard the airing of the program four to seven seconds so that, with the push of a "panic button," an operator may delete any profanity, personal attack, libel, or copyright infringement. Finally, twenty-four-hour taped logs, using very slow-speed recording ($15/32$ inches per second), give the station a record in case legal action or complaints arise.

These behind-the-scenes controls suggest the considerable extent to which talk radio has shifted from caller- to listener-orientation since the 1970s.[93] Less than one-half of 1 percent of listeners ever call in, and the advertiser is ultimately interested in reaching the listener-*consumer*.[94] One radio industry consultant considers each call-in the equivalent of a record on a music station's playlist: like a record, it must be carefully selected so as to not "turn off" the listeners.[95] The caller thus becomes a commodity, a product that must suit listeners as the station defines them.[96]

News and politically oriented controversy had been the topical mainstays of the "calls of the riled" format as well as of its most successful, "let it all hang out," hosts: Joe Pyne, Les Crane, Long John Nebel, Barry Farber, Bob Grant, Barry Gray, Brad Crandall, Ron Owens, and Owen Spann, among others. By the early 1970s, however, as the intense controversies of the 1960s—instabilities so effectively exploited in the rise of talk radio—died down, talk stations had to mine or invent new areas of controversy to maintain their ratings. In preparation for the eventuality of having few or no callers, hosts learned to enter the studio with newspaper clippings of presumed listener interest to support a monologue. They might also have an "expert phone list" of individuals who could be called to sustain a program.

By 1974, when some 113 stations had the talk format,[97] WERE Cleveland had begun a variation it titled *People Power*—aggressive, "soapbox" talk—and persuaded several other stations around the country to join in presenting "a radio explosion guaranteed to give you a drugless, psychedelic high." [98] Talk stations needed new ways to generate "legitimate" excitement, pleasure, and listenership. One positive development was the Federal Communications Commission's decision to drop proposals that would have required stations to fully record all call-in shows, make the tapes available to any interested parties for fifteen days after the broadcast, and (especially inhibiting for both station and callers) get and keep the name and address of each caller. [99]

The fact that such proposals were made suggests the kind and degree of fear lurking around the growth of the controversial radio call-in show. Apparently the government was reflecting the broadcast industry's own desire for more control over a form built on the spontaneity, diversity, and indeterminacy of personal narratives. Or perhaps the pressure was shifting to the federal regulators, now that the broadcast industry had assumed as much control as it needed to make talk radio "work" as an advertising vehicle. Significantly, the FCC's next intervention was related to the talk industry's post-1960s attempt at new, provocative, audience-grabbing material as well as a type of program that would cultivate young female audiences. That attempt was known as "topless radio."

"Female-only, two-way talk" was the title the form's practitioners preferred. KGBS, a Storer-owned station in Los Angeles, was pondering ways of expanding its midday talk audience, which in 1970 was primarily made up of young men. (This was unusual, but Los Angeles was a large and unusual market in that it had a number of talk stations to absorb older listeners, including talk powerhouse KABC.) Seeking to widen its youthful audience to include women, the station's new manager, Ray Stanfield, saw young *men* as the subject most likely to appeal to young women. The result was *Feminine Forum*, a midday call-in show intending, in Stanfield's words, to air "light, humorous conversations about the relationships between men and women." [100] From the broadcaster's perspective, the program's design would assure sufficient control while allowing uninhibited, sex-oriented conversation. Only calls from young-sounding women who remained anonymous were accepted, but the substance of the call was not screened. The success of *Feminine Forum*, hosted by former DJ Bill Ballance, led to widespread imitation and the KGBS show's syndication. It marked the beginning of the talkshow's intensely interpersonal focus, now epitomized by *Oprah* and *Donahue*.

Fifty to sixty stations nationwide were running such programs when FCC Chairman Dean Burch and Senator John Pastore announced that they were considering a test case against "topless" programming, which the FCC chairman denounced as "smut" during the March 1973 annual meeting of the National Association of Broadcasters. By that June, the trend was in decline. In an effort to justify these programs (in other than ratings terms) to critics and the regulators, station managers claimed that the phenomenon was consistent with other taboo-shattering developments of the era—television's *All in the Family*, increasingly explicit soap operas, the popularity of sex manuals—and a sign of progress and openness in providing women with a new kind of useful information unavailable elsewhere.[101] The managers thus invoked as justification the discourse of modernity deeply associated with participation, popular knowledge, progress, and transgression. But such claims, made as the feminist movement was gaining momentum, obscure the programs' shrewd design from an efficiency standpoint: they attracted young women to talk radio *without* losing young male listeners, who, although excluded from call-in participation, could nonetheless enjoy a voyeuristic, "safe," and even instructional relationship with the conversation and its participants.

The "shock radio" phenomenon begun in the 1980s seems to mimic "topless" radio's trajectory with respect to the regulators, and its appeal with respect to audiences. Although "shock" relies more on the comic, uninhibited "shock jock" personality rather than on audience participation, programs such as Howard Stern's morning show on WXRK New York have kept young listeners, especially teens, from abandoning radio (especially AM), which has an aging listenership.[102] The regulators responded to shock radio officially and strictly in 1989 by citing three stations for violation of the federal statute against indecency.[103]

As regulatory fears around indecency began to outweigh waning fears of civil liability, industry efforts to broaden talk radio's audience turned from "topless" to advice programs, particularly psychological call-ins. Dr. Toni Grant's show on the ABC talk stations epitomized the 1970s trend, and still does; psychological advice shows would continue to grow in the 1980s. That they were the industry's "safer" successor to female-only call-in programming is made especially vivid by the fact that in 1977 Grant's show replaced Bill Ballance's on KABC Los Angeles.[104] The psychological talk show could take special advantage of the anonymity provided by the telephone's low-resolution carbon microphone, which gives callers a sense of safety in revealing their most intimate problems. At the same time, the listener remains a voyeur—also safe.

The 1970s saw what had begun chiefly as a single format—older male-oriented all-talk or news/talk—fragment into several subgenres: midday advice, talk/service, and psychological talk (attracting female listeners); sports talk (attracting young male audiences); and "noncontroversial talk." The last was exemplified by the humorous, loyalty-inspiring Ludlow Porch in Atlanta, whose show featured "wacko" guests, and Herb Jepko, the host of Mutual's national *Nitecap*; callers widely considered Jepko "like a member of the family." *The Larry King Show*, which combines issue and celebrity interviews with unscreened call-ins, replaced Jepko in 1977 in Mutual's attempt to attract younger and more affluent audiences.[105] Meanwhile, the political news/talk "gripe" show, begun in the 1960s as a mainstay of the new format, was continuing to draw 1980s audiences with the rude, conservative, yet transgressive tone that would earn it the name "hot talk."[106]

Television Talk and Audience Participation

Both audience participation and transgression found their way, separately, into the television talkshow. During the 1950s NBC President Sylvester "Pat" Weaver's innovation of more casual, live fringe-time programming led to the celebrity talk/variety *Tonight* show and the news/talk *Today* show. Weaver approached the nascent medium with a progressivist optimism, seeing its "tremendous potentialities for upgrading humanity." Yet he also envisioned its best performer as a "communicator"—a word capturing a sense of interactivity—who had to be a "showman, thinker, commentator, narrator, and enlightener all rolled into one." In his role as *Today* host, Dave Garroway was conceived as just such a "communicator." Almost prophetically, Weaver foresaw the widespread use of satellite communications, instant and multisource random accessibility, the growth of fax usage, and, most significantly, interactivity. Television would be "a great electronic receiving *and* transmitting machine" (emphasis added). In a rejoinder to critics, who were claiming harmful effects, Weaver constructed television as ultimately beneficial in its *inclusiveness;* it would be "the greatest social force *and* the greatest selling force in American history." His pioneering of multiple sponsorship and the programming of fringe time with talkshows, along with his prime-time scheduling of inspiring "spectaculars" and "telementaries," were all consistent with his vision of inclusiveness. For Weaver, television had to "do good" while remaining profitable. It had to be a democratic form of cultural uplift and commerce—"the shining center of the home"— offering "every man" access to knowledge, pleasure, experimentation, immediacy, constant novelty, and the unpredictable. The very program names—*Today, Tonight*—suggest his attempt at breadth and immediacy. By 1954, after only two years on the air, *Today* was NBC's most profitable show.[107]

Today and *Tonight* relied on interviews combined, magazine-style, with various other bits—performances, presentations, news, and some audience participation—often in forms that took the host into the audience. Steve Allen, one of *Tonight*'s successful early hosts, was "a man in a suit and tie surrounded by [the] madness" of a show that cultivated the spontaneous and unpredictable.[108] Johnny Carson's occasional skit "The Edge of Wetness"—in which the cameras picked out close-ups of audience members about whom Carson narrated a soap opera send-up complete with melodramatic organ accompaniment—descended from the sorts of audience participation that went into the earlier shows.[109] The skit played with the audience's amateur status and its embarrassing incongruity with "good" (that is, professional) casting, as well as the clash of the audience member's face with Carson's narration. His characterization of each close-up imagined a secret, incongruous sexual liason with another audience "character," thus implicating strangers with each other in mock intimacy and drawing them into the spectacle with and through Carson in a comedy of forced interactivity. The embarrassment of amateur participation in a professionalized media frame provided the comic tension. Its use of "real people" in all their performative roughness exposed the implied constructedness—even phoniness—of the soap opera.

In yet another inversion, the "cast of characters" from the studio audience also doubled as their own spectators in the mortifying moment when they saw themselves "performing."

Their reactions had much in common with the famous "takes" Carson used to cover *himself* in an embarrassing performance moment, when a joke fell flat. The audience response that the take followed—an audible groan—was a useful part of his performance; spectators became part of the joke as well as its receivers, part of the production of the very product they were consuming. From the producer's standpoint, the efficiency of this—rooted in the eclecticism of the consumer-spectator-participant— almost goes without saying. Such studio audience participation helped materially sustain Carson's *Tonight* five nights a week for more than three decades. Reactions to a joke, even a bad one, became as productive as the limited number of "good" jokes that could be written over the same three decades. Such reactions constitute a dialogue, a form of talk between host and audience. Yet the surprise and pleasure of "The Edge of Wetness" lay not only in its violation of the "safe" spectatorial space of the audience members but in its ridicule of their amateur status. The broadcast institution negotiates the threat of interactivity by asserting its narrativizing *and* discursive control over it.

Arthur Godfrey and Art Linkletter easily made the transition to television with their relaxed, homey styles. *Art Linkletter's House Party*, known earlier as *People Are Funny*, was on television and radio for over twenty years. As a midday show, it addressed a largely female audience of wives and mothers. The sponsor was Parke-Davis, a pharmaceutical company whose products—Sominex and Geritol—Linkletter pitched from a wheelaround table. Like so many other talkshows involving a studio audience, *House Party* used a stage from which the host could direct his address simultaneously to live studio audience and home spectators. Both segments of the audience shared an interlocutionary axis, thereby strengthening their identification with each other.

An episode from the March 7, 1961, show demonstrates how it combined talk with elements of the game show to commodify the audience as consumers and "normal people." [110] The opener begins with a pan of the well-lit female audience enthusiastically talking to one another as if at a party. The women appear to be enjoying themselves, implicitly content in their roles as wives, mothers, consumers, audience members, and (stereo-typically) talkers. The show's title then appears in a crude drawing of a contemporary house.

As ingenuous, "authentic" performers, children too figure prominently here (and in other "house party" shows).[111] The first segment of this epi-sode concerns the on-stage reappearance of a "normal" three-year-old girl who has had eleven days of dancing lessons following the technique of instructor Fred Totten. After the screening of the girl's first *House Party* appearance and lesson, and some comic ad lib between her and Linkletter, the girl, under Totten's direction, dances. Following the ap-plause and laughter produced as Linkletter plays off the girl's confused exit with her winnings—a doll and carriage—Linkletter assures parents that despite the short attention spans of even normal children, they *can* be taught. *House Party* thus becomes an advice talkshow, drawing upon expertise as well as the experience of everyday individuals.

The second segment follows Linkletter pitching Sominex as a nonnar-cotic, "one hundred percent safe," and "non-habit-forming" sleep aid. He then walks into the studio audience to ask several women to tell him "the silliest things they ever did." Each participant gets an autographed copy of Linkletter's book, *The Confessions of a Happy Man*. As each woman tells her story (clearly, these participants have been preselected, and Linkletter seems prepared), the host engages in seemingly sponta-neous comic repartee. He assures them that such silliness is normal and that he has done worse; after all, "people are funny." From out in the studio audience, Linkletter then "bumps" the show's final segment—the daily feature in which he speaks with four school children[112]—before breaking to a commercial for Wisk detergent.

The sense of the "normal" projected by the show's participation con-flated normality with consumption, obedience, and—for women and children, at least—silliness. As subject, the participant was an amalgam: woman, consumer, parent, a "normal" and obedient person who did not take herself too seriously. If Edward R. Murrow's *Person to Per-son* fostered a sense of intimacy and voyeuristic pleasure through tech-nology by seeming to bring host and spectator into a celebrity's home, where the celebrity sat before a camera,[113] *House Party* offered the simu-lated sociality of a "party" by bringing the housewife into the studio—

and the advertised products into her home. The borders between home, stage, and marketplace—between spectacle and dialogue—seemed to have collapsed. The co-presence of the spectator's and the host's body and vocality, the performance space, and the media apparatus were all redefining "spectatorship" by inscribing aspects of folk culture and interpersonal rituals, "people are funny" storytelling and anecdotal personal experience.

The television audience participant's sharing of that experience, a practice avoided by the participatory game shows but begun in Linkletter's forays into the audience and in such shows as *Queen for a Day*,[114] was taken still further in CBS's *Stand Up and Be Counted!* This daytime program presaged *Donahue* in its structuring of audience participation, its personal depth, and its political overtones. Each thirty-minute show dealt with one "average" individual's personal dilemma; viewers sent letters describing their problems in the hope of becoming a "contestant." A live studio audience of some two hundred persons were seated before a stage with a front porch setting, the kind typical of an old Victorian house, with a couple of chairs behind the railing and an American eagle adorning the wall. Host Robert Russell addressed home and studio audience from the stage/porch—a symbolic space in which public and private could meet—saying that "the American way of life" involves dropping in on a troubled neighbor and helping her make a decision; he called neighborliness "a wonderful word" and "something in which *you* may participate . . . this show stars *you*, the audience." Claiming "I don't want to wave the flag, but . . . ," he would remind us "what neighbors do to neighbors elsewhere"—a thinly veiled Cold War reference as the eagle on the wall loomed over his shoulder. The introduction ended: "You may have a chance to win a half-million dollars in cash."

One 1956 program deals with a New Yorker, Gertrude Gurin. Her dilemma: should she use her inheritance for travel and "living it up" after spending her life unmarried while caring for her aged parents, or invest the money in her brother's business in the hope of a comfortable retirement? Russell interviews Miss Gurin on the porch, then invites audience members to come forward and "help our American neighbor reach a decision." He passes the microphone around to those at the railing, who are overwhelmingly women and who almost unanimously feel that Miss

Gurin should spend the money and take the trip. After they take their seats, the entire audience votes on the issue by "standing up and being counted." The majority agrees that Miss Gurin should take the trip. She will return next week to give her decision. Meanwhile, home viewers are invited to write in *their* advice; the best letter will win a Plymouth and a trip to any one of a number of American cities.

Last week's "neighbor," another middle-aged woman, then appears to share her decision about *her* personal dilemma: whether to marry and move out of the area where her roots are, or stay put and forgo the marriage. (The program strains to define each problem in simple either-or terms, and all participants must work within those terms.) She has decided on the latter, despite the recommendation of marriage from 77 percent of last week's studio audience and 68 percent of the letters. Russell then reads the week's prize-winning letter and awards the contestant her prizes: an air conditioner, an easy chair, and a refrigerator-freezer. "We hope you'll be happy forever," he says, and closes the show: "Stand up and be counted—its good for you, and its good for your neighbors." Once again, traditional ideology connoted by neighborly, nostalgic "front-porch" (interestingly, as opposed to "back-fence") social practices are linked not only with patriotism but with promotion, consumption, and an implicit cure for the 1950s housewife's domestic isolation. All are inscribed as typical and even desirable in American life.[115]

On other kinds of television talkshows, the transgressive strain reappeared—confrontation, controversy, emotion, political debate—but audience participation came to these somewhat later. In Linkletter's shows, *Stand Up*, and any number of game shows, audience participation traded on a well-lit, breezy ambiance of friendly, comic banter. They also played off the audience-participants' unpolished everydayness and amateur status, which was somehow more "real" and ingenuous in a mediated environment. "Shock talk" originally developed in the only place it could—syndication—because such shows were not bound to the same rigid broadcast standards as the networks.[116]

One network program, however, did show the way to greater emotionalism and controversy for the celebrity talkshow while also making it more promotional. *Tonight* during the Jack Paar era (1957–62), according to David Marc, was "a remarkably banal fantasy world of angry feuds and sentimental affections that became the subject of the show"; Paar used it "as a soapbox from which to denounce his enemies," particularly newspaper columnists such as Dorothy Kilgallen and Ed Sullivan. Sullivan accused him of exploiting entertainers by paying them only minimum union scale, though in fact they were more than repaid by the chance to promote their latest projects in a prominent forum hosted by a very popular, highly charged personality. To Marc, Sullivan's response suggests the degree to which Paar's *Tonight* threateningly blurred the distinction between the presentational, representational, and documentary television modes.[117] This blurring, amplified still further by audience participation, would become a key talkshow tendency.

Over his five-year tenure, Paar's list of guests ranged from ordinary individuals to celebrities to such major political figures as Robert F. Kennedy and Fidel Castro—a range broader than that of the current late evening talkshows, with the exception of *Nightline*. When Johnny Carson took over late in 1962, *Tonight* assumed a more easygoing demeanor. The program on which Paar made his first appearance aired on July 29, 1957; gave his first audience a peek at the unpredictable emotionalism that would become part of his appeal.

His opening announcer, movie character actor Franklin Pangborn, is also one of his guests and heralds the show as "live from New York" while standing at a microphone somewhere offstage. Paar's other guests are singer Helen O'Connell and actor Stanley Holloway (from the hit musical, *My Fair Lady*). Paar does not do a monologue; instead, the opening bit is Helen O'Connell singing a jazzy "Let's Get Away from It All" to Kokomo, the chimp from the *Today* show (an interesting instance of talkshow intertextuality), on a crude travel agency set. Following the song Paar walks on and talks with the "couple," making some deprecating remarks about his new show. There is another comic skit, some promotional banter with guests from behind his desk (at which he also demonstrates one sponsor's product, a Polaroid camera), and a piano piece by bandleader José Mellis. Thereafter, the show collapses. Paar keeps looking and asking for cues. He appears lost, then depressed, and finally overwhelmed, confessing that he is "just not up to" the show. The screen abruptly goes black. The risks of the semiscripted talkshow and the constant threat of its succumbing to chaos have been realized. Paar's emotional affect, presumably authentic rather than mere "play," is so crucial to his talkshow that it decides the premiere's abrupt ending.

Confrontation as entertainment developed in the late 1950s and early 1960s, when "insult humor" was gaining a foothold with the likes of Jack E. Leonard (who eventually replaced Paar for a short time before Carson's tenure), Mort Sahl (who briefly had his own talkshow in the mid-1960s), and Don Rickles. Mike Wallace's late-night interview programs, *Nightbeat* and *The Mike Wallace Interview*, typified the trend. The former aired in New York on Dumont's WABD and later moved to the ABC network; the latter was syndicated from 1959 to 1961.[118]

One surviving *Nightbeat* program is a 1957 interview with Hugh Hefner, who had recently quit *Esquire* to start *Playboy*. The set is simple: two chairs against a darkened background lend a strikingly somber and stark aura to the faces in close-up. Wallace's opening monologue is a mixture of commercials for Parliament cigarettes (during which he lights up) and the Chase Manhattan Bank, and a promo for *Looney Tunes*. Hefner then appears in the other chair and is needled by Wallace's confrontational questions.

> What is your conception of your magazine's editorial policy?
>
> Justify your use of the word "literate." In what sense? You talk about literature, but the magazine is mostly *sex*—double and single entendre. Let's not hide behind altruistic motives. Aren't you selling a high-class, dirty book?
>
> What's wrong with the other men's magazines?
>
> So what's the kick that *you* get out of it?

Wallace alternates questions about the magazine with personal queries that probe—and implicitly indict—the character of anyone who would found such a magazine. His critical tone and the intense, tight close-ups bear down upon Hefner; more often than not, the shot relentlessly dwells on him as Wallace's grilling persists. But Hefner keeps his cool. He defends the magazine not only from the market standpoint of providing an "indoor," urban, male escapist magazine—to compete with the numerous "outdoor" ones—but from his openness-about-sex-is-healthy philosophy. An excerpt gives a sense of their exchange:

W: Should this magazine be left out in the home with young children?

H: Sure. It's not harmful to children and not really dirty.

W: C'mon!

H: The danger in sex is when it's made a hidden thing. The magazine takes a *healthy* approach.

W: It takes a *lascivious* approach to sex.

H: When women's or general magazines treat sex, they're *less* healthy; they sensationalize.

Wallace ends by quoting from Gibbons's *Decline and Fall of the Roman Empire* to argue that encouraging indulgence in "indoor pleasures" and "soft living" implies civilization's decline. The show concludes with Wallace, addressing the camera, bumping tomorrow's show on the Egypt-Israel conflict—another topic, in his urgent words, from "out of the headlines." Then, as the credits roll, he looks at the latest *Playboy* centerfold and smilingly chats, microphones off, with Hefner—a framing suggesting that his adversarialism has been for "show," inauthentic. As Wallace opens the centerfold in full view of the spectator, the camera abruptly tilts up and away.

Ironically, just as *Playboy*, in its own commodified transgression, opened the middle-class home to sex, *Nightbeat* parasitically "exposed" that transgression for its *own* paratextual commodification. Wallace's questions strove for a sensationalized intimacy, a making public of the "real" (that is, private) Hefner. Journalistic interview became dramatic showdown. As a construct, the interview took advantage of the unstable boundaries between the journalistic and the dramatic, the private and the public. The Wallace-inspired "hot" talkshow also opened up another postmodern talkshow practice, a playing with the relationship between knower-enunciator and knowledge. While Wallace's unrelenting, probing questions and the equally unrelenting close-ups struggled to pry the "truth" free of Hefner's cool, seemingly dissimulating appearance in a modernist attempt to dissociate knowledge from enunciator, Hefner's performance worked their postmodern conflation.

Following Paar and Wallace were a number of 1960s talkshows trading on controversy and seeming to parallel the development of the news/ talk radio format and its "hot" political call-in shows. *Open End*, which became the two-hour *David Susskind Show* and ran in syndication for twenty-six years (1960–86), first courted controversy when it had Nikita Khrushchev as its guest in October 1960. The resulting notoriety quadrupled the show's syndication market.[119] Even outside of syndication, the ABC network in 1964 attempted to counterprogram Carson with *The Les Crane Show*, which featured a brash former DJ who played for controversy and also involved his studio audience through the use of a special shotgun microphone. The program lasted only a year, but it appears to have been the first television talkshow to combine controversy and confrontation with audience participation.

Although never an audience participation show, *Firing Line*, hosted by the pungent yet erudite conservative William F. Buckley, Jr., began in April 1966 and continues in syndication. During its early years it used a debate format—Buckley always represented conservatism—with a panel of questioners and a moderator. In so doing it echoed some of the "loudness" and polarization of other 1960s "hot talk" shows, in contrast to the more civil, "exploratory" exchange of ideas that it would become by the mid-1970s. The change was due in part to format adjustments and the replacement of guests who were "rhetorical flamethrowers" (such as Black Panther Eldridge Cleaver) with more restrained spokespersons. Buckley himself—a riveting performer who early on combined erudition, verbal facility, and an upper-crust demeanor with a no-holds-barred aggressiveness—also toned down as the contentious 1960s came to an end. Against the charge that the early *Firing Line* was too bloodthirsty, Buckley argues that it was merely reflecting its times.[120]

The 1969 debut of *Agronsky and Company* marked the beginning of a new political talk subgenre: the weekly half-hour "roundtable discussion of current events" by a group of journalists.[121] In the mid-1960s CBS News achieved a similar synthesis with its occasional Sunday afternoon, IBM-sponsored *Town Meeting of the World*. Produced by Don Hewitt and moderated by Charles Collingwood, each of these specials took the form of a debate on a given topic, staged between contenders on opposite sides of the Atlantic, who were joined by the Early Bird communications satellite.

On December 12, 1965, the topic is "Resolved: that the U.S. should honor its commitment in Vietnam." Collingwood moderates a tight, traditional debate between the New York-based affirmative team (a group from Harvard, including then professor Henry Kissinger) and the London-based negative team (a group of Oxford students and Sir Michael Foot, a Labour member of Parliament). Each team is in its own auditorium, surrounded by an audience of individuals who eventually get to question the team on the other side of the Atlantic. Each auditorium, as well as Collingwood's "control center," is complete with projection video screens and monitors displaying the other participants. With the Johnson administration stepping up U.S. involvement in Vietnam and that issue becoming more controversial, the show's debate and audience questions are confrontational, even rancorous. The connotations of the show's "control center" serve the broadcasters, suggesting that *they* are the mediating, controlling institution weathering controversies and crises. As sponsor, IBM technologically implicates itself in another kind of "information solution."

The Joe Pyne Show, originating at WTTV Los Angeles, was the most widely syndicated of the 1960s "loud talk" programs—it reached up to eighty-five markets—and its host, the most outrageous. Pyne was an ultra-conservative ex-Marine who invited guests to appear only to obliterate them and, occasionally, even his studio audience: "Go gargle with razor blades." On August 14, 1965, in the midst of the Watts riot, he pulled out a gun, yelling, "Let 'em come! I'm ready for 'em!" in response to a black guest's suggestion that a race war was at hand.[122] Like the Khrushchev show for Susskind, this one made Pyne's national reputation.

More sensation than political debate, these "loud" talkshows were primarily cathartic and transgressive; their historical value lay in their having pushed the limits of the de facto political and rhetorical censorship enforced through television's "standards and practices" offices. For example, *Alan Burke* producer Paul Noble claims that it was on his Metromedia-syndicated show that "penis" was first uttered on television. This risk taking paralleled that of 1960s political talk radio, in which controversial talk hosts such as Jerry Williams featured guests such as Malcolm X and always wondered whether they would be fired the following day.[123] Indeed, "loud talk" embodied *and* helped create what the 1960s were all about: political polarization, the casting aside of inhibition and authority, "do-it-yourself" participation, the emphasis on feelings, subjectivity, and personal style.

Paradoxically, the late 1960s and early 1970s were also the years when the daytime celebrity variety chat shows named for their hosts—David Frost, Merv Griffin, Mike Douglas, Dinah Shore—came into being and thrived among women audiences until the early 1980s. In this context, what now appears most innovative about *Donahue*—which debuted as a phone-in show on WLWD-TV in Dayton, Ohio, in 1967 and provided the prototype for current interactive talk/service shows—is the way in which show and host not only intermingled controversy, confrontation, audience participation, and product promotion but added the dimensions of service ("useful knowledge") and the compassion of an in-depth sharing of personal experience (evident in *Stand Up and Be Counted!*). Unlike the other 1960s controversial talkshows *Donahue* and its host could be confrontational yet sensitive and caring, still somehow "polite" in the Merv Griffin mold. As a synthesis par excellence of so many historical talkshow strains, it has been an effective daytime advertising vehicle for some twenty-five years. When it became a national phenomenon in 1979, the popular reception of its host positioned him as Joe Pyne's Other— the feminized, sensitive male who admits his insecurity ("folks, you've got to help me out") and "cares." He has a "boyish charm" and seems "nonthreatening" even while his show has been perceived as an explosive hybrid—"part psychodrama, part street theatre, part group therapy . . . something live, spontaneous, rawly emotional, and *real*." [124] Phil Donahue's predictable persona—his nonthreatening, caring affect combined with a passionate intensity—counterbalances the "shock" of many of his topics; it makes them, and him, acceptable to largely female audiences as well as to a prosperous broadcast industry that recycles current controversies in a cheap yet always novel audience participation form.

In the late 1970s the tremendous growth of *Donahue*'s popularity (by 1980 it was on 215 stations and delivering audiences of women aged 18 to 49 in "resounding numbers"), coupled with the aging of the Merv Griffin– type daytime talkshow's audience, forced a reexamination of the genre. Although still viewing talkshows in large numbers, women over fifty had become undesirable to sponsors. This spurred changes in daytime talk-show formats toward more provocative content, audience participation, advocacy of women's issues, younger hosts, and a magazine approach that blended light talk with satellite-delivered, on-location news and information. Group W's *Hour Magazine* epitomized just such a show. By 1980 young actor John Davidson had replaced Mike Douglas. Syndicators like Group W and Metromedia were struggling to do whatever they could to save the daytime talkshow by "evolving" it into a provocative, magazinelike "third generation"; if *Mike Douglas* and its like represented the first generation, *Donahue* was the second. After all, syndication executives had to acknowledge the fact that the daytime talkshow was "a lucrative, low-maintenance vehicle" too profitable to discard. Its efficiencies were essential for daytime blocks, when viewership—and revenues—were lower anyway.

The slowly built popularity of *Donahue* and the increasingly noted blurring of the line between news and talkshows—a phenomenon that Donahue had himself remarked—prompted programming executives to surmise, in 1980, that audience hunger for exciting informational programming would be a key 1980s trend. CBS News president Bill Leonard predicted that 50 percent of network programming would be informational by the mid-1980s.[125] With popular "reality" programs like *Real People* and *That's Incredible* mixing documentary information with entertainment, Leonard's forecast did not seem so far-fetched. The late 1970s also saw a decline in the late-night talkshow and its viewership, a tendency especially vivid in the stagnation of the dominant *Tonight* show.[126]

The shifting boundaries between broadcast "information" and "entertainment"—a shift already quietly occurring among interactive media forms in the early 1980s, breaking down the accepted distinctions between producer, text, and audience—would prove another key instability in the transition from modern to postmodern: from the modernist talk and entertainment practices of the lyceum to the talkshow and its play with a host of distinctions. Its seemingly endless capacity for participants, topics, and approaches indicates the form's ability to vary, adapt, appropriate, incorporate, and simulate. As a part of postmodern culture it "thrives on its own uncertainty" and "simulates society by shattering meaning in the reprocessing of cultural remnants."[127] The talkshow's development demonstrates the emergence of productive multiplicity and contradiction, and how the media industry uses each.

2

Constellations of Voices: How Talkshows Work

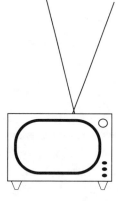

The productive instability of the talkshow is hardly an accident. It is a part of the industry's intentionality in developing and producing "infotainment" for a multichannel media environment in which the spectator with remote control in hand is a "grazer"—a random access "player" who "interacts" with an expanded set of channels. With the advent of cable and the demise of broadcast scarcity, asserts Robert Pittman, developer of MTV and *The Morton Downey, Jr., Show*, diversification is the strategy. Rather than displacing any news programs, *Downey* represented the growing diversification (already achieved in entertainment) of the news and information genre. It was "one more voice." [1]

Geraldo Rivera has said, "I'm Walter Winchell, Edward R. Murrow, Merv Griffin. I'm a TV talkshow host, an emotional man, a reporter, a journalist, a writer. . . . I do good." He is all those things, he says, because "the world has changed" and the definition of the journalist can no longer be so narrow. Phil Donahue has called talkshows and the tabloid news programs "new sources of information," arguing that "more information, from any side, leads to truth." [2] Geraldo sees the news becoming "more diversified, more democratic" with the appearance of his and similar shows, which pose a challenge to an elitism charging that such shows are not "real" journalism. [3] Even the editor of the long-established *Des Moines Register* has confessed a degree of tabloidization, arguing that to compete, newspapers also have to seek a "richer mix." [4]

As part of this "mix" strategy during his "loud" talkshow's heyday, Morton Downey, Jr., saw himself as "a good old American hot dog" among the "caviar." He accused those "caviar" hosts and guests of speaking "William F. Buckley English,"[5] whereas he was "just the dummy, and the audience is the ventriloquist. They put the words in my mouth. I speak for them."[6] Phil Donahue confirms that his show's producers "look for novelty" and seek to "expand boundaries," explaining that talkshows "sandwich the Persian Gulf between the male strippers." He has reminded his critics, "I'm not the *New York Times*. . . . I have to *generate* an audience."[7]

"The Old Formulas Don't Hold Anymore"

Donahue's remark begins to situate productive instability as an intentional talkshow dynamic. Novelty and the play with boundaries drive his production of an audience—the electronic media industry's ultimate product—because his show is *not* the *New York Times*. He implies an institutional discourse from an inferior position: the *New York Times* is established in a way his program is not; the *Times* carries an ongoing, preconstructed audience sufficient to its success. Institutionalization here implies certain identifying stabilities—a distinctly bounded tradition and academically valorized journalistic practice—which, for the *Times*, have been productive. They assure its circulation, maintain its advertising rates, and secure its hold on the best "establishment" journalists and news sources. Donahue knows his show is different. It must "work" the new, the inclusive, the changing—in other words, the unstable—to succeed in the current media environment. His program must make every effort to "expand boundaries" in order to produce an audience and sustain itself. He must constantly tap *and* create shifting spectatorial desire and affective alliance.

Yet it is significant that talkshow producers still incorporate establishment journalism into their practices in a further play with boundaries. *Downey* executive producer Bill Boggs, who said he picked the topics for the show, emphasized that he did not get them "from the *Star* or the *Enquirer* but from the front pages of the *New York Times*, the *Los Angeles Times*, and the *Washington Post*."[8] What here seems at first like a "high" rationalization for a "low" form could as convincingly be read as the talkshow's useful interplay of texts, voices, and social accents. Boggs himself furthered this boundary play when he characterized *Downey*'s productive mix of journalism and emotion, anger and issues, affects and ideologies as "confrontainment" and "3-D television . . . rock-and-roll without the music," transgressive, youthful, energetic, tied to popular cultural practices.[9] His new, hybridized terminology matches the program it describes and evokes a metaphoric breaking-through of television's two-dimensional frame.

The iconography of sports, town meeting, and spectacle, modernist transgression and subjectivity, rock-and-roll and premodern moralism all come together in the talkshow. Play with the general notion of communicative frames—the logonomic, metalingual, or situational framework in which an utterance occurs and which cues the reader how to decode it—proves to be one of infotainment's, and the talkshow's, most important productive instabilities.

If these kinds of "play" are fruitful for talk producers, they are a threat to media critics—a threat cutting to the heart of what "real" news is as distinct from "real" entertainment. David Halberstam, who once called *Donahue* America's "most important graduate school," has more recently called infotainment a "con."[10] Fred Friendly, particularly irked by the news reenactments or simulations used in such programs as *Inside Edition*, *A Current Affair*, and *America's Most Wanted*, has called this technique, along with the docudrama, a "fraud" crossing lines "that never used to be crossed." He wonders if the audiences that take them seriously (do they?) can distinguish news from drama, given the "blurred line between the real and the unreal."[11] The dispute over authenticity has extended to the politically organized radio call-in hosts, who were called "deceptive" by members of Congress angry over talkshow agitation against a House pay raise.[12] And as Chapter 1 suggested, tension between print and broadcast media has long existed in the United States. Newspapers' fears of broadcasting's erosion of their market underpin their moralistic condemnation of what they see as broadcasting's deceptive techniques and harmful effects.[13]

The inevitability of the talkshow's growth stems to a degree from the recent economics of broadcast production. At a cost of $25,000 to $50,000 per half-hour, the syndicated audience participation talkshow and tabloid news show are among the cheapest to produce. Young, low-paid, yet enthusiastic staffers—including bookers who locate the many guests—work in a highly charged, "can do" atmosphere.[14] Usually, a program is taped for airing in national syndication within a day or two. In markets of origin, however, shows are often broadcast live to permit phone-in participation, as is the Chicago-based *Oprah Winfrey Show* when in Chicago, although many *Oprah* shows are taped on the road in cities throughout the country.[15] These shows are timely, appear live even if on tape, and are readily changeable with respect to topics, guests, audience participants, and locales—uniquely able to take advantage of instability.

The kind, numbers, and organization of production staff make possible that capacity. Most shows have several of two particular kinds of personnel: bookers and producers. Bookers—also called talent executives, talent coordinators, or sometimes producers—spend endless hours on the phone seeking guests. Predominantly women, they juggle a stream of guest and topic possibilities in an effort to put together the right mix of personality and experts. Bookers must "be creative" and show "moxie" in their persuasive efforts. The daily unpredictability of the outcome of their efforts is evident in the frequent difficulty of finding guests—due, in part, to the sheer proliferation of talkshows. The ever looming threat of guest shortages came to pass, in one particular instance, during the October 17, 1986, installment of the short-lived *Nightlife with David Brenner*. Not one guest appeared, and Brenner ended up performing an extended monologue. Despite the constant requests for appearances made by parties anxious for self-promotional air time, bookers often face a challenge of finding the kinds of guests the shows need.[16]

The bookers for political talkshows have earned the label "powertots": the "underpaid, overworked 25-year-olds" who are "among the most powerful people in Washington: they get to decide who goes on TV."[17] As "lowly" as they may seem, they assert power over the powerful—lobbyists, think-tank experts, investment bankers, and so forth—whose media appearances can prove crucial to the success of their businesses. Like the talkshow's audience participant, the booker exemplifies boundary-violating inversion and an empowerment of women. The booker, who is likely to burn out by age thirty, has assumed a position of power in a time and context when decisionmakers from "inside the Beltway" rely heavily on the media. The booker thus becomes an institutional embodiment of what the interactive talkshow itself is: a localized inversion of the relationships between the powerful and the common, between the mass media communicator and the "feminized," supposedly passive spectator.

Working hand in hand with the booker is the producer. He or she— again, usually "she"—is one of several producers on the show who put together programs in rotation, since most participatory talkshows are five-day-a-week "strip" syndications or live local broadcasts. The "hub of creative ideas *before* the show" (whereas host and director "carry" the show as it is taped),[18] the producer develops an episode largely from a content standpoint (the show's format and host remaining more or less "fixed") and is responsible for all research, guest, and logistical arrangements. The *executive* producer oversees the program's "look," budget, and distribution. Complementing these producers are the director, who "calls" the show during taping; publicity and promotion people responsible for generating media attention for a particular show's topic (which is not usually known more than a few days in advance, creating a special challenge for a genre that is itself highly promotional and success oriented); and an occasional field producer for taped inserts recorded and edited in advance.[19]

Along with an institutional structure built to handle the participatory talkshow's fundamental resource—a chaos driven by the news, personalities, and the interactive "liveness" of the form—guest practices demonstrate the same ad hoc, contingent structure adapted to the unpredictable. Besides celebrities, who can be interviewed either as stars or as "private people," the participatory talkshow focuses on guests who are issue motivated, "average" people culled from either the headlines, support groups, or a list of stand-by experts. Especially valuable are "crossover guests," persons expert and articulate on several issues; they are the most efficient, adaptable, and often available on short notice. Agents and publicists pushing their clients for appearances are often unsuccessful in part because a client fails to fit the crossover profile. Richard Mincer, *Donahue*'s executive producer, encourages prospective guests who cannot qualify as crossovers to be *especially* unique or different, to take advantage of rather than repress difference.[20]

By the same token, the audience participation talkshow has taken advantage of the power instabilities in the contemporary media environment, particularly the Big Three networks' loss of audience share and the uncertainties of programming in an era of deregulation and corporate consolidation.[21] Network audience erosion, which has received substantial coverage in the trade and mainstream press, is one result of the proliferation of channels and choices created by cable and the rise of independent broadcasters, "superstations" carried by cable systems as distant signals, and the Fox "fourth network" offering original programs to affiliates comprising formerly independent (largely UHF) stations.[22] Such stations have long relied heavily on syndications, of which the talkshow is a significant part.

Interestingly, talk hosts have practiced an anti-network discourse for years, an "anti–big guy" line rife with populist overtones and consistent with a participatory form purporting to give its audience unique media access. Ironically, Phil Donahue talked this line even when NBC, in the late 1970s, began running short segments of his upcoming shows on *Today* each morning.[23] Geraldo Rivera more recently espoused a similar line when, in light of his syndicated talkshow's success, he pronounced, "The network monopoly on real life [programming] has been broken forever."[24]

If the rise of syndication and its all-important talkshows is both cause *and* effect of the vacuum left by the decline in network shares, the erosion of the "hard" news audience and its financial base parallels this decline. The drop in viewership of the major networks' evening newscasts resulted by the late 1980s in a destabilizing of their revenues and cutbacks in their news divisions.[25] After years of expansion, news programming produced by local stations came under increasing competitive and financial pressure during that same period.[26] Network and locally produced documentaries and editorials also declined.[27] Meanwhile, local cable systems, which are usually subsidiaries of national multisystem operators, began to supply news programs emphasizing a "hyperlocal" approach. Such operations are more limited in scope and budget than their broadcast competitors, but they nonetheless provide an efficient, affordable advertising vehicle for local businesses.[28] Cable systems also get a substantial community relations benefit from their newscasts—especially important to them after charges of poorer service and higher fees (following cable's growth and deregulation in the 1980s) put them under increasing government scrutiny and, by 1992, regulation.[29]

The news programming environment has been further unsettled by two other seemingly contradictory developments: the success of new forms of network news programming outside the well-worn evening newscast slots—"reality programming" in prime time—and the clear influence of the syndicated tabloid shows, talkshows, and related infotainment forms. The rise of tabloid television news has added a new type of program to the "access" slot (seven to eight o'clock in the evening) dominated by the game shows. Group W's *PM Magazine*, which began in the mid-1970s, and *Entertainment Tonight*'s debut in 1981 marked tabloid television's beginnings. By the end of the decade, Fox's *A Current Affair* (distributed via syndication rather than by the Fox network affiliation, which involves a specific package of shows over a number of evenings) and King World's *Inside Edition* had both broken into syndication's top ten.[30]

If "standard" broadcast journalism has suffered because of the proliferation of channels and the wider range of news formats now available, that "standard" journalism has itself been influenced by such alternatives. Appropriating talkshow techniques, more of the nightly network newscasts feature crosstalk, real-time, and often confrontational interviews (the influence of ABC's *Nightline* is also apparent here). As a result of their operational cutbacks, the network newscasts are focusing more and more on high-profile and longer, more analytical feature segments.[31] Perhaps the most controversial of the tabloid and talkshow influences is the network newscast use of reenactments or simulated footage to dramatize news events of which no footage is available. When ABC's *World News Tonight*, on July 21, 1989, aired a reenactment of a U.S. diplomat allegedly passing a briefcase of secret information to a Soviet agent, there was a ten-second delay in the appearance of the word "simulation" in the corner of the frame during the first network feed of the show. The slip prompted an outcry against simulations as unethical "tabloid techniques." [32]

One final and seemingly contradictory development in the news programming environment is that even as early evening newscasts lose viewership and revenues, the networks are expanding self-produced *prime-time* news, magazine, interview, and other forms of "reality" programming as a more profitable alternative to their usual entertainment.

Prime-time news shows allow the networks more production, cost, and copyright (and thus syndication) control—a control once the domain of independent package producers.[33] Inspired by the success of *60 Minutes* and, since 1988, its hour-long, in-depth *48 Hours*, CBS developed the short-lived *Saturday Night with Connie Chung*; ABC debuted its *Prime Time Live*; and NBC, its also short-lived *Yesterday, Today, and Tomorrow*. Despite being initially counterprogrammed against *The Cosby Show*, *48 Hours* is profitable because it costs half as much to produce—about $400,000 weekly—as an hour of entertainment programming. With $1.3 million of revenue per show, *48 Hours* generates about as much profit each week as it costs to produce. And though its viewership is relatively small, the numbers, according to the show's executive producer, are still "entertainment size" and growing. Its chances of longevity are considerable, and CBS owns all the rights to it—factors important to its future syndication or videotape distribution.[34]

Such distribution promises to become an ever bigger profit center as cable, independent "superstations," "fourth networks," satellite, and home video continue their expansion. The syndication prices commanded by such successful series as *Cheers* and *Cosby* rose to a point in the late 1980s where major-market stations winning the bid for them paid in the millions of dollars per daily, stripped episode.[35] As evidenced in the networks' ongoing congressional lobbying to change the longstanding "syn-fin" rules—regulations barring the networks from having a financial interest in the later syndication of shows they initially license from independent producers—the Big Three clearly want to get in on the syndication "action." Having ownership of program rights in perpetuity would grant them long-term profits from series they helped make into hits.[36] The networks have also established their own in-house companies to produce series and made-for-TV movies.

The broadcast and cable industry's understanding of spectatorship provides the groundwork for its programming strategies. A study by a major broadcast research firm, Frank N. Magid Associates, summarized in the September 1988 issue of the media business magazine *Channels*,[37] seemed to confirm what television programmers had suspected—that spectators use their remote controls to "zap" among dozens of channels.[38] "Zapping" takes its place with "zipping" (fast-forwarding) past commercials when home viewers watch what they have videotaped off-air; however, the study found boredom and a concern about missing "a better program elsewhere," rather than the desire to avoid commercials, as the main reasons for zapping.

The implications of all of this are considerable. Zapping is either an expression of dissatisfaction with existing programming or a new form of entertainment made possible by the more interactive use of television as the random "raw material" for the spectator's own unique program assembly. If the latter is the case, it may stand as an implicit critique of existing programming in that the play with program fragments through remote control—an intensification of the spectator's primary identification with the apparatus through interactivity—becomes a greater source of pleasure than a single narrative. It also suggests that forms of interactivity are gaining spectatorial preference, a disposition that the audience participation talkshow has tapped.

Along these same lines, the study found that what makes viewers stop "grazing" is "visual impact—something unusual catches their eye, or they see something that is familiar to them."[39] The most significant "tune-out factor" is programming that fails to hold viewer attention—an increasingly difficult task for the programmer and one that is likely to remain so, since those who zap tend to be younger viewers. Given the ease of zapping, the long-practiced programming concept of LOP—"least objectionable program"—has become irrelevant.[40]

Most curious, however, is the paradox in the finding that viewers say what is most attention-holding and thus grazer-resistant is programming that is either unusual *or* familiar. The programming challenge, then, points to the design of shows and formats that strive for not just one or the other but *both*. The talkshow, in its combination of the familiar-yet-different—its constantly shifting, news-oriented focuses and guests; its highly charged, ad-libbed performance; its unpredictable, chance elements intensified by spontaneity and audience interactivity—seems calculated to meet the challenge. It implicitly addresses the exhaustion of older, overly predictable narrative paradigms not only by mixing ever changing news material with entertainment but by blurring the lines between producer, text, and spectator as well as between program and commercial through its promotional aspect. The latter is becoming more and more important to advertisers as zappers continually negate their messages.

One advertiser response is to make commercials more "compelling" through unusual production techniques which, according to E. Ann Kaplan, involve a narrative non-closure that eliminates the necessity of having to watch the commercial in its entirety.[41] This response seems the opposite of the intended effect of the audience-interactive talkshow, which strives for the more sustained engagement of the spectator-participant under deliberately less "slick" conditions. More casual, user friendly programming, echoing what Donahue called the talkshow's "messy democracy," is a form that stands out from the "MTVing" of much of the rest of television. That the two styles coexist in the same turbulent environment to attract the zapping spectator demonstrates how the seemingly chaotic can be productive. "Uncanned," "news punk" programming has also been called "cut-through TV": shows designed to "cut through the bullshit" represented by the predictable formulas glutting an expanded set of channels. The producer of the audience participation crimestopper show *America's Most Wanted* has described it as television where "you [the audience] can make a difference." And viewer tips have in fact helped authorities apprehend a number of fugitives.[42]

Another broadcast industry boundary play to create more grazer-resistant programming is the use of radio as a model. Radio's outlets-per-market have been far more numerous than television's for many years; hence, competition has been far more intense and the audience far more fragmentary (radio grazing through in-car, pushbutton tuning has long existed). By the late 1980s, television managers were looking to radio's adaptation and survival for lessons, most of which have been centered in a concept of localism and greater audience and community participation.[43] Besides introducing the call-in show in the first place, radio has inspired the television talkshow's more intense, rapid-fire versions.

This is particularly evident in the syndicated *McLaughlin Group*, its CNN spinoff *Capitol Gang*, and others of the fast, combative subgenre of political talkshows that had evolved out of *Agronsky and Company* by the 1980s (*Inside Washington*, *Brinkley*). *The McLaughlin Group*'s host, John McLaughlin—one-time Washington radio talk host, Republican political consultant, and Jesuit professor—has consciously inscribed his radio call-in techniques to enliven the journalistic "discussion" in what has proved to be a key influence on the entire roundtable subgenre. He imposes strict limits on how much he or his panelists may say at any one time and gears the show toward "the spin of the week" rather than "complexity." He insists on "quickly identifiable labels" because his discussants' "cartoon roles must be immediately grasped."[44] Dramatic role playing across the political spectrum lies at the center of how the show works as grazer-attracting television. The quick switching between shots of the rapidly speaking, almost aphoristic combatants is orchestrated by McLaughlin's verbal cues. He is a hard-edged, high-volume host, rapidly shifting topic and address to heighten the sense of conflict. The show's effort to achieve the "heat" of political call-in radio is obvious. The opening voiceover frames the show as "unrehearsed." McLaughlin's moderating technique—based on the loud, abrupt interruption—is an adaptation of talk radio's "hang-up" technique, originally used to control anonymous callers. In his thorough look at political talkshows, *Talking Heads*, Alan Hirsch calls *The McLaughlin Group* "television's zaniest political talk show"[45]—a choice of words recalling the studied zaniness of current radio formats such as the "Z," or "morning zoo."

Productively confusing the distinctions between genres and even paradigms *within* a given genre is a strategy not only for tabloid programs and talkshows but for the station as well. By the end of the 1980s the independent "passive superstation" WWOR Secaucus, New Jersey—which is carried by many cable systems—had moved into the forefront of innovation, cultivating a greater localism, live, in-house production, audience participation, and "reality-based" concepts in an almost radiolike way. After MCA acquired the station in 1987 and moved it from New York City to New Jersey, a state long underserved by broadcast television, WWOR's overall ratings increased 40 percent. From being the commercial station with the lowest ratings in the nation's largest market, it had risen to number one in advertising billings by September 1989. It did so by expanding its news department and changing its newscast's format to include an informal "peek" behind the scenes: bumpers and teasers consist of documentary-like, hand-held shots of the newsroom as anchors, reporters, and staff informally discuss the upcoming newscast in a kind of "inauthentic authenticity." And, in October 1987, this same station developed *The Morton Downey, Jr., Show* as a local talkshow; it went national in May 1988.

The station's vice-president for news has vowed to bring entertainment values to what will remain "good, solid journalism" while "de-mystifying" the production process through reflexive techniques. Man-agement's language is revealing here. The general manager intends that his "new" news programming will "further erode the barriers between news and entertainment" with the purpose of making WWOR "stand out from the pack." [46] He contextualized it "as part of a counterprogram-ming strategy. It sure got us attention. It served that purpose extremely well." [47] If "uncanned"-looking programming is the grazer-resistant fare of the 1990s, the audience participation talkshow is among the best at generating or exploiting the productive instability that has become vital to gaining and keeping spectatorial attention. Long-time media consul-tant Paul Bortz best summed up these developments: "It's definitely no longer business as usual. . . . The old formulas don't hold any more." [48]

"I Don't Sing One Song": *Geraldo*

The title sequence *Geraldo* used in early 1990 (since replaced) began with dozens of postage-stamp-like, digitized video still-frames. [49] They seemed to be floating on a blue-purple background—some facing the viewer, others at an angle—accompanied by a synthesized rock-fusion score. Each floating "snapshot" illustrated a potential topic. One, for example, pictured an elderly yet healthy-looking couple smiling at each other, apparently enjoying their "golden years." Another suggested a naked teenage couple in sexual embrace. The snapshots reflected the di-versity of topics that *Geraldo* discusses and their "extraparliamentary" politics of interpersonal and "self" issues, intentional communities, and affective alliances. [50] That such topics shift daily demonstrates the talk-show's unique power to respond to the moment.

Although the show occasionally features celebrities, its guests and par-ticipants are usually "average" citizens with particular problems, stories, experiences, or expertise. The individuals represented in the floating snap-shots signified this everydayness as well as a wide experiential, intona-tional, and affective range. With the further connotation of high-tech sophistication conveyed by its digitized design, the opening linked urgent topics with both common people and the in-the-know, in ways expressive of the show's intention to offer the spectator-participant identification with all three. The dozens of floating frames appeared in no particular order. A sense of randomness, multiplicity, and diversity prevailed. This is part of the audience-interactive talkshow's premise, since its guests, topics, participants, and even locales shift daily. Such instability is here linked with a whole set of positive connotations: democratic inclusion, dynamic change, "pumped up" energy and affect, and constant novelty. Chaos becomes productive. Anything that can happen or has happened to anyone is fair game for the show, as is the individual to which it happens. He or she is eligible to be a participant.

Geraldo Rivera has explained that his success is a product of his performative diversity as investigative journalist *and* emotional man: "If the audience rejects the host, then the talkshow has no chance of making it . . . what the audience knew that the critics didn't know was that, just like most people, I have the full range of human emotions. I don't go through life crashing through doors."[51] A stated or implied "and" marks Geraldo's discourse and is indicative of his postmodern journalism. He describes his journalistic style as "responsible . . . passionate . . . involved." He also sees himself *in* and *as* his audience: "There's a populist aspect to what I do that's important . . . a feeling of almost surrogacy. . . . I represent them" in such a way that there is "a kind of feeling of being looked in the eye."[52] He also finds his audience "tremendously helpful" to what he describes as his "spontaneous . . . improvisational . . . rock-and-roll" show "because they come up with the questions that either you knew too much to ask, or just didn't think of." The chance aspects of audience participation are, for Geraldo, eminently productive.[53]

The last element of the 1990 opener was the appearance of the show's title: *Geraldo*. Like the title logos for two other talkshows—*Oprah* and *Sally Jesse Raphael*—it materialized signaturelike over the floating images, as if written by an invisible hand. Along with oral and interpersonal communication, a signature confers a sense of nonmediation. The high-tech computer graphic simulates a low-tech *look*; it resembles a handwritten signature at the bottom of a note from a friend.

When the title shot switches to Geraldo's entrance from beneath the audience gallery, he bounds up the ramp energetically, smiling, microphone in hand, wearing fashionable slacks and a pullover sweater. The spectator has the sense of entering the performance/participation space of *Geraldo* along with its host. We are "in" his space—narrative, discursive, and performative—and his subjectivity as he and we embark upon a seemingly modernist diegetic journey of discovery. It is "his" show, but he is "with" us, the spectators, and we are on a first-name basis with him.[54] As the program unfolds, however, his subjectivity does not always dominate in modernist fashion. Rather, a host of voices is heard in a relatively open and open-ended interlocution. The show's audience participation and reflexive qualities—its constant acknowledgment of camera and microphone—defuse the para-sociality of the interaction, making it both a genuine social interaction *and* an electronically mediated spectacle.

Geraldo has called his critics "elitists . . . lecturing down to the masses about what they should or should not like."[55] His show, by contrast, is dialogic rather than monologic, inclusive rather than exclusive. *Geraldo* and its host's discourse operate on the logical premise of "and" rather than his critics' modernist, exclusion-based "or." Geraldo sees the elitism of the "or" premise as "self-destructive" and the reason for the networks' deteriorating shares. He rightly regards it as hypocritical as well, since a news magazine like *Newsweek*—the coiner of the widely used term "trash TV"[56]—itself exploits what it sees as the sensationalism of *Geraldo* and similar shows. Geraldo calls his critics "professional ethicists" who are "frustrated" and "jealous" because "they're watching the world go by and having zero impact." They are "scared" of passion.[57] He thus imagines his intentionality as one of impact and feeling, an effectivity linked with affectivity and unattainable through established "objective" journalism. He rejects the notion that his passion and inclusiveness prevent him from doing "responsible journalism" or "doing good": "Responsible journalism should not be confused with objectivity . . . responsible journalism is fair reporting . . . you can still do a hot topic *and* be responsible" (emphasis added).[58] Again, "and" is the key conjunction in his largely conjunctive self-theorization. His inclusiveness productively destabilizes traditional generic and even ethical distinctions. Journalistically, he says, he is "marching to the beat of a different drum"[59] and "different programs have different responsibilities"[60]—rhetoric trading on his show's very "otherness." He also sees his show as *additional* to a daytime television environment formerly dominated by soap operas and game shows. Unfortunately, however, he cannot support his genre without attacking the others: even the tawdriest talkshow teaches something, he implies, but "you can't say that about the game shows they replace."[61]

The *Geraldo* episode I want to discuss aired on February 14, 1990—Valentine's Day. The host makes his way down to an area between the stage, where his guests are seated, and the audience gallery. Here, as in most audience participation talkshows, the steeply pitched audience area is an integral part of the set, lit and arranged—with respect to sightlines and camera coverage—almost as well as the guests seated on the stage. This is obviously important for visually representing audience members, who are initially integrated into the discourse through their applause, the visual backdrop they provide, and their appearance in tight reaction-shot close-ups. Eventually, some of them take the opportunity to speak when Geraldo acknowledges them: he moves toward and stands next to them, microphone in hand. A moment of interpersonal contact with what is initially the discourse's dominant subjectivity—Geraldo—becomes the condition for participation: an equality-connoting, side-by-side, face-to-face contact in which the spectator-performer simultaneously addresses Geraldo, the guests and studio audience, and a nation of television spectators. It is a moment, however brief, when a huge institution becomes accessible.

Geraldo hosts the show on his feet and often in his shirt sleeves, moving—sometimes bounding—around the full space of the set. Spatially, he spends most of his on-air time "with" the audience, in the aisles. His mobility between stage and audience space denotes dynamism, labor, and border-crossing. His mobile, responsive presence and microphone transform the spectators into performers, a parallel set of available guests, experts, experiences, and intonations. But Geraldo retains a special enunciative status. His intros, transitions, questions, comments, tape segments, conversational turn-taking prompts and cues, and his affect all orchestrate the conversation, the shift between story and discourse spaces, the audio track and the televisual picturization that follows it, and especially *him,* fish-in-a-barrel style.[62]

The camera locations around the set both represent and enable the inclusion-through-host. Two cameras are back with the audience and to the sides for shooting the on-stage guests; the television spectator can observe the guests from the same general position as do Geraldo and the studio audience. At least another two are located at either edge of the area separating audience gallery and stage, thereby offering visual access to Geraldo (one camera is always on him, assuring his primary enunciative position with the audience) and prospective audience participants. Often, one of these cameras is hand-held for greater flexibility. Such a use of setting and apparatus obviously blurs typical boundaries between audience, performer, and performance space, giving the show—somewhat like environmental theater and performance art—an interactive, liminal dimension.

The focus of this Valentine's Day program, which Geraldo announces to the camera with the audience behind him, is "Romeo ripoff artists": men who charm, then "con, fleece," and abandon the women they said they loved. Before and after each commercial break, Geraldo repeats this focus in catchy "tabloid" headline terms: "Our subject today is Romeo ripoffs," or "We're discussing when Cupid is a crook" (his address uses "we" copiously, extending the sense of inclusion). Such phraseology efficiently emphasizes what his program is doing: exposing the everyday emotional and financial victimization of women. In other ("tabloidese") words, the program looks behind the "Cupid" to the "crook." The discursive strategy plays with an appearance/reality opposition; it frames the show as an epistemological inquiry beneath "normal" but often deceptive appearances. Like the modernist detective-journalist story, *Geraldo* also inquires into the integrity of the sign: how does a woman "see" a possible con artist, the "ripoff" behind the "Romeo"? Geraldo's subjectivity provides a springboard, a guide to this inquiry.[63]

Talkshows like *Geraldo* are not only about their shifting topics but implicitly about the slippery *signness* of the object under inquiry. There is a gnostic recognition of subjectivity and the constructedness of the object, which itself can be culturally variable and multivocal (as attested by a single show's multiplicity of guests and participants). This is consistent with Donal Carbaugh's analysis of speech on *Donahue*, in which a discursive emphasis on self highlights "everchanging and resistant personal orders" over a sense of *social* order. This "deculturalizing" effect, while devaluing traditional social roles in favor of a "separate humanness" linked with the right to speak as an individual, also devalues the sign's stability, transparency, and cultural agreement.[64] Self (subjectivity) and its perception, more than the topic, become the overarching "realities" of the audience participation talkshow.

As "our" fair yet passionate journalist-detective-explorer, Geraldo undertakes what at first seems a modernist investigation. But Geraldo and the program's discourse make no special attempt to objectify the "facts" in a manner consistent with modernity's discourse.[65] Inseparable from the performer and his or her experience and affect, knowledge remains a discursive and performative construct. If *Geraldo* seems quasi-fictional in its obvious constructedness, it is also framed as "real" through its connotations of improvisational, news-based "liveness." That the show plays with both is further testament to its inclusiveness.[66]

After Geraldo directly addresses the camera to introduce the topic he introduces his guests, each of whom has been swindled by a Romeo rip-off artist: Sylvia, Linda, Karen, Kate, and Joan. As he makes each brief introduction in voiceover, the camera pans to the woman he is describing. She is visually rendered in point-blank chest shot, accompanied by a bottom-of-frame superimposition of her first name and a brief description of her experience—for example, "Linda: swindled for money." None of the women is smiling; their affects suggest the painful experience of victimization each is about to relate under Geraldo's sympathetic questioning. While they are all reasonably well dressed and attractive, their silent, close-up countenances become, at this point, metonymic of suffering as well as everywomanness. They tap an existential commonality; their stories will suggest how things can go awry and how hard it is to "read the signs" of a swindle when one is in love.

After the first commercial break, Geraldo introduces today's experts: the persons invited to appear by virtue of their extraexperiential credentials or a special knowledge from the position of helper rather than victim. Such credentials give the experts the modernist aura of objectified knowledge, a residual holdover from the culture of expertise. They have the "right" (socially sanctioned) degrees, the "right" positions of authority, judgment, and counsel; they are therefore recognized as legitimately able (they have "the right") to help the guests, whose knowledge is solely experiential and presumably more tentative. If the expert is an author, his or her book appears in a close-up, limbo shot as the host makes the introduction. The talkshow's promotional aspect resurfaces here in its link with expertise and commodified knowledge. Yet, like Geraldo, the experts do not hold a monopoly on knowledge. Instead, knowledge ends up dispersed among guests, experts, and host (himself a knowledgeable journalist and lawyer). As part of a single conversation inquiring into a particular question, each of the three parties represents a voice speaking from within its particular situation. Their combination is an intentionally polyphonic construction of knowledge. Likewise, modernist expertise and inquiry combine with the performative and the experiential.

The experts on this Valentine's Day *Geraldo* are a social worker who counsels swindled women, a detective from the Washington, D.C., police department who specializes in investigating con artists, and a New Jersey private detective who has helped "conned" clients. The detective and social worker are African American, as are two of the guests, Linda and Karen. The social worker presents a list of four telltale signs warning that a lover may actually be a charming con: he is often unavailable for phone calls, asks frequently about money, disappears for days on end, and fails to repay borrowed money. As she speaks, the four signs are also listed graphically on the screen. An expert thus contributes an objectified knowledge, semiotically separated from her as performer to underline its objectivity and distinguish it from the rest of the show's performed knowledges. Momentarily, such knowledge seems to be privileged.

Geraldo next turns our attention to Linda, who, under his questioning, relates her particular experience as a kind of "case study" illustrating the expert's points. Geraldo guides her narrative with such questions as "How did the subject of money come up?" and "When did you start to lose confidence in him?" She reveals that she fell "totally in love" with a man whom she thought sincere, only to find him behaving in accordance with the social worker's four telltale symptoms.

As the other women's stories unfold, the experts' prescriptions seem more and more qualified, even inadequate. The typical "ripoff Romeo" ultimately plays on a woman's emotions to a point where those feelings "blind" the victim to any objectified knowledge. Next to the far more complex reality of the guests' knowledge, which is primarily emotional experience, objectified knowledge looks increasingly absurd. The Washington detective's advice for preventing these financial "crimes of the heart" (Geraldo's words) is incongruously reductive: "Get a receipt."

When Geraldo asks why two of the women continued to date the "ripoff Romeo," they tell him that they were not yet reading him as particularly suspicious. Geraldo's reaction is one of incredulity: "C'mon!" But the detective comes to Karen's defense by acknowledging the dominance of the contingent and the affective in a complex situation. The unfortunate truth is that the vulnerable victim becomes aware only ex post facto: that is, as a result of altered contingencies and affects. "They're looking for romance, he's looking for finance" is the detective's catchy tabloidese for the difference in intent and perception of the two parties to a "Romeo ripoff."

Under Geraldo's conversational direction and affect, the show dia-logically shifts back and forth between expert analysis and individual emotional experience to demonstrate the limits of both in conversational performance. The postmodern "collapse of critical distance and the crisis of authority," in Lawrence Grossberg's words, are both evident here.[67] The women victimized by the "Romeo ripoffs" achieve an affective alli-ance more than they constitute clinical case studies or a legalistic prepon-derance of evidence, although both those modernist intertexts echo here, as do the confessional and the revival meeting. The women's redemp-tive "confessions" build a resistant community of "normal," passionate, and honest people—qualities also reflected in the host and the audience participants.

This sense of alliance is reinforced by the show's close, which gives ad-dresses and phone numbers for the use of viewers who may be able to help track down one of the con artists. *Geraldo* and other talkshows frequently end with viewer-activating, self-empowering information. *Geraldo* may commodify such alliances and resistances, but knowledge, community, and interlocution in postmodern culture can, in Dick Hebdige's words, circulate "on the other side of the established institutional circuits" through affective alliances: support groups, issue-based organizations, and intentional communities.[68] Spectatorship has been redefined as par-ticipatory: the viewer is encouraged to connect interpersonally, via tele-phone, in a collective self-help narrative. Participatory talk offers the possibility of the spectator's physical and communicative involvement in narrative and spectacle, thereby encouraging his or her perception of the media's efficacy and "friendliness." This, in turn, encourages a greater dependence upon the media; beyond offering distraction, pleasure, or information, the media project themselves as somehow "deinstitution-alized" through their seeming accessibility. *Geraldo*'s participatory cues and openings for spectators challenge their heretofore "safe" distance while giving them a sense of mastery, despite interactivity's "deeper" intrusion.

The episode continues with Kate, whose own "flip side of the choco-late candy box" (another of Geraldo's transitional tags) involved a man who ended up with half of her inheritance. The source of her own "blind spot" to his machinations (besides his charm), she confesses, lay in two closely occuring events: her father's death, and her start at a new job. She was unsettled, insecure, and especially vulnerable. Geraldo asks, "If he is watching, what do you want to say to him?" Her answer: "What goes around, comes around." The discussion returns to a concern for jus-tice and the empowerment of "everywoman"—a concern here realized through a spectacle of performative conversation.

After commercials for a denture adhesive and life insurance for seniors (pitched by Ed McMahon),[69] the remaining guests tell their stories. Like Kate before her, Joan was swindled when she purchased a condo, in *his* name, with $30,000 *she* inherited; again, trust and affection were vio-lated. Like the others, Joan became suspicious only after it was too late. Geraldo turns to the experts: "Are we blinded by pride? Shouldn't she have known?" The experts' response, paradoxically, is to deny the utility of expertise in the very midst of such affective situations. The detective says, "It's a con game, pure and simple. It crosses all socioeconomic and intelligence lines."

Geraldo's closing gesture is to give each of his guests a bundle of roses and a kiss, his Valentine's Day "thank you" for sharing their stories. As he does this we hear the detective, in live voiceover, enumerate the things one can do to build a criminal case against a "Cupid con artist." The orienta-tion of expertise has shifted from detection and prevention to therapeutic restoration and justice, from epistemology to ontology. Since the expert enunciates only in voiceover, he does not have the "last word"; rather we watch the emotional exchange of roses and kisses and hear sporadic audience "ohs" and applause.

Though *Geraldo* is an amalgam of modern and postmodern knowl-edge and structural modes, it is ultimately postmodern in its inclusion of both. Other participatory talkshows such as *Oprah* also inject the premodern: a Manichean moralizing rife with stated or implied "shoulds" that play well to what critics of the talkshow have called "the misery market."[70] Oprah assumes a number of roles and voices and makes jarring shifts in emotional register in her talk host performance. Her paratextual position as modernist success story also becomes mixed with her New Age philosophies. As someone who rose from humble, troubled beginnings to stunning material success, she is a signifier of progress, perfectability, and control.[71] Hers was a "dramatic transformation" that could be the very apotheosis of modernist growth and development: taking control of her talkshow and forming her own company, Harpo Productions; building her own studio and diversifying into feature films that voice the experiences of blacks and women, who were, paradoxically, once excluded from modernity. Such a trajectory is an acting-out of her belief not only in taking control of one's own destiny but in "taking responsibility for what you've earned."[72] Oprah sees herself as a consciousness raiser whose "good work" seeks to "bring people closer to knowing themselves." A much-cited example of success through self-help, she acts as a catalyst for the growth of others. She and her show represent a postmodern mix of the premodern (a repository of maternal wisdom and prescriptive solutions) and the modern (a living embodiment of progress and entrepreneurial control). That she and her show constantly alternate between these discursive modes to achieve a playful yet productive instability helps explain her appeal.[73]

The audience's participatory position is crucial. Before the viewer ever hears from a studio or call-in participant, most interactive talkshows use reaction shots of audience members listening to the guests or experts as the host questions them. The effect seems, at first, to complete the circuit of exchange; an imaginary construct, cast in the mode of news or documentary liveness, seems to allow us a privileged, unembellished look at each party to the conversation. The format puts studio audience members in a position of surrogacy. Their initial appearance positions them in terms of reaction. Their reactions, which become verbally elaborated as they eventually speak into the host's microphone, establish a discourse of the "normal," while the guests and experts generate discourses of the "problematic" or the "possible."

While the spectators are positioned reactively, they are also positioned expectantly. They, like the televiewer, watch the talkshow with a range of expectations. The audience joins the host's quasi-empirical, polyphonic inquiry as processors of the performed and spoken data. That the host controls the microphone, cameras, and shot-sequencing *through* control of the conversation (almost as if he or she were directing from the floor), that the host has a special mobility around that studio floor as well as "having the floor" in the sense of having the preeminent, direct-address voice (with Geraldo, we are "in" "his" show), only furthers this identity with him and the apparatus. We knowingly share Geraldo's glance and hearing, but we are not confined to them. The show's and host's multiaccentuality permits the pleasures of identification and inquiry despite audience differences in gender, race, class, education, lifestyle—the modernist categories of subject differentiation.[74] Affective communities of otherwise socially differentiated subjects can momentarily coalesce. The personal becomes political. The show taps affective investments that transcend multiple subject boundaries while using an ethic and aesthetic of "both-and" to "have it both ways" in a narrative that is complex and contradictory[75]—a constellation of voices.

"Hard Times for Wimps":
The Morton Downey, Jr., Show

If *Geraldo* plays with the boundaries of news and documentary, *Downey* played with the limits and structures of other participatory talkshows. During its twenty-one-month run and its national syndication of just over a year, *Downey* played itself out as a self-conscious inversion of the women's talk/service tradition epitomized by *Donahue.*[76] Downey, his creator—MTV originator Robert Pittman—and his producers constructed the show as an angry response to what they saw as television's glut of polite, liberal, feminized talkshows populated by smiling faces and "nodding, bobbing heads."[77] In the words of executive producer Bill Boggs, Morton Downey, Jr., had "broken the mold of the polite, neutral host," which, for Boggs, accounted for the show's controversy and offered a telling parallel to Geraldo's self-conscious breaking of journalistic molds.[78] When Boggs called *Downey* "3-D television . . . rock and roll without the music," he was not only explicating the show's boundary-expanding, hyperstimulating, and hyperreal intentionality as "confrontainment"; he was also excoriating the implicit two-dimensionality, the limitedness, of his talkshow rivals. Such a view positioned *The Morton Downey, Jr., Show* as a new and greater source of spectatorial stimulation—an assault, a breaking-through of the screen, a "bite" into the viewer, a dramatic oral productivity that metaphorically penetrated that viewer more effectively, more "loudly," than other talkshows.

The reproductive interplay of rhetoric and program concept is critical here. Downey's trademark loud mouth, both a trope and part of the performing body-in-space, was the site of and a metonym for a cheap yet powerful oral communicative capacity surviving in an era of electronic technology. The mouth is the primal medium, a part of the body at the core of interpersonal communication and logocentrism yet brashly asserted, through Downey, into the mediasphere. As universally available channel, the mouth is the "natural" site of emotion, self-expression, defiance, deception, taste, appetite, and pleasure. Its pretechnological universality connotes its authenticity—you can *trust* the loud mouth. Though universal, it is also the focal point of selfhood through speech. As a "loud" mouth, Downey's connoted a particular potency, a greater effectivity; it tried to cut through the clutter and make a difference. For Downey, potent speech became action, language became performative; his broadcast speech "kicked some ass."

Despite its attempt to be different, *Downey* resembled other talk or tabloid shows in incorporating participation with the intent of "making a difference."[79] But Downey was positioned as taking the spectator *beyond* the usual formulas, emotions, and issues of talk television to a place that may also have been beyond the limits of taste (of which the mouth, interestingly, is a biological site). That Downey typically called his liberal adversaries "pabulum-pukers" only extended his oral metaphors. It also positioned his adversaries as crybabies in an implicit yet startling inversion of the long-standing scholarly-critical discourse against television: the spectator as impressionable and easily manipulated child. *Downey* imagined its fan as neither childlike nor subject to television's "paedocratic regime."[80] Rather, it cast the supposedly liberal, high-culture *critic-scholar*—what Vice-President Dan Quayle, by the 1992 presidential campaign, called the "cultural elite"—in the role of the "pabulum-puker"—the solipsistic infant—in contrast to Downey's hypermasculine "adulthood." The show took on a carnivalesque and resistant aura. That Downey's loud, defiant, cigarette-dangling mouth had been rebuilt following an auto accident years earlier only underscored, metaphorically, its constructedness in performance. It became part of his costume.[81]

In its late-night venue and violent, sportslike ambiance, *Downey* seemed a deliberate corrective to the negative association of mass culture with the feminine, so well epitomized—for Downey and his producers— by the daytime talkshow. In his essay "Mass Culture as Woman: Modernism's Other," Andreas Huyssen demonstrates how aesthetic modernism's male-encoded, critical discourse devalued and opposed mass culture by labeling it "feminine." The modernist adversarialism of Downey's style, recombined as it was with the atavistic antimodernism of many of his political positions, thrust its masculinism upon a "feminine" television. Modernism was a misogynistic "reaction formation" against the seductive "lure" and pleasure of mass culture and its consumption, which were, ironically, the engine as well as byproducts of modernity and progress. While modern*ism* in this way constructed itself as adversary to modern*ity*, the former was, as Huyssen has established, "deeply implicated" in the latter. With *Downey*, key elements of adversarial modernism phallically invaded its perceived Other: television—an Other in which it was, paradoxically, quite enmeshed. This invasion, finally, was a postmodern appropriation and an "attempt to negotiate forms of high art with certain forms and genres of mass culture and everyday life." The Downey persona became one of Huyssen's "postmodern raiders of a lost past," [82] his hyperproductive mouth the sign of a residually modernist emphasis on productivity as a reaction to the "feminized" consumption of a mass cultural product. In effect, *Downey* was an institutional and textual rebuke to the woman's talk/service show.[83]

Like the predominantly male political and activist radio call-in hosts (Downey was once one himself in Chicago), *Downey* strained to restore participatory talk programming to a male imaginary, and to do so more "actively" (productively) through more, angrier, and "louder" (masculinized) audience participation. The loud mouth became a figural condensation of male talk—a potent, penetrating mouth and speech that *had* to be loud, it seemed, to overcome the clutter of "wimpy, sensitive" women's talkshows like *Donahue, Oprah, Sally Jesse Raphael,* and *Geraldo.* Just as a team of New York women cops became a series premise in *Cagney and Lacey* to join the male-buddy formula, *Downey* was a masculinist incursion into the issue-oriented television talk genre by way of "rude" political talk radio, 1980s shock radio, and Joe Pyne.[84]

In an interview the day *Downey* was canceled, senior producer Peter Goldsmith called the show's "yelling and screaming" its "methodology."[85] Significantly, Downey's most frequent putdown—"Zip it!"— linked suppressed vocality (the loud mouth's Other) with the clothed (hidden) body. But the open mouth is also the key metonym of consumption, the supposedly feminine site so strongly and negatively identified with mass culture. The *Downey* logo, therefore, was encoded with its "other" in a carnivalesque multiplicity of terms.

In that same interview, Goldsmith stressed that Downey, like shock-jocks such as Howard Stern, had performed the difficult task of drawing an audience of males under twenty-five "to watch a show about the issues." Young males have been an audience long sought by advertisers yet historically difficult to reach—a task at which the sufficiently potent *Morton Downey, Jr., Show* was, for a time, effective. The predominance in the studio audience of young, white men "from the New Jersey suburbs, Brooklyn, Queens, with a smattering from Westchester,"[86] provided an ample cheering section when Downey, on one show, called 65 percent of divorced women engaged in child custody battles "liars."

Although the nightly *Downey* episodes dealt with a host of relevant and pressing issues—from drugs to homelessness to dormitory parietal hours—the show's format, tone, and host were equally "about" defying its imagined Other: the discourse of the feminized, *Donahue*-like talkshow stigmatized as polite, restrained, sensitive, weak ("gray") in its excessive multivocality, and—worst of all—liberal.[87] *Downey*'s setting combined the sports arena and the prizefight (bleachers, cheering fans, and the host's gladiatorlike entrance) with the political debate and town meeting (podiums on two sides) and features of the daytime participatory talkshow (host mobility, cameras turned toward the participating audience, guest experts sitting on a stage up front). This combination inscribed not only the oppositional "male" intertexts of sports and politics but hegemonically plundered and negotiated elements of the "bland" feminine format it claimed to oppose. The show's "yelling and screaming methodology" issued not only from an imagined reassertion of the masculine in an equally imagined feminized medium but from the ideology of liveness and a spontaneity historically linked with avant-garde shock and transgression.[88]

Life also imitated art. Significantly, Downey compared himself and his show with the film *Network* and its Howard Beal character (played by Peter Finch), a news anchor who has a nervous breakdown on the air and becomes, for a time, a "mad as hell" prophet who is "not going to take it any more"; as a result, his ratings skyrocket. At the heart of the appeal of Beal's television persona is his shattering of staid, highly calculated television program practices. He suddenly breaks out of his hard news format one evening to "tell it like it is" and expose the "usual" news as lies. He must assume the label "mad" in order for those around him to explain and justify his breaking of television's "hard news" frame. Yet the industry, in keeping with its calculated, ratings-oriented ways, soon realizes that it can exploit Beal's ingenuous madness, his very on-air lack of calculation, in a way typical of a postmodern image economy that commodifies modernist spontaneity and transgression.

Downey appropriated a key aspect of Beal's semiosis: the affect of honest, passionate spontaneity approaching madness in its lack of repression and its striking disjunction with normal, "contained" television. Institutionally, however, television could barely contain the dangerous vehemence of either Beal or Downey. Though both deliberately played against the context of bland, predictable television in what has indeed become a strategy of productive instability, became a threat to an industry based on the calculated pleasing of large audiences. Both tabloid shows (Beal's was hauntingly prophetic in the 1970s of what would happen to "real" television in the 1980s) had truncated on-air lives.

Downey was generally described as having had a "working-class edge" as well as having been "antiauthority." In a 1980s context, Downey's defiant on-camera chain-smoking linked him with what is left of postindustrial America's youth and blue-collar cultures, the groups most likely still to smoke in large numbers. That Downey tried to be a country-and-western singer strengthed this link. His dress was also an affront to the 1980s upscale designer style. He usually wore a jacket and tie (never a suit), but his outfit resisted the careful, trendy coordination of the corporate manager; instead, it was uncoordinated and scrupulously "square." The brown shoes were clodhoppers, and the perennial red socks clashed with everything. Downey told media critic Edwin Diamond that his father, the famous Irish tenor who was close to the Kennedy family, once objected to Mort's attire, quoting Joseph Kennedy as having said that "only people with no class wear red socks and brown shoes." In a repudiation as Oedipal as it was a rejection of the liberalism and upward mobility typified by the Kennedys, Downey claimed to have worn the no-class combination from that moment on.[89]

Being the financially secure son of a celebrity apparently encouraged his checkered career and high-risk behavior.[90] But Downey was downscale in a way that further suggested his active dismissal of an establishment he regarded as liberal. Being the oppositional conservative he imagined himself to be involved opposing the fashion, taste, and propriety dictated by that establishment. Downey's motley clothing and on-camera rudeness, playing with and against the codes of corporate culture, reflected a third American generation, the child of the child of immigrants who resists a full modernist assimilation and social mobility by rejecting flattening notions of "class" behavior. Downey wore his alienation like a badge—a tactic solidifying his link with youthful fans who, in their precareer poverty and outsiders' relationship to corporate culture, were also free to dress unconventionally and behave with downscale aplomb.

The ritual corporate talk practices so valorized in the eighties, particularly the meeting, had become so pervasive, cautious, and group oriented that Downey's unbridled self-assertion seemed a conscious oral assault on those practices as well. His speech, like his dress, rebuked the cultural capital of the button-down corporate style. As the uninhibited "real man" who spoke "the truth," Downey offered an implicit corrective to the bland, jargon-ridden, technocratic speech of the workplace, the graduate-professional school, and their managerial group-think. As he worked through his hour show, he would loosen his tie, take off his jacket, and roll up his sleeves in an exertion that was as physical as it was "loudmouth," suggesting effort and labor in the old working-class sense. *Downey* thus carried the nostalgic connotation of a smokestack America that was somehow better; it meant higher productivity, better balance-of-trade figures, and the greater dignity (and buying power) of the average worker. The show resonated with a "before the fall" America.

It is no wonder that Downey's young, predominantly male fans "love[d] his attitude" and considered him "the coolest talkshow host" when he targeted the establishment professional—the educated expert imagined to be liberal—for his program's ritual "ass-kicking."[91] Anal as well as oral tropes abounded in Downey's discourse to create a carnivalesque play with the grotesque body. Though the mouth was the chief site of his performative productivity, "let's kick some ass" was his usual call to arms. In a program taped in Houston and dealing with drug pushers, Downey suggested that errant kids must occasionally "have a foot stuffed up their ass" rather than "just" be educated about the dangers of drugs.[92] In his show's premiere episode he held up an American flag and told the camera, "kiss my flag"—a substitution that playfully yet aggressively inverted highly charged paradigms and simultaneously linked nostalgic patriotism with rude, 1980s-style defiance.

For his youthful fans, Downey's antiauthority stance was embedded in the show's inversions. One youth described the show as being "like a school where the teacher *wants* you to scream and yell and act like a jerk."[93] The young male fan's educational metaphor reveals yet another inversion: the show became an upside-down high school classroom—a class-turned-pep-rally—run by a "real" man instead of, more typically, a woman or a man imagined to have been "feminized" and "liberalized" by higher education. As an affront to education's authority and procedural norms as well as to the culture of expertise (the host brashly challenged most of his guest experts), *Downey* questioned the dominant societal totem of professionalism and the credentializing role played by the educational establishment. Edwin Diamond, who appeared on the show as a "liberal" guest expert, described the experience as one in which "caution inexorably vanishes—along with logic, manners, and everything else you learned to do on traditional talkshows" (or in a traditional classroom). He characterized the young studio audience as a "beast" composed of "young white males and their girlfriends who don't read newspapers." Diamond's guest appearance had put him "in the belly of the beast" (consumed by the "loud mouth").[94]

Downey occupied a quasi-protected, liminal turf which, despite its host's seeming political single-mindedness, permitted multiple readings from multiple subject positions. While his defiant attitude, vehement affect, and implied if not stated outsider position seemed to underlie his appeal to young males, his parodic excesses—his exotic pushiness—seemed to account for his appeal also to older and even female spectators.[95] This bimodality of appeal suggests that Downey and his show were actually multicoded and negotiable in ways that were not apparent to the many critics who saw him solely in "power mouth" terms.

By the summer of 1989, sponsors, stations, and even audiences seemed to be abandoning *Downey*; the show was finally canceled on July 20. Station program directors had been describing the host as a self-parody and the show as "like leprosy." Even members of the broadcast industry once so "high" on *Downey*'s studiously "low" form were echoing the "trash TV" critics who had disparaged it all along as a "virus" or some violent form of mental illness that was "drowning out civil discourse."[96] Downey's unverified allegation that he was attacked by skinheads in a San Francisco International Airport restroom the previous April—widely reported in the press in images of the host with a swastika on his face and a botched haircut—only encouraged his abandonment.[97] His very name had become a convenient metonym for debased public discourse. For instance, during a televised New Jersey gubernatorial debate between Jim Florio and Jim Courter (part of a nasty campaign in which each candidate's television ads featured the other with a computer-animated Pinocchio nose), Florio expressed the hope that the debate would not "degenerate into the *Morton Downey Show*."[98] For some in his home state, Downey's program symbolized an "old," "on the waterfront" New Jersey. Ron Powers titled his scathing review of the talkshow "It Came From New Jersey," a monster-movie title recalling the old New Jersey as alien and monstrous.[99] And turning "he" into "it" made Downey a fearful, ill-defined Other as well as "otherworldly."

Perceptions of *Downey*'s incivility circulated in and through metaphors recognizing the sports intertext: it was called "brawl show," "prize fight," "wrestling match," and "Roman Coliseum."[100] Edwin Diamond's description of his experience as a guest on the show not only reinforced and drew upon these metaphors but bore out their relationship to the practices of the show's production. There were two separate green rooms:

one for the right-wingers, Reed Irvine and Charles Wiley of Accuracy in Media; one for the left-wingers, Diamond and Joe Conason of the *Village Voice*. Diamond likened this arrangement to getting ready for a prizefight. In fact, when he met Downey in the makeup room, the two touched fists, on Downey's cue, in the manner of boxers.[101]

When Peter Goldsmith came to the left-wingers' green room for their preshow warmup, with the sound of the youthful studio audience chanting "Mort! Mort! Mort!" in the background, he declared, "Our lions are ready for our Christians." He instructed his guests to interrupt one another in order to earn a place later at the Loudmouth podium. As a precaution against any eruption of violence, audience members had to pass through a metal detector before entering the studio. Before taping, a producer gave the audience a list of rules—no shouting obscenities, no crossing a red-tape line on the floor, no violence—only to have Downey declare, "Those are the *wimp* rules."[102] Even *Broadcasting* magazine's news item on the show's cancellation constructed its demise in prizefight as well as poverty terms: "Downey and Out in Secaucus."

Downey's credibility—indeed, the whole notion of authenticity—lay at the core of a paradox enfolding a personality and program that traded on supposedly being "real," at least on an expressive/affective level. Yet Bob Pittman explained that he was happy to cast Downey as host because he was "someone less polite and predictable" than even Watergate's own G. Gordon Liddy, whom Pittman had originally considered.[103] Talk about Downey made much of his inflated claims to a footloose and checkered past as singer-songwriter, political activist, lobbyist, fast-food and sports executive, alleged ex-con, DJ, and radio talk host. Such an unstable background seemed a deliberate publicity ploy calculated to position him as a school-of-hard-knocks outsider and thus more strongly identifiable with "the people," despite his privileged upbringing. Like an affluent 1960s college student who assumed the trappings of poverty to hitchhike across America, Downey made sure he had "been there." But as a former liberal converted to a rather inconsistent conservatism, he had "been there and back again" to become a unique variation of the experienced and "enlightened" amateur who could "have it both ways."[104]

Call 1-800-BE-ANGRY

As dozens of radio talk hosts from across the country organized in 1989 around their opposition to that year's proposed congressional pay raise and their call to boycott Exxon in the wake of its March oil spill in Alaska's Prince William Sound, they defined themselves in populist and oppositional terms. Their formal organizational gesture was the June 9–11 first annual conference of the National Association of Radio Talk Show Hosts (NARTSH) at Boston's Faneuil Hall; titled "Talk Radio and the American Dream" (after Murray Burton Levin's 1987 book), it displayed the scope of their rhetoric.[105] A consummate self-promoter, Boston talk host and conference organizer Jerry Williams anointed talk radio "the greatest forum for American citizens in history," even "the last bastion of freedom of speech for plain, ordinary folks." Claiming a diverse audience of alienated average citizens "disenfranchised by government by the elite" and calling themselves "the only ones who will listen," [106] the hosts described themselves as crusaders fighting out-of-touch public officials who listen only to PACs and whose unresponsiveness is typified by their sending the complaining citizen "a form letter thanking you for your support." [107]

Talk radio activism achieved its critical mass in December 1988 when Ralph Nader called *The Jerry Williams Show* to protest a proposed 51 percent congressional pay raise. At about that same time an anonymous caller phoned Roy Fox in Detroit (on WXYT-AM) with the same complaint. The pay raise issue spread rapidly as a talkshow topic. Some twenty talk hosts nationwide organized a protest, urging listeners to write or call their representatives. Thousands of letter writers enclosed teabags in a gimmicky reference to the Boston Tea Party. The outpouring of protest forced both the House and Senate to back off from the proposal in February 1989.

Although the talk hosts triumphed, if only temporarily,[108] broadcast executives feared reregulation by an irritated Congress. Republican Michael Oxley of Ohio probably reflected the prevailing sentiment on Capitol Hill when he accused the campaign of being the "most unfair" he had ever seen. "Disk jockeys," he continued, whose "total I.Q. wouldn't reach the top number on the FM dial," were working up the electorate . . .

giving them false information."[109] FCC Commissioner James Quello accused the crusading talk hosts of being on a "messianic binge" and their broadcast managers of shooting themselves in the foot by airing these personalities and their causes at the risk of raising the specter of their own reregulation.[110]

The hosts saw themselves as providing a compensatory link between people and politicians—in Jerry Williams's words: "We fill a vacuum"—at a time when the "usual" channels, the constitutionally provided representative processes, had broken down. The Faneuil Hall conference setting became, as Williams himself suggested in his opening remarks, emblematic of the ties that talk radio was forging with American political traditions and ideals: freedom of speech, revolution, and the perceived intentions of the Founding Fathers—intentions lost in the growing bureaucratic distance between the "plain," private, ordinary citizen and the public official.

Williams expanded talk radio's role beyond feedback and advocacy and into the journalistic. Talk radio for him was "a window on the world for millions," giving "information on an unprecedented scale never known before in the world." Mike Siegel of KVI Seattle made a claim for uniqueness: he and his colleagues, though "denigrated, demeaned, and attacked" by their critics, were providing "a form of communication that is not found in other media." Phoning in to the live June 9 broadcast of the conference's opening, Morton Downey, Jr., called the participatory talkshow "the last forum for the disenfranchised, the powerless."[111]

Despite their broad claims and even broader egos, the talk hosts' discourse of being "the most" (informative and participatory) and "the last" (bastion of free speech) for "the least" (the "little guy") is a string of pugnacious superlatives juxtaposed to the counterclaim that they are merely catalysts and not instigators, which offsets their threatening status with a measure of deniability. Like television's Geraldo or Downey, the radio talk hosts also want it both ways. Jerry Williams once said on the air that his job is "to blow the whistle," a self-positioning that assumes serious public responsibility.[112] But on another occasion he told a college class that what he really does as a broadcaster is no more or less than *sell*.[113]

The question of power constantly lurks in and beneath the hosts' self-definition. They construct an ambivalent, deniable position with re-spect to power and the media's sociopolitical effects. Sensitive to charges that they are "a lot of people with questionable credentials manipulating people's emotions,"[114] they claim to defer to "the people" and limit them-selves to the role of communicative "helpers." Mike Siegel, a principal organizer of the Exxon boycott, described it as having "grassroots" rather than talkshow beginnings. His callers urged him into a leadership role, he said; the boycott "wasn't because of me, but because I represented the points of view of millions of people." Williams claims a similar role in the congressional pay raise opposition; the hosts were merely "the bugle boys and girls." "We have no power," said one, "it's when *you* light up the phones."[115]

But with the major networks and newspapers labeling their first conference "a conspiracy" of "hometown demagogues" with a "hidden agenda,"[116] the organizing talkhosts became understandably sensitive. Williams told his June 9 listeners that ABC/Capital Cities had refused to let its hosts attend because, according to a company spokesman, the "uni-fying of talkshow hosts is an unfair concentration of media power."[117] Williams rightly pointed out the hypocrisy of such an assertion, remind-ing the conferees and his listeners of the power of the networks as well as of the *New York Times*, the *Boston Globe*, and the *Washington Post*: "[Columnist] David Broder at the *Washington Post* just can't control everything." Thus, the hosts cast themselves in an oppositional role as another group of persistent "little guys" homologous with their audi-ences: the "plain, ordinary" citizens with and for whom they claim to speak. In Mike Siegel's words, "We don't manipulate or coerce. We're just the means through which the public is heard."[118]

As "means," however, they construct themselves in powerful, hyper-masculine, sometimes violent language. Jerry Williams: "The essence of talk radio is to give people a punch in the solar plexus." It is also "a weapon, a provocateur."[119] Bob Grant of WABC New York said he and his show got involved in the 1990 New Jersey tax protest in order to "throw the bastards out" in the upcoming election.[120] The hosts' rheto-ric offers a renewed, physical-visceral *contact* with politics and power which the "little guy" has lost. They purport to put "plain folks" muscularly back "in touch" with the "out of touch" politicians. Their words translated into significant action again on October 27, 1990—Taxpayer Action Day—when talk hosts around the country helped organize anti-tax and anti-incumbent rallies in 241 of the nation's 435 congressional districts.[121]

Legislators in Massachusetts complained about "government by talk show" during the state's 1989 budget debate and the tax cut crusade led by talk hosts Jerry Williams and Pat Whitley and *Boston Herald* columnist Howie Carr (who sometimes appears on Williams's show).[122] By the year's end a major series in the *Boston Globe* had singled out talk radio hosts—"'governors' on the airwaves"—as one of the major reasons for the "poisoned politics" of Massachusetts, a politics so poisoned that the state and its government seemed incapable of dealing with a towering budget deficit. Rather than truly and reasonably inform, said the *Globe*, the "self-styled" "pseudo-populist" talk radio "governors" treat the facts as "eye-glazing minutiae" standing in the way of a good story; with cynicism as their "principal value" and bombast as "the order of the day," they denounce most persons on the public payroll as "hacks." The result: an avalanche of phone calls to the State House.[123]

It may have been a negative effect of such low regard for elected officials and state employees that late in 1990 the Republican governor-elect, William Weld—himself a relative political "outsider" whose campaign benefited from the talkshows' anti-Democrat rhetoric—was in the ironic position of having trouble hiring people for his new administration.[124] Another telling irony is that the same politicians who complained about talkshow "governors" rarely refuse—in fact, they *seek*—talkshow appearances. Like the talk hosts, they too seem willing to cross borders and "have it both ways" in their own exercise of a persistent yet strangely productive contradiction in American political life: the fuzzy, crossable line between the political inside and outside. By now, both sides of the line are very media-dependent.

Long aware of their demeaned status in the eyes of the "elite" media (although that contempt seemed to be easing by the time of the fourth talk radio conference in 1992),[125] the talk hosts saw themselves as under siege in the same way they see the political process envisioned by the Founding

Fathers as threatened. One host described himself as a member of "an endangered species." Such rhetoric reinforces the hosts' identification with the postindustrial spectator-participant as tenuous *worker*. Like that worker, the call-in host is subject to the instabilities of the information economy; he or she, too, can suddenly and all too frequently be out of a job.[126]

The talk host who can become an object of identification for the listener-participant on the basis of perceived dystopian similarity, however, can at the same time embody utopian possibility. The caller speaks anonymously; the host's identity and personality are known to all. Likewise, the caller assumes a position of modesty and anonymity; the host is often a well-paid, high-profile celebrity rewarded for taking the expressive risks that most callers cannot, except anonymously. The talk host thereby becomes an ideal contemporary worker: the outspoken, brash individualist in a time of corporate anonymity. In the words of Jerry Williams's Boston colleague Gene Burns, the talk host is "the last generalist in a world of specialists."[127]

Television talk hosts have their shirt-sleeved, loosened-tie image; radio hosts display their labor through a uniquely lengthy time *on the air*—fifteen to twenty weekly hours of exposure and effort—so demanding that to be successful at it has put them at a premium and escalated their salaries.[128] Their sustained interactive availability subjects them to intense scrutiny by the public, the competing media, and even their own employers—so much so that they *must* "read" as credible and genuine. The talk hosts thus also trade on a self-description of authenticity. Some who attended the first conference matter-of-factly boasted about having been fired for taking particular on-air stands. Steve Wexler of KGW Portland, Oregon, resorted to the usual superlatives and called talk radio "the most sincere form of radio that exists"—in other words, a manifestation of the grand, modernist claim to authenticity.

The first NARTSH conference took pains to project its membership as broadly representative with respect to race, gender, and viewpoint on particular issues—a tactic calculated to diffuse the "conspiracy" charges leveled by the press and media executives. African American talk host Joe Madison of WXYT Detroit assured Williams and his listeners that "in talk radio, there is no color, there's *voices*," and—in a populist flourish putting him solidly in the discursive company of the whitest and most conservative hosts—"the only color of freedom in America is green, unfortunately."

One female talk host waxed optimistic about the increased (though still paltry) numbers of women in talk radio while admitting that they need to become more assertive. Later, feminist talker Carole Hemingway of KGIL Los Angeles engaged in a heated on-air debate with Baltimore's ultraconservative Lester Kinsolving over what she saw as the dearth of women in talk radio. By including and airing their verbal scuffle the conference, like the genre, promoted itself as inclusive while retaining a largely masculinist mystique: most of its hosts tend to be well-paid, white, middle-aged, and politically conservative men.[129] Their marginality and "outsiderness" make for an affect they wear as they also play at being insiders, "governors of the airwaves." In yet another productive contradiction, they are both good citizens and bad boys in the images they project. In their growing political organization the talk hosts want to be part of a better, more truly representative system, even as their shows—in Murray Burton Levin's words—have a "subversive effect," are "the very few delegitimizing voices of America," and project America's "proletarian despair" and "crisis of confidence."[130]

The talk hosts' organizational efforts are an attempt not only to raise their status and political clout but to overcome their regional confinement. Regionalism may limit a national public's awareness of them and militate against any national impact, but it nonetheless gives each one a productive social accent identifying him or her with the *local* audience. By organizing nationally, then, the talk hosts seem to be immersing themselves in yet another productive contradiction: poising themselves somewhere between the localism vital to their daily appeal and modernist universalism. While their standardization is still tentative, their regionalism has already established itself as a fundamental dynamic: it is what makes their participatory form work.

Hyperlocal Boy Makes Good:
The Frank Rizzo Show

Nationally, there are so many talkshows and hosts—literally thousands—that they defy generalization. The micropolitical regionalism of talk radio fragments it as an object of study, as does even a single show's constant, daily shifting of guest, topic, and caller. Such fragmentation is a postmodern "condition." But one closely examined case can demonstrate some of the other ways in which talk radio "talks" us into postmodernity.

On November 4, 1988—the day former Philadelphia mayor Frank Rizzo, attempting a political comeback, lost the city's mayoral race to incumbent Wilson Goode—Rizzo began his radio career in that same city as host of *Frank Talk* (subsequently retitled *The Frank Rizzo Show*), an afternoon call-in program on WCAU-AM which he always ended with the words, "Goodnight, Wilson, wherever you are." The show left the air on August 15, 1990, when he announced that he would again run for mayor. In the interim, the station's afternoon drive-time rating for listeners over age twenty-four shot up from thirteenth to first, thanks to the tremendous popularity of Rizzo's show. The *New York Times* said he had achieved "one of the most amazing overnight successes in local broadcasting history," despite those "who said he would flop because of what they considered his history of bombast, botched grammar, and one-dimensional liberal bashing."[131]

Rizzo's fifth mayoral candidacy ended suddenly with his death on July 16, 1991. In examining the dynamics of his popularity in Philadelphia, I suggest that his play with locality in his talkshow performance was a key dynamic in how he "worked"—in both senses—as a media and political figure. Just as he "read" as "local" yet at the same time "*more* than local," he was "worker" and "*more* than worker," media performer yet anti-media, insider yet outsider to the system—all in a postmodern play with meaning and deniability.

The management of WCAU attributed Rizzo's success and the higher profile he gave the station to the belief that he was, in the words of the station's vice-president and general manager, Chris Witting, "a great communicator" who "had lunch with the Queen" but "never lost the common touch": in other words, the local boy who made good and went national, even international, but still kept his sense of locality. Witting also correctly explained Rizzo's success as "based on his politics," which "brought us a whole set of listeners we never had before"—white ethnics.[132] Station manager Gregory Tantum called Rizzo "the highest-profile person in Philadelphia," one who could focus on "what people talk about . . . drugs, crime, politics."[133]

Rizzo himself attributed his appeal to being "another voice, a conservative voice," and with his having "another philosophy than the liberal media." He saw his central role in "do-gooder" terms—not in the stereotypical "liberal" sense but in the sense used by Geraldo and other talk/service hosts: helping to solve people's problems, which was what he felt he did best.[134] Like Geraldo, he defined himself in populist terms: "I think there's another message people want to hear. There's a lot of issues that should be directed to the rowhouse people. The little people. This is the group I relate to." Even though he earned $200,000 annually as a talk host, collected another $45,000 in a city pension, and lived in the city's wealthiest district, he once confessed that he had moved to Chestnut Hill because his wife wanted to, adding, "I don't even know my neighbors." He projected an irrevocable link to the white, ethnic, working-class South Philadelphia neighborhood he came from.[135] Rizzo may have slept in Chestnut Hill, but he rejoined South Philly from three to six in the afternoon every weekday, recreating that neighborhood symbolically and sociopolitically.

Rizzo was long identified as a protector of the white, urban, immigrant culture of Philadelphia's rowhouse neighborhoods as black immigration and "white flight" transformed those communities. Rising from beat cop to captain, then to inspector in the 1950s, and finally to police commissioner in 1967, he acquired the label "toughest cop in America." His police department underwent Justice Department, *Philadelphia Inquirer*, and Public Interest Law Center investigations for police brutality; the American Civil Liberties Union accused him and his department of harrassing blacks, hippies, activists, and homosexuals—those he once called "bleeding hearts, dangerous radicals, pinkos, and faggots." Rizzo answered these charges by pointing out that his city "wasn't burning" in the late 1960s when he was police commissioner, while others were.[136] He also boasted that Center City Philadelphia boomed during his 1970s mayoralty.

His loss of the 1988 race seemed symptomatic of his transformation "from legend to bruised legend." He threatened to leave Philadelphia— "his world"—if he lost.[137] Instead, he stayed as talk host, recreated that world through mediated conversation, and became his listeners' "radio mayor"; in fact, many of his callers still addressed him as "Mr. Mayor." He traded on his historically rich connotations, affect, and multiple, shifting identities: bruised legend, tough and heroic cop, champion of the working class and the white ethnic, problem solver, father figure, good neighbor, survivor, ex-mayor, undereducated success story, nostalgic preserver of a community and a way of life, right-wing hothead, and grammar-botching liberal-basher. This multiplicity, activated and negotiated in the context of a participatory media form, became the source of his show's power. His shifts among these roles in talkshow performance—shifts that constantly redefined and even inverted his enunciative frame—were central to the productive instability of his performance and discourse. So was his tentative and implicitly oppositional relationship to radio as apparatus and, in his words, "liberal" institution—despite *his* using it and its using *him* in a uniquely productive postmodern double coding, a contingency born of commodification. His program's mix of premodern, antimodern, and modern codes—the utopian and the dystopian—combined in a discourse that could be called postmodern.

Rizzo's show usually began with an angry monologue lasting five to ten minutes. On March 12, 1990, he rails against the previous week's subway accident in which three persons were killed and dozens injured.[138] It has since come out in the news that the motorman tested positive for drug use. As Rizzo speaks, his South Philadelphia accent strains under his increasing anger. He advocates mandatory drug testing for all SEPTA (transit) workers—in fact, for all employees to whose care the public is entrusted. He lambasts the ignorance of the law evident in the district attorney's charges against the motorman; Rizzo "corrects" them and recommends that the DA undergo some in-service training. He offers up the accident as yet another instance in which poor municipal government has harmed Philadelphia's "good, hard-working people." He reads about the accident from a local newspaper, thereby inserting himself as a neighborhood journalist, a credible repository of "the facts," yet able to criticize that very coverage *and* the current municipal administration at the same time. In this single, semi-extemporaneous performance, Rizzo plays a multiplicity of locality-based roles simultaneously and consecutively: impassioned advocate and critic, "expert" ex-cop, former (and possibly future) mayor, political outsider *and* insider.

The first caller he takes is John, a county worker from Wilmington, Delaware. Like many callers who do not call Rizzo "Mr. Mayor," John addresses him as "Frank." John states his support for Rizzo's get-tough drug-testing policy after thanking the host for sending him a WCAU coffee mug. As a county employee, John thinks workers should have to take an unannounced drug test: "I'm not guilty about anything." What ensues (transcribed here from the taped record) is a ritual of mediated interpersonal identification celebrating common ground in a way that raises shared locality, even familiality, to the abstract level of common ideology.[139]

R: Exactly. And it amazes me that they try to hide under the First—ah, what is it, the First Amendment, er, Second Amendment . . . First Amendment, I think it is. But anyway, what's just—if you're—

J: Yeah—

R: —a person that's responsible, again, for the lives and well-being of other people, it would seem to me . . . in fact, I would not hire them. If they refused to take a drug test, I'd fine them.

J: Yeah. Yeah, that's—hey, that's the only way, man.

R: Exactly right.

J: Say, you're talking about people's lives.

R: Exactly right.

J: Now let's say they killed, what, four people?

R: Three people died. It was a, a load of them injured. I think the number still in the hospital, don't hold me, is about twelve or fifteen—

J: Yeah.

R: —but it could have been a lot worse.

J: That's right, Frank.

R: And it was—

J: Just the same—

R: Take that poor lady, a domestic out workin' hard all day, trying to make a buck, *dies* on the way home after scrubbing someone else's dirt, you know?

J: Yeah.

R: Now these are the things that upset me to no end.

J: And then—

R: And that creep's on coke at five o'clock in the morning, all right—

J: Yeah.

R: And I had to laugh when I listened to some of the statements made by—I, I can't get over it, they get away with it—it was some of the top guys in SEPTA, saying, "Well, we don't know whether it impaired, don't know whether that contributed to the accident." That's nonsense! I've had them in my career, many, many of them that were under the influence. You know, alcohol's just as bad, almost as bad.

J: Sure.

R: Ah, in my opinion, cocaine, drugs, crack are just—got a little edge on alcohol. They're both bad. Booze or—the examination should not only be in the area of substance use but also alcoholics. If they're alcoholics, they should never be in a position where they can go *ape*. And that's what happened. That motorman was stoned.

J: Sure.

R: He don't know that other noise. You know, like you're driving your car—I used the example the other day—your muffler drops. You hear a noise you're not familiar with. You pull over to see what it is.

J: Right.

R: Or, you're driving along, you hear a noise—that's not—bingo, you pull over. Ah, when you're stoned, nothing affects ya. You know, you're flyin', you're on your way, you know? So when this cr—guy, who wants to use coke and then he wants to operate a train—

J: Yeah.

R: No way! And this is what has happened to us. This is, John, what the social engineers have done to us, pal. The old values that made us strong and secure, the values of hard work, the values of dedication, the values of what's right, what's wrong—they went down the drain. We've let the do-gooders push us around. Now, politically, we have to stand up and take them on. You want a drug pusher rehabilitated? Fine, I do too. But I'll tell you this—and I would have no problem if they're rehabilitated—to give them another job. But never operatin' a train.

J: No.

Rizzo then goes into a condemnation of the local drug czar (whom he calls an "a-s-s-hyphen-hyphen-hyphen")—for thinking he can ease the drug problem by replacing street lights: in Rizzo's words, by merely "changing light bulbs." If Rizzo were police chief, the drug pushers would be off the street "in about three days" because he would tell his officers "how to handle 'em." He compares the drug war to World War II—"we can't give up"—and drugs to another form of slavery, "like a Hitler or a Stalin." Unabashedly mixing his metaphors, Rizzo criticizes the police commissioner, intellectuals, city services, and "social liberals" as he works himself into a highly charged state that prevents John from inserting more than a monosyllabic comment. Finally, John thanks Rizzo and tells him to "keep up the good work; you really inspire a lot of people." Rizzo reminds him and his listeners that his show provides news unavailable from the liberal press and that "if you don't like what I'm sayin', you can shut me off."

While purporting to offer vital information, Rizzo has built an intensity of affect to a point where dialogue becomes an extended monologue whose substance is reinforced by the listener-participant as co-present "yes man." Knowledge becomes a function of affect, reactive and inseparable from its enunciator, despite its journalistic framing. Rizzo has also shifted between his multiple roles just as he has between mediated, monologic performance and interpersonal exchange, using the latter as a mere vehicle for the former in what seems like bullying framed as dialogue.

The next caller, George, disagrees with him about the SEPTA operator; George thinks the accident would have happened anyway. Rizzo screams back at him, interrupting his argument in fits and starts: "I disagree!" "Did you hear what I said?" "Do you understand me correctly?" "You and I are not on the same wavelength." Impatient and arrogant, Rizzo argues on the presumption that his opponent has failed to listen, to grasp the "facts"—in other words, as if he were somehow "from out of town," displaced from the locality and logic of Rizzo's talkspace, which is the "real" Philadelphia. Rizzo does not acknowledge the possibility of an opposing *argument,* only the probability that the communication has broken down at his opponent's end. Rizzo's interlocution transposes the question of difference from the level of meaning to the level of process, frame, and performativity. He implicitly acknowledges himself as the better communicative performer: given his local experiential grounding, his views "must" be correct. His performance depends on his local accent, his botched grammar, and his long-time neighborhood experience—all marks of his hyperlocality playing effectively with *and* against his national stature and "white knight" persona.

After a commercial, Rizzo reads another article about last week's SEPTA accident. This triggers a flashback, a story about an injury he had suffered as a cop years earlier:

> Boy, I'm tellin' ya, I remember when I fractured my hip in a fire. I was in pain, great pain. The most horrible pain you could endure. And I got to Hahnemann Hospital and the doctors were workin' on me and they didn't want to operate on me the—because it was late in the evening and the, the surgeon had worked all day—Dr. Arnold Berne, who was one of the surgeons— and they put me in a holding room and they had a, they hit

me with morphine, some other drugs. Believe me, the pain left
me immediately. I was flying all over the place. I know what it
feels like. Euphoria, they call it. I had no pain that whole night.
Blood transfusions, the other things they give ya'—IVs. But I
had the opportunity that most people have never had, to use
high levels of morphine. So, when anybody tells me that I'm
not an expert in drugs, but I know a lot as a cop, and I know
what they do. I had a guy one time with drugs with an ax killed
his five kids and his wife and we got him under the influence of
drugs. Don't tell *me* what they'll do to ya.

The monologue confirms Rizzo's expertise in a way acceptable to his audience: it is local and experiential, deriving specifically from work experience rather than formal education. He reasons inferentially, on the basis
of his experience as cop, while also imparting his privileged knowledge
and experience to the "little guy" listener—the "decent, hard-working
citizen" of Rizzo's symbolic South Philly neighborhood—who, he pre-
sumes, would not likely have had a legal reason for using a high-dose
narcotic. He identifies with his perceived audience member along regional, class, ethnic, and ideological lines and at the same time clearly
recognizes his authoritative distance and *privileged* experiential status.
Frank Rizzo, in "looking after us," is "like us" and at the same time "not
like us." He makes a virtue of his difference: *his* drug experience is twice
transformed from "bad" to "good": first, because it resulted from his
selfless public service; second, because it is reconfigured into yet *another*
public service by his telling of it as a cautionary talkshow tale.

Like many call-ins, *The Frank Rizzo Show* produced information,
entertainment, trepidation, and pleasure through a constant dialogism
and quasi-improvisational mix of the predictable (format, host persona,
initial topic delineation through newspaper clippings) and the unpredictable (callers who agree or disagree with him and sometimes shift the
topic). Whether they agreed or not, callers became Rizzo's touchstones,
his foils. He played off and with them—in his words, had "fun." [140] The
callers became local particles of chance colliding with Rizzo's own issue-
and ideology-oriented agenda to vary the show—but only within a certain shared construct or vision of Philadelphia: the great place it once
was, the mess it had become, the great place it would again be once

Rizzo returned to the mayor's office. His performance relied on that implicit "what if"—what *he* would do for Philadelphia if he were mayor—a promise of utopia lying beyond the "fallen" city.

His constant shifts in role and frame, a productive instability fostered by the participatory format and the local political setting, sustained narrative surprise. This moment-to-moment play with identities and metalingual frames, spurred by the improvisational format and the unpredictability of audience participation, permitted, in Dick Hebdige's words, "a new principle of assemblage" going beyond the postmodern's "entropic connotations" to "open up new meanings and affects." Such play not only accomodates but thrives on subjectivities like Rizzo, who could perform as a conservative in a medium that he at the same time condemned as "liberal." Like his audience, Rizzo and his producers used the participatory talkshow's instabilities to produce from "the other side of established institutional circuits" by commodifying its very Other.[141]

Another source of Rizzo's productive instability was his tentative, even oppositional, relationship to radio as apparatus and institution, a relationship cultivated over his years of press exposure and embraced even while he was on the media's payroll. His performance was roughened, in what seemed an ingenuous reflexivity, by his awkward on-air transitions. His cohosts (who stayed very much in the background while Rizzo was taking calls) would come on-mike to cue him to a commercial, a newscast, or his next caller. After a long pause, Rizzo often asked, "Lisa, what do I do now?" "Who am I speaking to next?" Typical of the participatory talkshow's reflexivity and extemporaneous roughness, Rizzo's performance was studiously "un-slick." Though his anger flowed with a spontaneity that seemed eminently authentic, his transitions—expressive demands made of him by the medium and its practice—were abrupt and tentative, a performed nonendorsement of media practice. They became intonations that could only endear him to his media-critical fans, distancing him from the suspect, "liberal" medium within which he nonetheless spoke.

Such awkwardness reinforced his political, affective, and ideological authenticity. It made him appear superior to the medium and its standardizing, technological constraints; it implicitly questioned radio's ethic of professionalism and expertise. Occasional cohost and producer Ruth Weisberg, credited with keeping the show "professional," understood this so well that such a reading may have been a result of the program's—and Rizzo's—intended effect. She described her role as "like being a lifeguard letting someone swim out far and not drown. I'm very tuned in to him. I'm on him like a hawk." [142]

That Rizzo reproduced himself as an anti-media professional—another "enlightened amateur" with whom the listener-caller could identify—while also being an integral part of the institution and apparatus was a productive contradiction; it generated audiences from an otherwise media-suspicious constituency of largely white, working-class listeners who, the station admitted, had not previously been available to it. This particular instability was rooted in a play with frame, the metalingual situation of the communicative exchange cuing the interlocutors how to decode it. Here, the "how to" shifts between the professional-institutional (the commodified, standardized call-in format) and the spontaneous-ingenuous (the passionate, moralistic expressiveness of the host). The former is deeply implicated in modernity; the latter is pre- or even anti-modern. *Rizzo's* dialogical interweaving of them was a product of the constant disjunctions, contradictions, and inversions of the show's pastiche of historical voices. Rizzo rebuked modernity even as he utilized one of its major tools—mass communication—to target a narrow sociopolitical audience.

In *Rizzo* the talkshow's "act of disjunction" and "bewildering immersion" were not entirely dystopian, in Fredric Jameson's sense of the terms.[143] Like postmodern architecture, *Rizzo* was a discursive space that did more than "let the fallen city fabric into its being." It incorporated the voice of utopian, modernist possibility ("wish fulfillment and dream, a glimpse of the good life," [144] and what Rizzo meant when he said, in show after show, "We'll have our day") *as well as* the dystopian "fallenness of the American Dream" noted by Murray Burton Levin: talk radio's "confidence gap," its "delegitimizing effect," "sense of stalemate," and "chronic disenchantment." [145] It is the talkshow's intertextual inclusiveness and contradiction—its very *clutter*–that now makes it audience-delivering, "clutter buster" programming.

3

Making Sense and Nonsense: Talk about the Talkshow

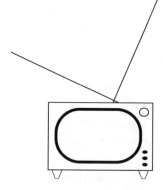

Boston radio talk host Jerry Williams calls talk radio "the greatest forum for citizens in history." Laura Jackson, producer of the Philadelphia psychological advice program *Family Matters*, boasts that her show provides a therapeutic network of people helping one another—a community that would not exist without the program's call-in participation. Yet *Talk Radio*'s author and performer, Eric Bogosian, labels his film's talk host character a "sociopath" and sees the 1980s growth of the genre as a "fad." During the early months of 1989, some members of the Massachusetts state legislature frequently objected to "government by talk show" while others appeared as guests on those very shows to promote their particular stands. A *New York Times* television review used the language of psychopathology to dub Donahue, Geraldo, and Downey "neighborhood delinquents," journalistic imposters who "drown out civil discourse."[1] Most empirical research has portrayed talkshow viewers as almost equally remiss—isolated, deficient, incapable of the "real" face-to-face, interpersonal communication for which the talkshow provides a deceptive substitute.

As these responses suggest, the reception of the talkshow is as varied as the shows themselves. Television critic William A. Henry III has condemned them for "demeaning one of the profound moments in life, the moment when noise becomes speech and then communication." He blames this result on their "blurred distinction" between interpersonal and mediated relationships, "journalistically researched facts" and "mere chitchat," and individualized "emotional 'truths' " and "provable"

109

scientific knowledge—blurring that supposedly confuses the viewer. He also faults the talkshow "for sanctioning prying and gossip, for transmuting communication into commerce, for legitimizing the tradeoff of a personal revelation for a book or movie plug." [2]

The concept of "blurred distinction," a concept so productive for the talkshow and the broadcast industry's development of it, lies at the heart of Henry's—and others'—condemnation of the genre. It is a concept based in the talkshow's intense contingency. That such shows seem to "take the pulse" of America in their intertextual recirculation of almost anything is because the talkshow has emerged as an institution central to that pulse. The language of talkshows is indicative: one makes an "appearance" on the talkshow "circuit." The talkshow constitutes as well as creates a vital circuit in an image economy, making it at once a cause *and* effect of that economy. Its unique intertextuality always requires its completion by *another* text, one already recognizable in its preexistent "textuality." The interview lies at the heart of this.

Whether used in the talkshow or in standard news programming, the interview is a singularly productive procedure: it manufactures information in ways that may be useful or entertaining or both. It also manufactures an event wherein the signifiers of performance—personae, setting, linguistic (representational) and behavioral (presentational) codes —carry meaning beyond the dialogue. The interview did not become a journalistic practice until the mid-1800s, at a time when the newspapers' pursuit of the news became vigorous in a competitive environment. What Daniel Boorstin called the "graphic revolution" was under way. It was also a time when newspapers sought to attract readers by emphasizing the newsgathering process itself, such as the use of technology like the telegraph, in their stories and layout. Later in the century, "making news" would assume still more aggressive forms—the staging of events, for example.[3] But the interview would retain its important place and even come to occupy the status of "pseudo-event."[4] The interview's connotation of contrivance has much to do with the presence of the reporter, a presence that inscribes the producer of the news within the product itself. As early as 1869 *The Nation* decried the interview as "the joint product of some humbug of a hack politician and another humbug of a reporter."[5]

As the historical forerunner of the talk host, the reporter and his or her self-inscription in the story textually encodes the newsgathering process. As a key part of that process, the reporter had emerged as its principle actor by the late 1800s.[6] The vocation of reporting gained status, evolving from job to an esteemed profession or even a "calling." It became glamorous; increasingly it required a college education. Reporters became as famous as the figures they covered—much like today's talk host or news anchor. While committed to the "facts" in ways echoing the growing value put on expertise in politics, scientific management in industry, and realism in literature, late nineteenth-century reporters also knew they had to be colorful and entertaining.[7]

To a large extent, the contemporary talkshow derives from this evolution of news practice and the status-conferring inscription of the reporter in both process and product. The reception of the contemporary talkshow depends upon whether or not it is perceived as news, as real rather than imaginary. Generally, the talkshow has become something the press, filmmakers, and academicians love to hate. Its play with discursive boundaries and identities, with chaos and contingency, have made it threatening to critics desperate for clear labels and stable structures—in other words, for a representational "purity" the talkshow will not allow.

The Bad and the Boneless

George Bush might very well have been addressing "confrontalk" shows and their hosts when he pleaded for "a kinder, gentler America" in 1988, kicking off a presidential campaign that would prove, ironically, to be among the most vicious on record. A *New York Times* front-page article declared 1988 a year "when civility really took it on the chin."[8] Besides being the moment of the "confrontainment" talkshow, the year was a time when "nastiness came into its own and became a commodity." Besides the Bush-Dukakis animosity, the piece cited the rise of "attack" comedians, ethnically insulting board games, and a kind of biography known as "pathography." It advanced three possible explanations: the negative effects of the media; the unrestrained, supposedly therapeutic venting of emotions (typical of the talkshows) encouraged since the 1960s; and the ascent of feminism, which both encouraged men to "take the gloves off" and left a familial vacuum in the teaching of manners (since women, whose job it had been, were increasingly entering the work force). The author, Lena Williams, found the media effects explanation especially plausible, given the ability of negative political advertising and the bombast of a Morton Downey, Jr., to "override the cynicism that years of conventional television programming and advertising have bred." If television was a "funhouse mirror"—as Todd Gitlin, cited in the article, maintained—then, according to the *Times*, ever greater exaggeration was a perpetual necessity.[9]

Although this discourse is hardly surprising, in 1988 or today, it *is* notable that the once innocuous audience participation talkshow and its host have become bad objects, implicated in what much of the "traditional" press has come to see as manipulative pseudojournalism harmful to the spectator's civic health. Along with the academic and psychological establishments' reception, the popular press response is important because of the talkshow's affinities with journalism. Obviously, talkshows and more conventional news programs can overlap considerably or see themselves as making competing claims to "truth" and "useful" public service. But the talkshow's disputed and multiple identity is actually quite productive, allowing competing claims to and about its "form" while generating a debate newsworthy in and of itself.

Empirical research into the talkshow was not undertaken until the 1950s, a time when critics and other "experts" regarded the talkshow as suspect at worst. Reviewers accused the most facile of the talk hosts of thinking no more than "an inch deep."[10] They doubted the hosts' talent, substance, and even their masculinity, chat being solidly associated with women. Jack Paar and his early *Tonight* show were, according to a 1958 story in *Time*, models of "organized planlessness." The article located the show's appeal in its (feminine) unpredictability. It put Paar somewhere between innocence and sophistication and characterized him as principally feeling and reactive, adding that "feeling takes the place of talent." The reviewer meant "talent" in the traditional sense associated with actors, musicians, or dancers; the notion of the media personality as a true performer or artist was beyond serious consideration. The best the *Time* article could do was regard the host as some combination of "low pressure" comedian and passive "personality"; it called him "self-effacing," hesitant and even shy, "amiable."[11] (More recently, Paar has been called an "anti-hero" who was "ahead of his time" in that he "brought an edge of quirky individuality to a previously neutered format" and "broke the rules" with risqué humor, deep emotional involvement in his subjects—he was notorious for crying before the cameras—and petulant threats to walk out—which he finally did, to end his talkshow career.) [12]

There were similar descriptions of *Today*'s first host, Dave Garroway. He was "cool . . . as languid as possible about everything," an attitude expressed by his "general bonelessness both in physiognomy and in point of view." [13] He was also called "a little fey," [14] much as 1930s and 1940s radio talker Alexander Woollcott was dubbed "a darling old male squealer." [15] Having watched Garroway as I grew up in the 1950s, I find the description approximate. But to call him "boneless" not only assaults the talk host's gender identity but makes it a threat to stable cultural meanings. Garroway's perceived androgyny devalued him and his genre. The implication that "real men" have points of view as well as angular features reflects the modernist privileging of masculine subjectivity and expressive assertion, even in "feminine" mass culture.

Arthur Godfrey, the most prominent 1950s talk variety host, was "hot" by comparison, but he made every effort to be equally endearing. Steve Allen, *Tonight*'s first significant host, fell somewhere between the "cool" Garroway and the "hot" Godfrey. That he was also recognized as a comedian and musician lent him the atypical talk host credential of "talent." Such hosts represented the "good time and happy consumption of the networks's entertainments and the sponsor's products." [16] But the talk host as bland and soft "nice guy" is a discourse that continues even to this day. Critic Richard Corliss called Merv Griffin and Mike Douglas "two of the nicest guys you'd ever want to chair a Rotary luncheon," and Donahue "a gentleman" who "behaves real nice to everybody." [17] The critics seemed to imply that though such "men" could be trusted with housewives during afternoon "talk time," the very image of their "bonelessness" implied a general threat to masculinity. In other words, by being so sexually non-threatening, the talk hosts actually *threatened* the male critic.

The talkshow host as a combination of student and educator is another persistent discursive strand with "feminine" connotations. The witty yet sometimes pretentious Dick Cavett was described as receiving his own liberal education while providing one to his audience through his 1970s PBS talkshow.[18] David Halberstam has called *Donahue* "the most important graduate school in America."[19] But Donahue as host has also come to represent a kind of split personality; he "is profoundly courteous and equally violative of all our middle-American morals" and "struggles against passing judgment on either the tormentors or the tormented, except by the implications of his aura of saintly liberal tolerance."[20] He is "nonthreatening," has "boyish charm" and "consummate sensitivity," is loved by women, yet is "live, spontaneous, rawly emotional, and *real*."[21]

The deep-seated American historical association of talk practices with women[22] may have crept into gender-stereotyped receptions of male talk hosts simply because the first talk personalities on widely available networks *were* men; women were hosting daytime "gossip" programs that were primarily syndicated, local, or the less prominent network offerings. The innuendo around the male talk host's gender identity and the talkshow's association with female spectatorship in a homophobic society deprecates the talkshow in ways reminiscent of soap opera criticism.[23] Such a discourse perceives the host as neither actor nor performer in the usual sense; critics therefore judge him and his show as somehow more "real," more available to the spectator in raw terms.

But what such terms *are* remains in question. The host's role and identity, along with the talkshow's situational frame, remain fluid and open, inviting charges of deviancy. Critics scrutinized the host as a threateningly naked, unpackaged, feminized personality—until such hypermasculine assault talkers as Joe Pyne, Alan Burke, and Morton Downey, Jr., came along to reconstitute the gender terms. Supposedly unencumbered by any recognizable role or talent, the host is unique in his "raw," unprocessed exposure and therefore more directly "visible" than, for example, the actor or dancer whose body becomes an instrument, or the musician who plays one. Any perceived deviance on the part of the host, it follows, would be more readily apparent. Add to this the talkshow's tightness of fit around the host's "unconstructed" personality, coupled with its apparent spontaneity, and one begins to understand the emergence of the next significant discourse about the talkshow: its unique ability to create an "illusion of intimacy" or "para-social relationship" between spectator and personality.

Intimacy at a Distance: The "Harmful" Talkshow

The familiar terms "illusion of intimacy" and "para-social inter-action" are the products of the first substantial consideration of the talk-show and its host: the 1956 essay "Mass Communication and Para-Social Interaction: Observations on Intimacy at a Distance," by Donald Horton and R. Richard Wohl.[24] Its appearance marked not only a turning point in the critical discourse on the "personality program," its host, and its spectator but the first in-depth, clinical-academic consideration of them. Published in the professional journal *Psychiatry*, the essay's implication of the talkshow's harmfulness assumes the legitimizing language of Freud-ian and social psychology, arguing the spectator's particular vulnerability to the talkshow's unique address. That the essay is still widely and un-critically anthologized in communications texts makes it a continuing influence—and this influence makes a reassessment necessary.

Admittedly, some of Horton and Wohl's observations remain quite astute, even predictive: the talkshow's "designed informality"; its dou-ble game of contrived spontaneity;[25] the ambiguous role of the host-personality, whom they call a "persona" (as distinct from an "actor").[26] They rightly perceive the program's hybrid nature, its textual position somewhere between the theatrical-fictional and the documentary or jour-nalistic. In the talkshow, they suggest, these two "worlds" are "in continu-ous interplay."[27] They recognize the power of the familiar inherent in the reliable, day-after-day, affable direct address of the host-personality but extend this power to what they see as its establishment of a "para-social" relationship—a blurring of boundaries—between them.[28] They are also highly, and appropriately, aware of publicity's role in promoting both the show itself and the guests appearing on it. In each case, the institutional objective is to "coach" the audience so as to "strengthen the illusion of reciprocity and rapport" and thus "offset the inherent impersonality of the media themselves."[29]

The essay rightly suggests that the personality program—the 1950s *Tonight* hosted by Steve Allen is its most frequent example—represents a unique problemization of the spectator's position: watching a talkshow is more "self-conscious" and "relative" than watching a dramatic pro-gram because the spectator does not fully suspend disbelief under the sway of the personality's "apparent face-to-face interaction with the home viewer." [30] The personality's performance is more "open-ended" with respect to the viewer's "answering role." To create closure, the viewer must play the role by imagining his or her family and friendship experiences. These "primary relations . . . characterized by intimacy, sympathy, and sociability" are engaged, and just as they seem natural in the spectator's primary relations, so Horton and Wohl see them as "naturally" carrying over to the "para-social" personality.[31] But this carryover is, finally, dangerous because it constitutes a less voluntary response than the spectator would bring, say, to a dramatic-fictional program involving a *willing* suspension of disbelief. Conditioned for years by the intimacy associated with family and friends, the spectator unconsciously transfers these responses to the talkshow.

The Horton and Wohl essay ends up in service of a dubious, effects-based stance inherently suspicious of the talkshow's formal specificity. For the authors, the talkshow is "real" to spectators in a way the play, novel, feature film, or sitcom is not. That even the psychologically "normal" spectator may be hoodwinked by the talkshow into the "twilight zone" of para-social relations and a greater belief in the "reality" of that interaction—"experienced as of the same order as, and related to, the network of actual social relations"—is a condemnation of the genre as deceptive and hazardous. Moreover, the hazard is even greater for the abnormally isolated spectator.[32]

By arguing that the talkshow, unlike a dramatic program, resists interpretation as the usual "fantasy or dream," Horton and Wohl are anticipating the need for Christian Metz's more recent concept of primary identification with the medium. Yet their 1956 essay sidesteps the apparatus altogether. For them, there is only secondary identification—with personalities—because talkshows are so reflexive they disable our imaginary investment in the medium. Horton and Wohl argue that the talkshow encourages the spectator's belief in an unmediated closeness to the performer, but they never explain how that performer so easily "passes through" the apparatus when cameras and microphones are readily apparent. They credit the cleverly adapted, chat-over-a-highball performance style of a Steve Allen or Dave Garroway as *the* cause of the "illusion of intimacy." The essay also neglects the spectator's implicit awareness of the talkshow's reflexive codes and conventions. If viewers are aware of liveness, direct address, the practices of the host-personality, greater intimacy, guesthood, studio audience, and so on, why should they be any *less* aware of the talkshow's interpersonal conventions?

The authors cite instances of "extreme para-sociability"—a condition in which a "psychologically active" audience member "passes over into the more formal, overt, and expressive activities of fan behavior"—to demonstrate the talkshow's negative effect on an admittedly marginal set of media-dependent individuals.[33] Yet they also believe that the talk-show's para-social nature may even have a societal *benefit* by providing the "normal" viewer a rehearsal for social mobility through conversational modeling or "role enactment."

Then, too, they burden the talkshow with an ideological effect from which other program genres are apparently exempt: ordinary people who appear as guests are treated as "persons of consequence" but only in terms of their everyday roles "as husband, wife, mother, as 'attractive' middle age, 'remarkably youthful' old age, and the like."[34] In this way, these programs make the participant-spectator a "model of appropriate role performance" (implicitly keeping each in his or her social place) while at the same time demonstrating "the fundamental generosity and good will" and the accessible, "human" side of the big corporate broadcaster and sponsor.[35]

The essay reflects an alarm over unstable identities prompted by the media's deepening inclusion in the spectator's everyday life. The authors would like to separate out and define that which has actually become inseparable. They atavistically long for a clear "fourth wall," a reestablishment of the defining either-or aesthetic boundaries between performer and text and spectator, a renewal of the clear distinction between public and private. If, as they say, the talkshow is a "simulation of conversational give and take," it becomes a suspect, tricky, and inferior substitute for "real" interpersonal communication—the privileged and thus "healthy" relationships its audience lacks.[36] They imagine the talkshow fan suffering deprivations similar to those with which 1940s empirical research stigmatized the female soap opera fan.[37]

The privileging of "real," interpersonal communication at the expense of the talkshow's "simulation" of it has continued as a dominant strain in the empirical research into the talkshow.[38] One example is the widespread acceptance of the term "para-social," which tends to conceptualize the talkshow in favored interpersonal rather than media terms. While deprecating the media, it also indicates the perceived boundary confusion: *is it interpersonal or mediated?* Most subsequent U.S. research has been functionalist, arising out of the uses-and-gratifications perspective of social science. The dominant object of study has been the talkshow audience. As research was getting under way in the 1970s, call-in talk radio, which had exploded as a popular program and format type in the 1960s, became the center of concern. Relying heavily on survey methods, studies sought to discover the talkshow "user" and his or her particular uses of talk radio; they gave minimal attention to program content (as they would call it).[39] In the early 1970s the talk radio industry itself engaged audience research beyond the usual ratings data for the purpose of constructing a favorable audience profile for "topless radio," the female call-in shows whose explicit sexual content aroused FCC attention.[40] Although results over the years have shown the audience's greater diversity and "normality," the discourse of the lonely spectator in need of a compensatory para-social "fix" persists.

Comedy Kings and Para-Social Subjects

Talk about the talkshow has found its way well beyond academia and the press. In discovering the talk host as dramatic material, popular fictional representations have extended and amplified the research and journalistic "takes" on talkshows. Two theatrical films—*The King of Comedy* (1983) and *Talk Radio* (1988)—and the recent television series *Midnight Caller* wrestle with what the talkshow "means" in the context of contemporary social problems. Even in its most benevolent representations, the talkshow and its host occupy a tentative, murky netherworld where they remain ill defined and thus threatening. Where positive portrayals of the host survive, they turn him from "bad boy" into heroic good citizen—honest, caring, street-smart, a working man of action. There seems to be an ongoing struggle to define the host *and* genre in terms of good and evil, a struggle suggesting an identity crisis that is both semiotic and political.

Martin Scorsese's *King of Comedy* is a disturbing fictional treatment.

Although the film's *Jerry Langford Show* is not precisely the call-in type, its concern with fandom raises the same issues of the para-social and the spectator's attempt to cross the proscenium and enter the text. Its black humor, ironic reversals, and relentless criticism of the media, celebrities, and fans came at a time when media deregulation, merger, and acquisition were coinciding with the television talkshow's 1980s revival. It also coincided with the advent of media terrorism, making the film a key indicator of the talkshow's centrality to all sorts of nagging questions and to tensions between ill-defined notions of public and private, subjectivity and "reality," "nature" and artifice, the "vulnerable" spectator and the media institution, participation and exclusion, celebrity, fairness, and exploitation.

As much as the character of Rupert Pupkin seems a portrayal of Horton and Wohl's lonely talkshow fan, he ultimately turns the tables on that notion of spectatorship. His contradiction of it calls into question the spectatorial stereotypes that dominate the media research discourse. The contradiction hinges on two of the film's narrative constructs. The first is Pupkin's dual status as active talkshow fan in hot pursuit of autographs and other contacts *and* as aspiring comic and talkshow host-performer. The second is the narrative's reversal of the public performer and private spectator roles originally embodied by Jerry and Pupkin.

Before Pupkin becomes "the king of comedy," the viewer is never sure who he is or what he does for a living in New York City. He may be a film courier or some other media industry functionary, but the narrative elides his day job as unimportant, initially positioning him instead as a "fan" in the word's original sense of fanatic devotee. Another of Jerry's fans, Marsha, is wealthy enough not to have to work; fandom is her sole vocation. Pupkin has done her favors such as giving up his place in the autograph line. One evening, however, Pupkin adroitly manages to force his way into Jerry's limousine as he leaves the studio. He takes the star's handkerchief away from this strange, interpersonal star-fan encounter, and it will later become his "verification" of his "real, intimate" ties to Jerry. Riding together to Jerry's midtown apartment, they momentarily reverse roles: the talk host becomes his fan's dependent, captive audience—a captivity that foreshadows the later scene when Pupkin, with Marsha's help, kidnaps Jerry.

This sudden, real-time, face-to-face "intimacy" is no longer "illusory" as Horton and Wohl meant it. Pupkin reveals an intense, even impatient drive to celebrity as a stand-up comic and the *chutzpa* to gain attention by a bold move. He seems to understand the promotional function of the talkshow perhaps better than Jerry himself, who advises him to develop his act in the traditional way by working "up the ladder" in the clubs. Pupkin's figural status becomes overloaded to a point where definitions collapse into the near meaninglessness of multiplicity. Representing spectator and performer, ruthless ambition and manipulation, he is a pathetic and ingenuous individual whose ambition seems to exceed his talent. It is the talkshow, a fluid and ill-defined form, that allows him to transform himself from spectator to performer, from the putatively passive recipient of media effects to "the king of comedy"—the *producer* of those effects upon subjects.

The opening scene also introduces a debate about "how things are done" in showbiz, what makes a good comic performance, what makes a good talkshow: in other words, about the "rules" the industry supposedly follows. Pupkin operates on a new rule of media ambition: sensational newsworthiness in the form of a terrorist act such as kidnapping, which exploits the vulnerability of the media to the criminal and the sensational. The film's point here is plain: there really are no rules, no pat formulas, for how media can or should work. The talkshow epitomizes this condition.

Pupkin's big "break" not only breaks what Jerry believes are the showbiz rules but also marks a major break in the film's narrative structure. The status of *The Jerry Langford Show* is pivotal; the film implicitly recognizes the talkshow's paratextual and parasitic nature. It is a genre that is "part of" and "in between." It becomes a tenuous public space, a deliberately ill-defined field wherein performer-personalities (neither actors nor comedians, perhaps not even talented) can contend and define themselves for public acceptance. In this framework where rules and roles become plastic and even the talk host alternates between spectator and performer, who is the spectator? Insofar as the talkshow establishes an "illusion of intimacy" and takes participation for granted, is there a spectator at all?

Pupkin hopes that one appearance on Jerry's show will be his quick ticket to national success, allowing him to bypass the years of arduous small-club dates that are supposedly the "rule" for getting on in the business. He violates the constantly invoked showbiz rules in an intuitive recognition of the incoherence and schizophrenia of postmodern conditions. In a way parodying the long-standing American tradition of using talk practices as a means of self-improvement and self-advancement,[41] Pupkin's use of the talkshow plays as an ironic, grotesque distortion of such institutions as the lyceum, the chautauqua, and the Dale Carnegie course.

The public stage is so crowded that getting attention has become increasingly difficult. Pupkin proves himself a master at overcoming these constraints through expert media manipulation rather than comic talent. He is so unfunny that the film's title rings with irony. Yet his publicity stunt—kidnapping Jerry and ransoming him for a talkshow appearance—gets him that appearance, a prison term, and then a best-selling book about the whole affair in which he was "king for a night." After his release he becomes a major television talk host who supplants Jerry and whose unfunny jokes get sincere laughs. He becomes the broadcaster, the controlling agent, the producer of alleged effects.

The media feed on one another for usable material, and the talkshow epitomizes this practice, consuming and producing for its own sake as an inexpensive advertising vehicle. It shatters the "master narrative" of "rules." Performativity reigns: do what works in your interest. The talkshow also embodies an ethic that values career strategy over inherent talent. Promotion becomes the ultimate form of self-construction, the talkshow its principal vehicle. Any sense of "real" talent is irrelevant; one "stages" one's life so as to appear on another stage. Though the public and the private seem to merge, the public is finally privatized because the interests of the self-seeking performer and the cannibalizing institution win out. In *The King of Comedy* the spectator seems to "win" only when he or she becomes the performer by *also* using the talkshow.

The cynical inversion of the film's ending—showing the opener of Pupkin's own talkshow in a flipflop of the opening—seems fitting. Pupkin has committed "patricide" and cannibalized Jerry in a faintly Oedipal trajectory to bring about his own success. Having a show bearing his name is the imprimatur of that success.[42] The circular aspect of the film's narrative, beginning and ending with a talkshow opener, enriches the reversals occurring in the middle. What seemed so bright, casual, and spontaneous about the talkshow early in the film is revealed, by the time Pupkin has his own program, as oppressively calculated; the film's spectator now knows what goes into the "illusion of intimacy" and how much is economically at stake. Even more than the talkshow, the entire media industry is exposed in its self-cannibalizing amorality and its exploitation of incoherence. Because the talkshow can provide an open door enabling the likes of Pupkin to cross from spectator to performer, and because it plays loosely—sometimes recklessly—with authenticity and intimacy, it epitomizes the media's duplicitous power.

As he crosses the boundaries separating spectator from media text and institution—the very institution supposedly governed by Jerry's "rules" —the character of Rupert Pupkin inscribes a narrative point of view that *also* confuses boundaries. At the film's beginning we see Pupkin as a man with all the stereotypical symptoms of Horton and Wohl's "fan-actic," one who has become para-socially dependent upon the talkshow's "illusion of intimacy." As the narrative proceeds, we focalize through Pupkin and shift unannounced into first-person, subjective sequences that put us into Pupkin's head and fantasies. These fantasies are fictional narratives-within-a-narrative which, ironically, become "real": Pupkin having lunch with Jerry at Sardi's to discuss taking over his show; the two of them meeting in Jerry's office so that Jerry can tell him what a great comedian he is; Pupkin's loudly applauded stand-up routine performed on a makeshift set in his basement. These abrupt focalizations not only project us— the film's spectators—into the fantasies of a television spectator but give us an illusion of intimacy through which *we* witness Pupkin's similar illusion about Jerry. In this way, the film cleverly—almost duplicitously— destabilizes our moral position as "involved" spectators, pointing up the hypocrisy of our own (spectatorial) sense of superiority to Pupkin. Authenticity and the high ground belong to no one. Pupkin's schizophrenic moments, so vivid in his own head, become reality in a characteristically postmodern way. The spectator cannot be sure of narrative "self" or "truth," the subjective or the objective.

After three of these fantasy sequences, the scene in which Pupkin and his girlfriend take a train to Jerry's country house, only to be tossed out, seems shatteringly real. Pupkin learns that his earlier, "real" interpersonal contact with Jerry, in his limousine, was itself filled with lies; Jerry had told him to phone his office only as a way of getting rid of him. Jerry calls him a "moron" to express what the film, up to that point, has led its audience to think about him: that he is a pathetic loser, self-deluded and ambitious far beyond his talent or prospects. But just as the Pupkin fantasy motif is shattered, his "loser" image also begins to crumble. The next scene abruptly makes us complicitous with his successful scheme to kidnap Jerry and get his big break. The "lie" or "illusion" becomes the operant, performative "truth," just as the postmodern "simulacrum" supplants the very question of the "real."

For someone who was apparently suffering self-delusion to the point of losing touch altogether, Pupkin turns out to have been eminently and boldly "realistic." His sizable ego, evident in his fearless intrusions on Jerry and, prophetically, in his own huge signature in his autograph book, assaults the common research notion—begun with Horton and Wohl— of the talkshow fanatic as lacking self-esteem. What appeared to be Pupkin's fantasies turn out to have been practical rehearsals for his eventual celebrity; his "schizophrenia," good practice for his participation in the image economy. Pupkin embodies the speculation that the talkshow's one benefit may be its preparation of the upwardly mobile individual through his or her para-social conversation with those embodiments of success, the stars. But though Pupkin does achieve the "new role possibilities" of which Horton and Wohl spoke, at the same time he resembles the spectator who is trying to "escape from an unsatisfactory and drab reality."[43]

Still, Pupkin is hardly very isolated or socially incompetent, as distasteful as he may seem. The film, in fact, depicts Jerry as more isolated. He wanders alone about his large, cold, high-tech midtown apartment; only servants are with him in his big country house; he walks alone down the midtown Manhattan streets to the studio. Significantly, it is his very aloneness that makes him so vulnerable to being kidnapped. Perhaps this reflects the negative effect of the media upon the *performer* and *institution* as opposed to the spectator, who is usually the one portrayed as victim. If so, the central cause-effect issue for social science media research is turned on its head. The talkshow's instrumental position in celebrity culture throws the common presumption of the human subject's vulnerability to media power back on itself. The talkshow, and the personalities who host it, are *themselves* used—exhausted—in their endless dependence upon promotional guests, novelty, and staged intimacy.

This added dimension of the talkshow's inherent reflexivity is as self-consuming as it is self-revealing. The film places the talkshow at the center of a process by which meaning is destabilized and multiplied. One is constantly fooled as "the rules" and accepted distinctions and practices collapse, exhausted—but *productively* and *deliberately* so, given a postmodern economy that trades on this mediated instability for ever new products which, performatively, "work." As the new "king of comedy," Pupkin, who is several "selves" rather than one modernist, "authentic" self, is the latest successful product of the latest rule-breaking practice: promotion through talkshow and terrorism. Under postmodern modes of production, there is no longer a single route to success or even a single set of rules.

Confused Identities, Ambiguous Roles: *Talk Radio*

As talk host, Jerry Langford is likable, funny, easygoing, approachable—the very qualities that encourage Pupkin to believe he can enlist the star's help in his comedy career. Offstage, however, Jerry is no more likable than Pupkin; his "nice guy" is exposed as nasty through Pupkin's persistence. The "bad boy," confrontalk host emerged in the 1960s as a conscious alternative to the "nice guy" hosts that Morton Downey, Jr., later attacked as too polite, "a bunch of nodding, bobbing heads . . . but everyone doesn't love each other." [44] "Nice guys" are still around in the persons of Phil Donahue, Jay Leno, Arsenio Hall, and others, but the audience participation talkshow also has its "bad to the bone" male hosts and "punk" formats.

Still another type has evolved, however, perhaps best described as the "good citizen," the host who selflessly provides a public service. Temperamentally, he or she is somewhere between nice and nasty: bluntly honest, but genuinely concerned at the same time. The "good citizen" is a wise counselor, an investigator in the manner of journalist or cop, a kind of "fallen angel" anti-hero, and a vociferous advocate when necessary. The 1988 film *Talk Radio* offers a telling representation of the nasty talk host who nonetheless imagines himself as "good citizen" in providing the "service" of exposing our demons. What is significant about fictional representations of the "bad boy" hosts, apart from their vengeant over-masculinity, is their outlaw connotations—overtones that enable the narrative investigation of legal and ethical questions as well as issues of media responsibility, public versus private, news and serious debate versus entertainment, voyeurism versus performance, and power versus its lack. Also significant about such representations is the talk hosts' own role confusion and symptomatic schizophrenia—conditions superficially masked by their loud, angry, hypermasculine affect. The host "lives"—and pays the price for—the identity crisis that has become a productive part of a postmodern economy dependent upon semiotic instability for creating novel consumables and constant market stimulation.

Talk Radio has existed in two forms: a play written by Eric Bogosian and produced in Portland, Oregon, and New York, and the film directed by Oliver Stone and written by Bogosian and Stone.[45] The film expands considerably upon the play by shaping the protagonist, radio call-in host Barry Champlain, more like the assassinated Denver talk host Alan Berg. New characters are added (an ex-wife, for one); a flashback shows early points in Barry's career; some of the action—relocated from Cleveland to Dallas—occurs outside the radio station; and Barry, like Berg, is gunned down by a right-wing fanatic.

In both versions, Barry's late-night call-in program are central. As a tight performance space—opened up, in the film version, only by windows overlooking an impersonal nocturnal Dallas—the studio setting permits an intense scrutiny of the host, the broadcast industry, the medium, and their motives. It also allows a particular look at his *Night Talk* audience-callers, this time through the twin frames of medium and host. As station KGAB's slogan says, Barry is "in the heart of the Lone Star state," just as he is at the center of a heartless panopticon that works both ways at once. Though the powerful, fire-breathing talk host surveys Dallas and its problems with his authoritative, controlling aural "gaze," his listener-callers are also observing *him* from the safe distance of anonymity; they see *his* insecurity and near nervous breakdown. The personnel and apparatus—the confrontalk host and producer, their computerized call selection, the cutoff button, the sponsors, the syndicators—

can manipulate the audience to their own ratings advantage, but the audience comes through and bears down on Barry. The narrative illuminates perspectives on the talkshow, its host, and what they "mean." By the end, Barry's listener-callers and even his co-workers have constructed their own interpretations of him. The clash of these interpretations—the host's, the audience's, the industry's, the author's, the director's—draws attention to the talkshow's ambiguous identity in the public sphere. Like the film, the genre itself thrives on such ambiguities.

Dan, Barry's executive producer, assumes a highly rationalized business perspective but is aware that it can easily be lost. He sees Barry's save-the-world sense of mission as naive and considers it a source of trouble, obscuring the "reality" that being a talk host—even an angry, world-saving one—is only a job, an "act." Dan reminds Barry that his job is "to hang up on people" and that his host persona—his on-air identities as victim, war veteran, hippie, Ph.D., and airplane pilot, all constructing him as a Renaissance man—was Dan's own invention.

In the play, Dan describes the development of a talkshow in terms of a card game; along with calculation, chance also plays a role in achieving success. Until he had Barry, his "joker," his station lacked a "full deck"— a metaphor that also warns of confused identities and madness. Dan sees talk radio as a game played strictly for ratings. He depends on Barry for success but still regards him as a commodity, currently useful but always potentially expendable. The play's metaphor then shifts from game to vehicle, and Barry becomes Dan's "train": "Talent comes and goes. Like trains in and out of the station. Trains wear out, they get derailed, they crash. Sooner or later, they're out of commission. The faster they go, the harder they crash." [46] These shifting metaphors suggest the host's unstable meaning, an instability conducive to economic utility, especially for Dan, but perilous to Barry, the talkshow "worker."

If Dan seems secure in his views about the talkshow, Barry is profoundly torn. He is expert at milking conflict, drama, titillation, or putdown out of any caller; through his projection of attitude, he can dramatize almost anything. But when his call screener, Stu, sends him "stiffs"—callers he cannot "work with" to "keep the show moving" Barry gets angry. To him, the callers are raw material he can entertainingly—even playfully—"work" to extract dramatic value for cathartic, enlightening effect. Barry's work is in fact an affective "play" with chance fragments, represented by the callers.

Just as he controls an audience, Barry determines the format; a spontaneous, "alive" show paradoxically means following *his* mode of production—one centered in the maximum exploitation of his callers through attitude rather than any consistent ideology. If Barry "stands for" anything, it is "anger." The narrative develops the anger—and confusion—more than his left political leanings, which are culturally underscored by his position as an isolated, from-out-of-town Jew in Texas. In controlling his show and his callers, he loses control of himself. He is an egoist who deflects his self-hate onto an audience he despises precisely because they *are* his audience—a dilemma he is only beginning to recognize.

For the most part, Barry believes his show to be a sincere, straight-shooting public service, a necessary and courageous voice in the land of the scared. He regards his audience as not only afraid but ignorant, voyeuristic, unhappy, and morbid: "You frighten me! I come up here every night and I tear into you, I abuse you, I insult you . . . and you just keep calling." He accuses the audience of reducing his program to sensational trivia, denying his own complicity in this result. For Barry, the audience is "a pack of baying wolves"; yet he remains "a voice in the wilderness."

The film's narrative and mise-en-scène reveal what Barry fails to see: his real isolation, fear, and lack of self-esteem, which so uneasily coexist with his angry-young-world-saver persona. Attaining some degree of self-awareness, he engages in a long, final tirade to his despised audience, accusing them of misreading him: "You don't know who I am, what I want, what I like, what I don't like in this world. I'm just a voice." His voice—his radio persona—is a mask created by role, institution, and apparatus. Barry's self-revealing rant at the story's climax, his acknowledgment at last that he is simply doing a job, occurs only after a young prank caller who visits him in the studio tells him that the program is "only a show," hardly worth the seriousness Barry so tempestuously invests in it. As he leaves, the young man unexpectedly snaps Barry's picture with a camera previously concealed. In the sudden gunshotlike flash, Barry's brazen facade ruptures, revealing the true depth of his fragility and hyperconfused identity. Yet in response to his conclusion that the evening's show has been a failure, his screener and producer dismiss it as "just one show," eminently disposable in the long tradition of the daily (or nightly) talkshow.

While part of Barry believes that his job, despite its contradictions, *is* important—it is, after all, *him*, his sincere performance—another part believes it merely performative. Utterly alone during his final monologue (having rejected his ex-wife's attempt to reach back and support him), Barry acknowledges this performativity: "I'm a hypocrite. I ask for sincerity as I lie. I denounce the system as I embrace it. I want money, and power, and prestige. I want ratings and success. I don't give a damn about you, or the world. That's the truth."

Or is it? Barry's "truth" here is that of the riddle about the man from Crete who says all Cretans are liars. As *Talk Radio*'s audience, *we* are caught in an endless circuit of signifiers that denies *us* the possibility of truth and knowability even within the film's narrative. Later in the monologue Barry tells us (in discursive/enunciative terms, we are at this point aligned with his radio audience), "I say what I believe in. I tell you what you are. I have to. I have no choice." He concludes, "I guess we're stuck with each other"—an existential admission of a postmodern contingency and impurity.

One key paradox for Barry is that the compulsions and contradictions of his character are, through talkshow performance, inseparable from the "jobness" of his public role. The performance effort involved in being a talkhost—usually requiring more live, on-air hours per week than almost any other job in radio or television—associates the talk host with workers and work in a way no other electronic performer (save, occasionally, the journalist) can. At the same time, the exposure factor intensifies the host's aura of knownness: the spectator *feels* that he or she really knows the host, who is presented as authentic—supposedly unmediated by any fictional role—over a prolonged period and under conditions of apparent intimacy. In these exceptional conditions of spectatorial identification, the talk host seems to work with and for the common individual, the "people," however he may titillate and abuse them in what Barry sarcastically calls "a public service." It is a labor that denies the laborer a protective degree of detachment from his work; through performance, he *is* his work. Barry is caught in the talkshow's productive contradiction. As the performer whose job, in Dan's words, is "to hang up on people," Barry hosts a "mere show" that is nonetheless doubly dangerous, demanding his use of powerful, weaponlike words to raise significant issues and his near-total self-exposure.

In his introduction to the published play, Bogosian says, "Nothing invigorates the mass media the way reality does." A "special drama" can suddenly become available because "we know real people are involved." The author here senses a key talkshow dynamic: its apparent reality cues its audience how to decode it, thus expanding the deceptive possibilities of its reception. Bogosian shows a critical understanding of confrontalk exhibitionism and its blurring of what once were distinctions. His confrontalk host, an "indignant and enraged crusader" who supposedly "sees through all the lies and hypocrisy" and "tells it like it is," ends up giving the real issues short shrift in the interest of sensation and ratings.[47] Bogosian's sensitivity to the debate around the interactive talkshow—a debate centered in the genre's merging of news and entertainment, reality and fictional drama, text and audience, sincerity and artifice—spurs him to go a step further and investigate the form's meaning and appeal. He locates both in a kind of addiction. Host, audience, and institution are bound together in a love-hate relationship they cannot control. The industry and host will resort to anything novel to maintain the audience they "love" yet despise. The audience, in turn, is attracted by the dramatic, especially if it is made to seem "real." Each looks to the other to fulfill a lack. The consumer economy's addiction to novelty has no meaning other than its constant need to stimulate its market, to reattract the consumer to the commodity.

As the assassin's bullets cut Barry down to end the film, the tensions between provocative entertainment and news remain unresolved. "Art" and "life" have intermingled. Barry is caught in confusion's crossfire: the productive multiplicity and contradiction, the "expanded field," of the talkshow's meaning in postmodern media culture.[48] Representations of the talk host such as *Talk Radio*'s suggest a schizophrenic information worker—a new, postmodern subject—adaptable to the hazardous yet productive conditions of the image economy, one that can somehow survive the merger of public with private, transgression with complicity, intimacy with anonymity.

This economically productive crisis of subjectivity and representation has become a large part of what the talkshow, as fictional or discursive image, now "means." That crisis in turn projects the as yet unfathomed fear, promise, and power of a new interactive medium that is nonetheless still encrusted with some of the conditions and meanings of the "old" one-way mass media. When Barry blasts his listeners' fear, which he accuses them of hiding behind their anonymity and voyeurism, he reveals what may well be an interactive medium's present dilemma: its discourse and reception precariously walk the tightrope between "genuine" interactivity and exhibitionistic-voyeuristic performance, between conversation and specularity, between the personally revealing (in two-way, interpersonal communication) and the hidden (the one-way, mass communication paradigm embodied in the anonymity of the receive-only audience). He condemns his audience: "Marvelous technology at our disposal—instead of reaching up to new heights, we're going to see how far down we can go, how deep into the muck we can immerse ourselves. The only thing you believe in is me." As the repository of audience belief, Barry is caught in the middle of this double game and is finally destroyed by it. The neo-Nazi who kills him pushes him off the talkshow performance tightrope, out of the talkshow's unstable symbolic construct, and into "reality." For the assassin, Barry and *Night Talk* were never merely a performance; they were singularly real.

The film equates the Dallas night cityscape with the studio's blinking, forbidding, high-tech atmosphere. The medium and its public are self-reinforcing in their icy alienation, mechanistic degradation, and commodification of both work and leisure. The film's visual design—isolating Barry in the studio as if in a glass cage, precariously suspended high above a nocturnal steel-and-glass Dallas—effectively develops this motif. Oliver Stone stages Barry's long, excruciating monologue, which is the film's climax, by spinning the camera, and Barry at his mike, around in circles—an obvious correlative to the vortex of productive confusion and the circuit of shifting identity in which Barry as talkhost and we as spectators are caught.

As we turn again and again, we see in the background the industry principals in whose merciless "fishbowl" he is. *Night Talk* may be *his* show, as others keep telling him in a desperate denial of their own complicity, but he is also *their* product, and both audience and producer *need* him. To his audience, he provides a "public service": "You're afraid of the bogeyman but can't live without him. . . . I'm here to lead you by the hands through the dark forest of your own hatred and anger and humiliation." To his producers, station, and syndicator, he is a valuable asset. When, after what turns out to be his final show, Barry tells Dan that he may not show up the next day, Dan confidently responds, "You'll come in tomorrow—you always do." Dan understands all too well that Barry's final on-air words refer to the broadcast industry as well as to his audience: "I guess we're stuck with each other"—a state of postmodern "fallenness." Though there seems to be no exit, there is always death.

The advent of interactivity and generic hybridization dissolves accepted role distinctions and destabilizes each "separate" facet of the communication process—spectator, producer, text, generic frame, message, media cause, societal-subjective effects. The advance of media technology in the home, office, and automobile as well as on the air itself has been one factor in the emergence of interactivity. The exhaustion of traditional genres encourages new forms based on "reality" and audience participation, as well as further hybridization. By setting its narrative within the broadcast industry, *Talk Radio* interrogates institutional and textual dynamics that now interweave spectator and text, information and gratuitous titillation. *The King of Comedy* did that by examining the industry through someone who aspired to it and who, in so doing, learned its sometimes duplicitous and relentlessly promotional process.

This crisis of representation is also an institutional crisis. The 1980s mergers and acquisitions in the media industry find a parallel in the talk-show: entertainment acquires news, gossip merges with the debate of serious issues, and text and producer literally acquire the audience in interactive ways that alter the traditional "darkened room" definition of the scopophilic spectator. Incorporating the audience into the program as spectator-participants not only cuts costs and increases economic efficiency through attractive "reality programming"—made all the more attractive by what the industry sees as its resistance to random-access, remote control "grazing"[49]—but deepens the media's reach in a way consistent with such business developments as telemarketing and direct mail advertising. These are among a host of increasingly advanced techniques of targeting and domestic intrusion eroding the distinction between public and private spheres.

Television Looks at Talkshows

Of television's few fictional representations of talkshow hosts, *Midnight Caller* and *The Larry Sanders Show* are among the most recent. The first was *The Joey Bishop Show*, a half-hour situation comedy in the early 1960s. *The Larry Sanders Show*, an HBO sitcom starring Garry Shandling as a desk-and-sofa talk host—a role he has really played as a one-time guest host for Johnny Carson—had its debut as this book went to press. Shandling plays the late-night host as a smarmy "bad boy" who knows—and exercises—the promotional power and exposure of the celebrity talkshow. Reviewers focused immediately on the show's obvious blurring of the line between reality and fiction, achieved not only by Shandling's casting but by his celebrity guests' playing themselves. One episode of *The Joey Bishop Show* activated the tension within and between generic frames and the talk host's identity.[50]

Joey, a bachelor in his thirties who still lives at home with his mother (a situation strikingly like Rupert Pupkin's—the father is somehow absent) and who is already jittery in anticipation of his talkshow's debut, learns that his first guest will be Milton Berle. Because he has not yet established himself as host, he fears that Berle will overwhelm him and take control of his show. During a rehearsal, technicians and producers order him around the set in what proves his initial experience of humiliation and loss of control; it establishes the episode's problem as rooted in Joey's insecurity, his lack of situational definition and authority as talk host.

Gender and intergenerational tensions, projected from a masculinist standpoint, underpin the narrative. Milton Berle—widely known as "Mr. Television," "Uncle Miltie," and "the father of television"—poses a paternal threat to the younger, unseasoned Joey. In his domestic relationship with his mother, Joey projects a dependent boyishness despite his age. The night before Berle's appearance, Joey has a nightmare in which Uncle Miltie, dressed in a grotesque zoot suit and acting his most outrageous (much as he did in the early days of television), reduces Joey to the role of foil. In an imagined playing-out of Joey's worst fears, Berle commandeers the show and leaves the host soaked, his clothing tattered, in a ritualized slapstick humiliation. When Joey wakes up in a cold sweat, he goes downstairs to find his mother still up, reading. She reassures him with some homespun advice implying his immaturity: he has "absolutely nothing to be afraid of," she tells him. "Believe in yourself. If you believe in what you do, you can't miss."

Berle's actual appearance turns out to be modest and low-key, and Joey keeps control of his show. His tenuous ego, like the equally tenuous talkshow form, remains intact. The episode uses the common talkshow paradigm in which the host and guest retain their own names and "play themselves." Joey's insecurity as talk host has to do with the improvisational genre's play with borders and identities. Its weak boundaries make it vulnerable to the encroachments of other genres (slapstick) and threateningly "stronger" performers (Milton Berle—"Mr. Television"). This threat is built into the talkshow's very identity, giving it the capacity to shift and fragment in production circumstances that are both planned and spontaneous. The pleasures the late-night talkshow offers its audience, intimacy and the unpredictable, become a threat for Joey (the "good boy" talk host). A deeper ideological implication is that the talkshow, interpenetrated as it is by "outside" personalities and texts, is somehow too feminine for a "real man." The host must play the passive giver of hospitality and the foil to ego.

Although NBC's *Midnight Caller* (1988–91) hardly avoided the confusions associated with talkshow and talk host, it did attempt to reconcile them to the metropolis by granting the talkshow a vital function in solving social problems. Jack Killian, the "Nighthawk," whose show airs from midnight to three in the morning on a San Francisco station, combines panoptic "good citizen" with transgressive "bad boy." He is kind and gentle but tough when necessary; self-aware and wise but also world-weary; solitary and self-doubting in a way reminiscent of Barry Champlain but without sacrificing ego altogether.

The series worked on the premise of a thirty-ish San Francisco ex-cop who becomes the popular host of a late-night call-in show yet maintains his police ties. The dark, isolating studio setting, steeped in night and netherworld, had the look and feel of *film noir*—an intertext appropriate to the circumstances under which Killian left the force: he had accidentally shot his partner in the line of duty. This aspect of his past was central to many episodes, explaining why Killian was willingly drawn into the detective hermeneutic structuring those episodes.

Significantly, the late-night call-in host and his privileged involvement in the life of the city borrowed from the cinematic and literary intertexts of police detective, private investigator, and journalist. Killian achieved a semiotic approximation of each of these, combining the narrative and motivational qualities of all three. The integration of police investigation and important public issues (especially public safety), the information and service effected *through* him and his talkshow, and his amateur gumshoeing informed by his former career and colleagues—all testified to his multiple role. He also resembled his three prototypes in their high-risk occupations, their existential action and outsiderly isolation, their terse, tough outspokenness, their disillusioned affect, their world-weary wisdom, and their working-man veneer. Like the protagonists in many Fritz Lang films, Killian was a "double" figure inscribed in a detective hermeneutic. His marginal, "in-between" public status—between amateur and professional, detective and counselor, "normal" and marginal—permitted his special mobility and liminal status.

The talk host has come to symbolize a new kind of participant-observer who is simultaneously private and public, a knower and performer who is both marginal and mainstream. Like his three character intertexts, Killian moved between normal social world and underworld in a particularly fluid way; but the price he payed was the taint of his contact with the marginal, the demonized. He was, to varying degrees, flawed, corrupt, haunted, even failed. He occupied a "quasi" or "para" position. Like his cinematic and literary counterparts, he was a "working man"—the gender specificity here is notable—linked closely to his occupational intertexts and their all-consuming, around-the-clock workload. He performed under great pressure, personal drive, and public scrutiny. He provided the spectator with a vehicle for identification in that his identity was so strongly linked to his job. Call-in host, like detective, reporter, or private investigator, is an occupation fusing the personal, the private, and the public in exceptional ways. The radio talk host as represented by Killian presented the tightest fusion yet.

While the similarities between Killian's talk host and his fictional prototypes are considerable, there are key distinctions. The host is far more public. His or her occupational performance is media spectacle; the production and distribution of knowledge occur in on-air performance, whereas journalist, private investigator, and detective are producers of knowledge in a time and space usually anterior to its public distribution. As producers of knowledge, they engage in a modernist inquiry into truth and the world through the answering of a hermeneutic question. The "whodunit" affords an authorial opportunity to scrutinize the subject of the knowledge as well as its object, the perils of subjectivity, and the process of knowledge production, but rarely is there an abandonment of belief in an external, discoverable, empirical truth. The modernist hermeneutic has a fundamental faith in the world, its readable signs, and truth as knowable, even though the subject's perception may be clouded. But, because the talk host's construction of knowledge is simultaneous with mediated public performance, the ultimately knowable externality of truth can be questioned. Knowledge becomes an interested, performative commodity inseparable from the personality or institution producing it. The talk host produces knowledge by linking subjectivity, institution, apparatus, and even the spectator, through interactivity. Knowledge is reconflated with the knower. Killian also crossed boundaries by living his work. He became a "postdualistic" self who overcame the rationalized and alienating separations of industrial modernity: he and *his* immediate concerns *were* his talkshow and his work.[51] In Killian, the modernist detective became the postmodern call-in host. Like Barry Champlain's, his residual modernism was ruptured by the "impure" situation of contingency, shifting identities, floating signifiers, public-private performance, and the "double game" of multiple codings.

The use of his talk show in each episode made *Midnight Caller*'s animating conflict at once personal and public. As personal as it often seemed, Killian's use of "his" air was never self-indulgent; underlying it was an ethical, greater-good motive. His verbal sparring was only in the public interest; his antagonist was usually a threat to public safety. Killian also used "his" air to fortify his allies, empower society's victims, or console those whose "antagonists" were largely internal: drug users, or people torn psychologically. Through Killian's talkshow-within-a-television-show, the voices of the narrative's major characters constituted a spectacle within a spectacle as they pervaded the nocturnal cityscape of San Francisco and the "theater of the mind" of its inhabitants. Everyone involved in a story—whether in a bar, keeping late hours at the office, or lying in bed listening—was a spectator as well as an actor through Killian's mediation. The omnipresent radio voice as narrative device, used in just about every episode, recalled Fritz Lang's similar, spatially unifying use of media in many of his films. Killian's talk radio availability to each episode's principals—indeed, to people all over the Bay area, however isolated or disconnected from one another—suggested the modernist control technique of the panopticon. But like Barry Champlain, Killian was all-seen as much as all-seeing, panoptic as well as an inversion of the panoptic, in an eerie postmodern dual status that inscribed modernity as but one of its voices.[52]

Also characteristic of each episode was a final scene in which Killian, alone at the microphone, delivered a brief, thoughtful closing to his radio show—"words of wisdom" thematically appropriate for the episode. This epilogue, evincing genuine concern and a hint of sadness, ended with the words "Good night, America, wherever you are."[53] This lonely sign-off suggested an America lost, unknowable, of indeterminate social and moral location; Killian's impossible job was to make contact with, find, and guide that America. Since meaning is a "location" or determination that is "lost" in postmodernity, Killian's sign-off seemed appropriate, even poignant. At the same time, the show's depiction of the talkshow as medium showed it as "disentrenched" in Hal Foster's sense: fluid, questionable, impure.

If the character of Killian deserves so much attention, it is because the talk host has become such a rich symbol in and of contemporary America. Actor Gary Cole played Killian as likable "bad boy" with long hair, quick retort, scruffy jeans, and leather jacket. He came across as part detective, part older brother, part widower—a streetwise, compassionate survivor who had "been there" and "knows," but who knows his own limits as well. One was his personal relationships. He lived alone, the perpetual bachelor. His public title, the Nighthawk, furnished an apt metaphor: alone, hovering over the fray, nocturnal, seeing everything, "visible" to everyone yet still, to a degree, isolated. Given the detective narrative of most episodes, the Nighthawk's privileged observational position—transposed to the ear through an extensive network of callers—made his talkshow an instrument of surveillance. He surveyed the city and bound its disparate parts together in a way that offered a "postdualistic" unity to its alienated inhabitants. Yet though detached, he was at the same time involved, connected, even compromised by past and present alliances from the margins *and* the mainstream, just as the city's inhabitants were also involved with him, and each other, via call-in participation.

Killian's working-man image was also important. His blue-collar dress and around-the-clock efforts for his callers and their well-being projected a distinctly nonalienated worker, one whose work and life were insepa-rable. But even engaged in his work, he seemed apart in other respects: alone in his darkened studio, talking to an audience not "there" with him; alone in his bachelorhood. Curiously, paralleling Killian's integration of work and life was his work's integration of him into the community, an integration that coexisted with and yet seemed to contradict the several ways in which he was also an isolated figure. In his hands, the audience participation talkshow became an artifact seemingly sculpted, as it was happening, by the host's thinking-on-his-feet labor.

The Infotainment Debate and the
Ethics of Representation

Since their beginnings, call-in shows have had problems with libel: hence the use of tape- or digital-delay and call screening, now nearly uni-versal. They have also had problems with FCC regulations and broadcast-ing's statutory law on obscenity and the Fairness Doctrine (before it was repealed).[54] What the audience participation talkshow has evolved into— along with tabloid, "shock," and hybrid news/talk/magazine programs like *Prime Time Live*—seems at least in part a consequence of 1980s de-regulation, based in the belief that "what sells is the right thing to do." The talkshow raises the legal-ethical questions of communicative con-trol, knowledge, truth, credibility, and representation.[55] Somehow sens-ing this, the talkshows' own publicity machines as well as their popular press reception play with their multiple identities of "bad boy" and "good citizen," "reality" and "entertainment," interpersonal "talk" and mass-mediated "show." Undecidability, so effectively tapped in film and tele-vision fiction, has likewise become the stuff of journalistic controversy.

That talkshows borrow from other discursive practices has long been acknowledged. *Geraldo* and *Sally Jesse Raphael* resemble inquiries. *Donahue* lies between inquiry, confessional, and (to one student of the talkshow) a "communion" of participants.[56] *Oprah* has been called autobiography and cathartic New Age therapy session.[57] Political radio call-in shows are inquisitions where one can "hear America snarling" and where "bashers" "cut off heads."[58] New York talk hosts Bob Law and Barry Farber describe their shows as "journalism."[59] Although, as Farber reminds us, such cross-referencing of forms has become typical,[60] the reason for it lies in the very insecurity of the genre; the talkshow's need to portray itself in terms of other, better-understood, more clearly defined, and higher-status forms is an ongoing attempt to secure legitimacy. The talkshow has come to occupy a thankless position; as eminently useful, efficient, and integrated into public discourse as it (and even its fictional images) has become, it still gets "no respect." Why? Because its rule- and boundary-blurring efficiency in response to an accelerated image economy is frightening, a harbinger of chaos, to the many who fear the media's power but who also fail to see that the talkshow productively *structures* chaos, just as chaos structures *it*.

Television critics in the print media have developed the convenient terms "tabloid" or "trash" television to disparage talkshows, syndicated news shows usually scheduled in the access slot, and other hybrid "infotainments": *A Current Affair, Hard Copy, Inside Edition, America's Most Wanted*, and even CBS's *Rescue 9 1 1*.[61] Most include some audience participation. *Hard Copy*, for example, ends its program with audio letters from viewers who phone in to its answering service. *America's Most Wanted* takes viewer tips in tracking down fugitives. As sensational news programs that mix dramatic re-creations with actualities, offbeat human interest stories with "real people," home video footage and celebrity "dirt," these shows interweave audience participation with "slicker" material. Syndicated fare such as the game show depends, of course, on a highly structured type of audience participation. But even daytime soap operas and syndicated "cult" programs like *Star Trek* have experienced a high degree of extratextual audience participation in the form of local fan clubs, national conventions, newsletters, fanzines, and spin-off merchandising.

One instance of reception that epitomizes the late 1980s good citizen–

bad boy debate around the talkshow and tabloid television was a ninety-minute PBS seminar program aired in the spring of 1989, when *The Morton Downey, Jr., Show* was near its peak. "The Other Side of the News: Entertainment News or Entertainment?" was a roundtable hosted by former CBS news chief and current Columbia University journalism professor Fred W. Friendly; it originated from Columbia and opened the American Society of Newspaper Editors' annual convention—a set of institutional frames already obviating the traditional journalistic standpoint from which "trash" television has been defined and within which the "problem," as Friendly sees it, has been engaged.[62]

Friendly's panel pitted journalists and editors from prestigious newspapers (the *Los Angeles Times*, the *Washington Post*, the *Des Moines Register*) against Morton Downey, Jr., Phil Donahue, Geraldo Rivera, Larry King, *60 Minutes* producer Don Hewitt, station group owner Stanley Hubbard, television critic Tom Shales, *Downey* originator Bob Pittman, and even an editor from the *New York Daily News*, F. Gilman Spencer (included, perhaps, to indicate that the broadcast media were not alone in being labeled "tabloid"). A media critic as well as moderator, Friendly set the tone and direction by laying out a series of questions and exhibits: clips of sensational moments from *Downey, Geraldo, Donahue,* and *60 Minutes*, plus a shrill radio ad for the *Daily News* and one of its sensational front pages.[63]

Friendly's seminar itself became a highly charged version of its very target—the talkshow—by using its ingredients and reproducing its shouting matches. To uproarious laughter, a mockingly disdainful Downey commented that he found all the shouting "extremely distasteful"—a clear hint of his awareness of the irony. Friendly's choice of talkshow clips was also ironic—using provocation and sensation to incite the televised discussion of those very tactics. The roundtable could not help being yet another talkshow, though one implicitly claiming journalistic and even moral superiority in the kinds of questions it asked, the accusations it made, and the "lofty" venue (PBS) in which it was broadcast. If the seminar was a necessary paradox, it was (unlike the talkshows it confronted) one that could not be comfortable in its contradiction.

Friendly began by asking his former Columbia journalism student, Geraldo Rivera, "Who are you?"—who, professionally, his models were and what kind of work his program represented. Gropingly, Rivera replied that he sees himself as a cross between Edward R. Murrow, Walter Winchell, and Merv Griffin, justifying this combination by explaining that "the world has changed" and traditional categories such as "journalist" have become too narrow. Showing a clip from a *Geraldo* program on sexual surrogacy, Friendly contended that it focused on titillation and avoided the more socially significant aspects of the subject that "real" journalism would have pursued. Geraldo pointed out, to the considerable amusement of the live audience of newspaper editors, the hypocrisy of emphasizing this clip in a PBS seminar. This exchange marked the contour of the debate that followed and demonstrated that none of the talk hosts and journalists seated around Friendly's table really held the high moral ground; all were in some way tainted, complicitous with their Other, or caught in their own contradictions.

Morton Downey tried to lift himself above the debate by describing himself as an "advocate" whose show was also "news." Geraldo made the related point that his show is "news" precisely *because* it deals with stories that are neglected by the *New York Times*. *Downey* creator Bob Pittman defended his show from a wider perspective: because the advent of cable, deregulation, and the proliferation of channels had ended broadcasting's initial condition of scarcity, *Downey* was an instance of diversification, not elimination; if *Downey* had replaced anything, it was entertainment, not news. Pittman asserted his confidence in the audience's ability to judge for itself and pointed out that *Downey* was a new way of getting information across to the young, whom the traditional news shows were not reaching.

Concurring with Pittman, Phil Donahue went a step further: the value of his talkshow, he argued, is that it not only reaches but activates its audience; in his words, it may prove to be "your last best hope when the cops arrest your sister." Like all talk/service hosts, Donahue can point to a mailbag full of viewers' letters recounting how his show prompted them finally to act and solve their problems.

Don Hewitt, attempting to occupy a tenuous middle ground between the "trashmongers" and the print journalists, declared, "There's no one in this room who doesn't deal in trash." Donahue's response: "Trash? Those were *good* stories!" Indeed, most of the debate centered on questions of definition: what *is* news? talk? entertainment?—*ontological* questions. But Friendly concluded the debate by defining it strictly in *ethical* terms, trying to strike a balance between "what's a right to do" and "the right thing to do." He and some of the print journalists proposed as corrective a kind of paternalism: the "journalist," whoever that individual is and whatever form his or her informational program may take, must assume a professional distance and decide what the public *needs* to know, not just what it *wants* to know.

Historically, "journalism" has retained a special status derived not only from a professionalizing education but from particular ways of reporting and presenting the news. Such ways linked the reporter with the culture of expertise that along with the traditional definition of the journalist emerged at the end of the nineteenth century. As a specially trained expert who dealt with and decided upon "facts," the reporter also had a duty to interpret those facts, since they could be tainted by private interests and their public relations. When the social sciences began increasingly to portray the public as irrational and thus vulnerable to manipulation, journalism became one of the professions that "developed a proprietary attitude toward 'reason' and a paternalistic attitude toward the public."[64] "Reason," of course, included "reasonable" debate and a form of presentation based in an "ideal of objectivity" that was primarily an outgrowth of 1920s and '30s journalistic developments.[65]

Herbert Gans, in his 1979 institutional study of news media decision- and product-making, observed a strong reformist, Progressive-era undertow in the newsroom: a notion of socially responsible capitalism (which will not simply "do anything" for profit), a faith in the wisdom of the expert over the politician, and a suspicion of anyone resembling a populist demogogue.[66] When Downey and Geraldo describe themselves in populist terms, or when Friendly (as he did in the 1970s) calls Donahue "the people's journalist," the traditional press's hostile reception thus seems inevitable.

Nonetheless, the clash between the talk host and the "traditional" journalist is, in another sense, merely the current manifestation of an intrajournalistic conflict dating back to the 1890s, "the moral war between information journalism and story journalism."[67] In that era, the *New York Times* embodied the information model; the *New York World* typified the story model. Information journalism—the "genre of self-denial" and "abstraction," in which facts are interpreted "without an inherent, psychologically significant order"[68]—correlates most closely with the model implied by the journalistic critics of the talkshow. Like story journalism, however, the talkshow "plays intentionally on connections to human experience" by invoking the "less respectable" faculty of feelings. The result of these two models in the 1890s was a "moral division of labor between newspapers." To media historian Michael Schudson it was also a "cover for class conflict": the *Times* information model was "adapted to the life experience of persons whose position in the social structure gave them most control over their own lives. Its readers were relatively independent and participant. The readers of the *World* were relatively dependent and nonparticipant."[69]

Although the talkshow is clearly derived from working-class-oriented story journalism, the contemporary talkshow audience's class orientation is less clear than its gender address. The scheduling of most television talk/service shows during the daytime may suggest that they reach the low-status shift worker, the mother-housewife at home, the student, or the elderly—though this ignores the prevalence of the time-shifting VCR. In any case, the legitimacy-based conflict between journalism and the audience participation talkshow reiterates the omnipresent high culture versus popular culture debate provoked by postmodern boundary crossings.

The press reception of the Friendly program—like most of the newspaper coverage of the June 1989 meeting of the National Association of Radio Talk Show Hosts—was amused at best, damning at worst. Walter Goodman's blistering *New York Times* review of Friendly's "encounter session" called Donahue, Downey, and Geraldo "television's pre-eminent noisemakers," "neighborhood delinquents" who are "insecure" about what they do despite "all their assertiveness." They finally got their chance in Friendly's forum, he said, to present "rationalizations" for their "touching desire . . . to be accepted as journalists by real journalists"—not only by those on the panel but, presumably, by Goodman himself. To Donahue's admonition that the mainstream journalistic professionals "trust the collective wisdom of the people," Goodman responded that such thinking has been typical of "panderers over the ages." He rightly sensed a contradiction in talk hosts' claiming that what motivates their successful "reality" formats is "collective wisdom" and the "democratiz-ing of life" but confessing at the same time "a very significant competitive problem" that "straight" journalists are not supposed to have.[70]

While Goodman was properly wary of the talkhosts' grandstanding about their proclaimed, save-the-world motives, he stigmatized them by couching his contempt in the language of psychological dysfunction: their "split personality," their "delusions of mission." If Downey declared him-self an "advocate," Goodman regarded it as "the advocacy of a bully . . . drowning out civil discourse" and at the same time "advocating mainly himself," so that he and his ilk could earn the "good livings" that "real" journalists like Goodman only dream about. For Goodman journalists may be poorer, but at least they do respectable work and avoid identity confusion, whereas talk hosts need a psychologist "to help them be proud of, or at least live with," their lucrative work, whatever it really is, and to bring them "gently around to some acquaintance with reality." Goodman implied that the boundary confusions of the talkshow could support only one diagnosis: madness.[71] Like others in his position, he could not see how productive that "madness" is for the mediated economy—except, perhaps, in terms of how much more lucrative hosting a talkshow can be.

Ellen Goodman's column on the Friendly show broadened the focus and did what so many other critics have done: it condemned the television *medium* as the ultimate source of trashiness. Interestingly, her column, a syndication like the talkshows, must compete nationally for space in local newspapers, just as talkshows must compete nationally for off-network broadcast time on individual stations—an institutional comparison that never occurs to critics intent on distancing themselves from television and talkshows. Ellen Goodman used Friendly's PBS seminar to scrutinize the tabloid and "brawl" shows she would otherwise have found unworthy of her time. The implication is clear: most such talkshows are too "trivial" or "low" as forms of popular culture to merit discussion in and of them-selves; Friendly's forum was another matter. Still, Goodman called the discussion a "free-for-all" that mirrored the "trash television" problem by being "entertaining" and "only marginally informative." Oblivious to the value of the program's vivid condensation of the whole "trash" contro-versy, she ascribed the "brawl" shows' deficiencies—chiefly, their "bias" against civility and complexity in favor of a highly charged, sportslike conflict—to the television medium itself. To her, the problem was rooted in the specificity of a medium that can terminate any threat of complexity "with the words, 'I'm sorry, we're out of time.'" She found *Nightline*—a culturally "high" instance of the talkshow—equally guilty. Only the printed word could provide "a better shot at subtlety."[72]

Locating the talkshow "problem" in notions of the medium's rather than the genre's specificity has typified a critical discourse emphasizing the dangers of negative audience effects, made all the more insidious by audience participation. Oprah's New Age philosophy is "often loose—and dangerous"; her "comfortable truths do not entirely cohere . . . they are, nevertheless, perfect for the age of the soundbite," says Barbara Grizzuti Harrison in a *New York Times Magazine* feature.[73] But such "contradictions work for her" by establishing her "kinship with an avid audience, whose perplexities they reflect; they insure that she will be regarded as spontaneous, undogmatic." Harrison locates Oprah's principal contradiction in her self-described "ministry," which believes, on one hand, that one cannot be anything one wants because, in Oprah's words, "nothing is random"; yet, on the other hand, "all things are possible" and "goodness is always rewarded" when one is "obedient to one's calling." Oprah's contradictions do indeed work for her in ways consistent with a postmodern productivity—a point lost on the critic.

Along with Oprah's mixed messages, Harrison also finds the show's *format* dangerous. The participation of the mostly noncelebrity guests and the audience gives spectators an "experience" that people "like" to have and that "saves them from having to think." Spectatorial involvement lulls us into believing that we are "doing something . . . whereas in fact we are coddled in our passivity." Again, predictably, such a problem is "intrinsic" to a medium Harrison sees as beguiling as Oprah's "easy questions"—questions her executive producer says "ordinary people would ask"—and her "easy answers." To her, *Oprah* aims to have viewers see themselves in others, in the suffering guests, but Oprah herself consciously projects the viewer. The appearance of spontaneity, identity, and involvement masks the actual condition of a passive, unquestioning reception of a program that is more about Oprah than anything else. Harrison sees *Oprah* using the "unhappiness of others" as a basis for a falsely experiential exercise in caring, a nonactivity that *appears* active and empathetic to millions of "lonely and uninstructed" spectators.[74]

Harrison's critique trots out the old questionable assumptions about media exploitation, the vulnerable, feminine/child spectator, and the fearful tendencies supposedly inherent in the medium.[75] Her portrayal of television's overwhelming, deceptive power and the spectator's vulnerability is even more simplistic than she accuses *Oprah* of being. Oprah's mixed messages are another example of the "postdualistic" hybridization of the self in postmodernity: Oprah is maternal yet also a successful business woman, a modernist who believes in control yet who is also passionate and moralistic.

Predictably, in a discursive environment pervaded by a bias against the electronic media in general, talk about the talkshow as dangerous has also emerged from the psychological professions. A July 1989 feature article in the *Boston Globe* asserts—with little hard evidence—the "growing" sentiment among mental health professionals that talkshows are "bad for you."[76] Some psychologists and guests who appeared on talkshows to discuss psychological problems complain of feeling "dirty" and "guilty" afterward. At the root of their complaints is their self-perceived fragility and lack of control over the programs' sensationalizing direction, which results in an "emotional insensitivity" to them. Despite these charges, many mental health professionals still believe in the efficacy of the participatory talkshow to the degree that it purveys vital psychological information to people who have no other source. Some see the matter as one of taking responsibility for the "extraordinarily powerful tool" of television by establishing ethical parameters for the medium's use by psychologists. The American Psychological Association has already adopted standards for its membership's media involvement and has been working on guidelines specific to talkshow appearances.[77]

Despite the scare talk, some press voices have defended the audience participation talkshow in its infotainment and confrontalk forms. Besides calling *Donahue* America's "most important graduate school," "pure television" in that it is "live, spontaneous, rawly emotional, and *real*," "part psychodrama, part street theatre, part group therapy," sensitive, intelligent, and the triumph of local station talent and syndication over the big networks,[78] defenders of these shows endorse them as ensuring a vigorous debate usually absent from mainstream journalism. For example, in a *Wall Street Journal* op-ed piece, former NBC news president Reuven Frank took the occasion of a fight that broke out on *Geraldo* in 1988 to support such shows as "the current bastions of the vigorous contention of ideas." Because they represented "the ultimate expression of the Fairness Doctrine," they did not deserve to be used as an excuse for reregulation. Long a journalist, Frank recognized journalism's limitations: by seeking facts, journalists "tend to lose sight of ideas clashing." Talkshows such as *Geraldo*, even in their simulation of news events (he mentioned the reenactment of a murder on *Downey*), "openly and healthily" inform the public in a forum presenting ideas and their advocates in conflict. The program that resulted in Geraldo's broken nose—one that brought together the leader of the White Aryan Resistance Youth, the head of the Congress of Racial Equality (CORE), and a rabbi—was "a new opportunity for the public" to see what such people "really" are.[79]

A college professor's op-ed piece in the *Wall Street Journal* defended *Downey* by comparing it to Speakers' Corner, where, as a nineteen-year-old airman stationed near London, the author first became interested in issues and debate. If the vehemence of the scene was part of what initially engaged the young man, "the initial ugliness" was soon "overwhelmed by the force of new ideas and a synthesis of old ones." He admitted that recognizing *Downey*'s value to its youthful audience "requires philosophical tenacity" but argued that ultimately such a show offers at least one compelling way into the practice of political discussion.[80]

One must note the "faint praise" aspect of these defenses. To say that the interactive talkshow deserves legitimation because it is attractively educational and involving for audiences who are mostly women or youth purportedly in need of more education is to call it a kind of necessary evil. It becomes a "low" form of information that is nonetheless useful because it gets through to those whom "higher" forms do not reach. The lowly talkshow's lofty critics here grudgingly attribute to it some social and political utility for those somehow "beneath" them.

In the light of the ways a critical and largely print journalism has received the talkshow, how do the hosts and producers of those shows construct themselves through their own publicity? The industry has long referred to the interactive television talkshow as the "talk/*service*" subgenre, one that offers relevant and useful information. The hosts commonly identify themselves with the "people" and insist, as Geraldo did to Friendly, that they are "doing good" by presenting compelling information, viewpoints, or guest "experiences" often ignored by mainstream journalism—and doing so in a format that speaks directly with its audience. To them, such formats fight the overprocessed blandness of most television.[81]

Both television and radio hosts claim that their participatory shows—and even they themselves as models of personal success via the talkshow—are a form of spectator empowerment. Oprah Winfrey responded to the charge of exploitation by citing, among others, a letter from a woman who, after watching one of her shows, finally walked out on her abusive husband after seventeen years. Information, empathy, activation, and being "in touch with America" are central to Oprah's self-definition: "I'm called a 'talk-show host' because I understand in my heart that there is something deeper, stronger, and more important going on with the people who are affected by the show."[82] Even the most acerbic "hang-uppers" claim a degree of empathy with "the people" which, because of call-in participation, makes them uniquely effective. Like Oprah, many say they "make a difference in people's lives."[83] This very claim to a special effectivity has prompted the talkshow's supporters to see it as truly participatory and redemptive; its detractors see it as intrusive and dangerous.

As portrayed in research, criticism, and fiction, the talkshow's confusions of identity and role, its disorienting defiance of established aesthetic standards and distinctions—from gender to genre to the status of the interactive "spectator" (a term that no longer seems adequate)—all point to how the talkshow epitomizes a crisis of representation that has as much to do with politics and ethics as it does signs and meaning. However, it appears as a "crisis" because the residue of established boundaries persists in much of our "official" critical consciousness—in the journalist, researcher, dramatist, filmmaker, and critic. Instead, like Rupert Pupkin, the talkshow loosely adheres to the new set of "rules" in the expanded field of a postmodern image economy whose productive instability—its *play* with established boundaries—is exactly how it *works*.

Postscript

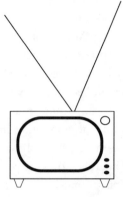

A New Sense of Place

By the winter of 1990, *America's Funniest Home Videos* had become one of the most popular shows on television. It is a combination game and participation show for which viewers send in amusing video clips to compete for cash prizes: $10,000 to the funniest, as judged by a technique used back in the 1950s in *Stand Up and Be Counted!* and *Queen for a Day*—the studio audience's electronic vote. The finalists are seated in the audience.

Judging from the homey set, we have been invited into the host's living room to watch some home videos. Most of the entries rely on the slapstick humor of "odd" behavior, often involving children or animals: someone's pants fall down; a dog clings to a dustmop as it rides across a kitchen floor. Sound effects often accompany these "home bloopers" for comic emphasis, and host Bob Saget narrates a carefully planned commentary.

The supposedly "accidentally funny" home videos are, in fact, only partly "home" and not always "accidental."[1] The professionals appropriate the amateur. The calculated—the broadcast industry—takes and "plays with" the ostensibly unplanned. As in the talkshows, chance meets structure and professional meets amateur in such a way that the producers can manufacture spectacle of "prime-time" quality using chance elements and audience participation as raw materials. In so doing, the professionals return home video to the viewers, reprocessed and somehow "improved." Through this loop, the professional commodifies the domestic. The host's scripted voiceover frames the clips as decidedly amateur and incomplete. With a wireless microphone, Saget, like Donahue, moves around his studio audience, soliciting ad-libbed comments, which

149

he milks for laughs. His discursive and presentational control derives from his power as appropriator. That control, however, is not complete; the participant's voice still comes through.

The talkshow's constant play with a constellation of voices, like its play with boundaries, has been central to how it works. Sports talk plays with the sports news. Talk host Jay Sorenson of WKXW Trenton—the talk station through which the 1990 New Jersey anti-tax campaign coalesced—tells heated callers that his anger is only "play"; he is merely "playing" with the issues.[2] Despite this seeming denial, his own activism in the New Jersey anti-tax crusade reminds us that he more than "plays" with issues. American politics has had a long history of combining its serious ends with playful and participatory means—rallies, stage shows, barbecues, and partisan choruses, to name a few. That talkshows are part of a powerful private industry makes their addition to that list as controversial as it is inevitable. Talk host Bob Grant, who was involved in that same anti-tax campaign, plays with and against his own fans, the most devoted of whom accompany him on annual overseas tours. He tells them, "Your lives must be empty, absolutely empty"—the talk host's mockery of the compensatory "para-sociality" for which he is supposedly "responsible."[3] Nationally syndicated talk host Rush Limbaugh is notorious for suspending his radio persona so well between the serious and the comic that he is "probably both."[4]

But call-in radio's "work" *and* "play" with heated issues has a real impact when, for example, its tax-bashing leads to deep cuts in public services such as education, as happened in Massachusetts.[5] The talkshow's productive instability—its entertaining "double games"—can destroy what is left of the common good, and can do so even more effectively because it appears to involve its public directly, "democratically." Talkshows walk the fine line between a renewal of the public sphere through discussion that transcends private interests, and the deeper privatization of public life. This productive instability *can* but does not necessarily have to become broadcast irresponsibility. But talk radio deserves criticism when its feedback loop amplifies dangerous misconceptions into high volume—and influential—noise. The talk host has the bottom-line responsibility for knowing the facts, and reasonably projecting the implications, of issues, especially the "hot button" ones. When Massachusetts call-in radio undertook an anti-tax and anti–big state government campaign in the late-1980s, reviving the 1970s label "Taxachusetts," its rhetoric side-stepped the fact that, during the 1980s, Massachusetts had moved to the rank of only a *moderate* tax burden state; it ranked twenty-ninth in per-centage of tax bill to workers' earnings (in 1981, it had ranked sixth). Fortunately, those anti-tax efforts—focused in a binding 1990 ballot ini-tiative known as Question Three, which would have rolled state spending back to 1988 levels—were rejected; the legislature passed $1.1 billion in tax and fee increases, which, by 1991, helped balance the Common-wealth's budget. One talk host at the center of the anti-tax fervor, Bos-ton's Jerry Williams, used the occasion of "his" defeat to mitigate the very talkshow power he and many of his colleagues so often proclaim: "It just goes to show that everyone who said we have this overwhelming in-fluence was wrong." Other talk hosts, however, including WBZ Boston's Peter Meade and Ted O'Brien, along with a host of interest groups, some comprised of representatives from Massachusetts business and industry, questioned or opposed the referendum.[6]

Since home video is a vernacular and domestic practice, and thus part of what was once the private sphere, *America's Funniest Home Videos* seems to colonize that domain through a diffused, available, and everyday-life-penetrating technology that takes its place alongside the growth of the deregulated telephone industry;[7] cable's penetration of more and more homes; the interactivity of addressable converters (allowing cable systems to target individual homes), and pay-per-view; the expansion of person-alized, mobile, miniaturized reception through Walkman technologies; 800 and 900 telephone numbers; and home satellite dishes. The media are now expanding their markets by moving temporally and spatially inward; a greater invasiveness is coupled with an accelerated product life cycle. This inward move draws the spectator into a fluid text as coproducer and participant. Rather than suffering what Joshua Meyrowitz calls "no sense of place,"[8] the media consumer now occupies—for good or ill—new cyberspatial "places." The electronic media may have blurred what were once interpersonal situational boundaries, but they have also created whole new interactive "places" that are no less distinctly "situational."[9]

Like a cyberspace, the talkshow's audience participation brings about the deeper interpenetration of public and private spheres. The spectator-participant may now coproduce his or her own narrative inscription in a further realization of the mass-mediated reproduction of work in leisure observed years ago by Max Horkheimer and Theodor Adorno.[10] Commercial broadcasting's audience participation transforms—but does not necessarily reduce—the self, politics, diversity, and even resistance and leisure into labor and exchange value. While such programming still gives voice to the everyday anonymous citizen and the subcultural, the broadcast industry is able to reinscribe these voices in what becomes a strange undecidability, a mutual contamination—another "double game" that "works both ways." The financial economy and the cultural economy have become mutually dependent, almost indistinguishable.

Rather than epitomizing the "tyranny of intimacy" and collapse of conventionalized public culture envisioned by Richard Sennett in *The Fall of Public Man*, or the triumph of private interests in the erosion of the public sphere envisioned by Habermas, the media's interactive cyberspace is qualitatively *different* from the separate public or private spheres conceived in modernity.[11] It is, instead, a liminal space somewhere between or beyond the two. The call-in show makes public spectacle of private passions even as the caller remains to a degree private, hidden behind the masking, low-resolution apparatus of the telephone. It also makes *private* spectacle of *public* passions. While modernity's public sphere may have collapsed as such, so have some aspects of the private; talkshows display the personal in performance. Notions of "public good" and disinterested "civil discussion," however, must persist. My view is that a new sense of "public" must develop and prevail.

The common promotional address of talkshows underscores their drive to absorb the spectator cyberspatially. A news announcer for Philadelphia talk radio station WCAU begins his newscast by saying, "These are the stories you'll be talking about." Using a grainy, exaggerated *cinema verité* style, a 1989 promotional spot for *Donahue* depicted a radio "talk jock" at his microphone as a voice over told us, "If you're talking about it, you'll hear about it on *Donahue*." The show's most common 1990 promos depicted Donahue in close-up, addressing the camera in what appeared to be his well-lit studio, excitedly describing his next show through a series of questions about the topic; his final words often included "you": "We'll find out where *you* stand on the next *Donahue*."

A 1990 promo for *The Oprah Winfrey Show* consisted of close-ups of three speaking individuals which dissolved from one to the next. The first, an anonymous, "average" man—a surrogate spectator-participant—said that the show teaches him something. The second, Oprah herself, said that we need to get control of our lives. The third, an anonymous woman, said, "It felt good to talk about it." The three statements, taken together, promoted Oprah's (and *Oprah*'s) therapeutic themes of self-control and self-improvement for personal success.[12] The spot's inscription of the spectator-participant next to the host herself, however, not only serves as a metonym for the show's participation (the subjects get to speak *with*— on the same plane as—Oprah-the-success-story) but puts the spectator into the spectacle.

Sociologist Jerold Starr makes the point that industrial capitalism's survival depended on the split between public and private spheres. During times of market contraction, the private sphere—home, neighborhood, informal and interpersonal exchange, the domain of intimacy, personal loyalty, sentiment ("where feeling counts"), "the communal and the spontaneous"—provided a "compensatory network" counterbalancing the market and its "cold rationality."[13] The audience participation talkshow revives elements of that domain, making public that private space "where feeling counts" while also commodifying it and its spectator-participant.

Starr also locates premodern and preindustrial impulses in the radical politics of the 1960s—impulses that favored interpersonal communication out of a suspicion of corporatized media entrenched in the increasingly suspect project of modernity. This political and countercultural movement sought to install the ad hoc, the communitarian, the "feeling" qualities—associated in modernity with the private sphere—in the public-political realm. There emerged the extraparliamentary political speech of talk radio: *Joe Pyne, Donahue*, and their wide spectrum of marginal guests, intentional communities, and interest groups. In response, the audience participation talkshow has incorporated those 1960s impulses in a disentrenchment of the modernist encoding of broadcasting's technology even as it has used that technology. In this way, the talkshow typifies the postmodern: it "uses and abuses, installs and then subverts, the very concepts it challenges."[14] In Robert Venturi's words, it "has it both ways" in an both-and aesthetic—and ethic.[15]

Observers of the postmodern condition such as Jean Baudrillard, using words that seem to apply perfectly to the talkshow, regard the media as causative of the condition. For him, the "ecstasy of communication" brought on by today's media pervasiveness has transformed the "real" world into simulation, into useless, meaningless image: "body, landscape, time all progressively disappear as scenes." Public and private space gives way to "gigantic spaces of circulation, ventilation, and ephemeral connections." The "scene" or "spectacle" of what was once the "real" has become "*obscenity* where the most intimate processes of our life become the virtual feeding ground of the media . . . an obscenity of the visible, the all-too-visible . . . a pornography of information and communication." And he might be describing Rupert Pupkin or Barry Champlain when he declares us to be "in a new form of schizophrenia" because the media put us in "too great a proximity to everything." With "no halo of private protection," we are "living in the greatest confusion." As "schizos," each of us is "a pure screen, a switching center for all the networks of influence."[16]

Though some of these observations seem consonant with my study, they do not address the way talkshows reclaim voice—speech and the originary *logos* it has long represented—and, with it, body, to the otherwise more ethereal, fast-paced, patchworked media of MTV, ten-second ads, and shrinking news soundbites. This is exactly the media trajectory the 1992 presidential candidates seemed to be resisting in their increased reliance on talkshows as a kind of in-the-system bypass operation.

Media historian James W. Carey reminds us that the United States developed out of a vision of expanded communications held by early leaders such as Jefferson and Madison *and* out of a historical moment when "a space in between the oral and written traditions" was opened up.[17] While affirming a vision of democracy that seemed possible only if the republic remained small in geography and population, the Constitution and the *Federalist Papers* sought to overcome such limitations through what Carey calls the "transmission and transportation" solution. Constitutionally protected communication technology was trumpeted as being able to bind a larger democracy together and make it work. At the same time, this new republic's greater size would restrain government power. Technology became "not only an artifact but an actor," pushing spatially outward yet temporally backward in "a journey of restoration as much as progress." The "talk" "show" furthers this restoration by reinserting the oral culture of the village into mass communications and the nation-state. It juxtaposes the "transmission and transportation solution" to "the ancient theory and practice of the voice." [18]

Despite its seemingly amoral pastiche, the talkshow can aspire to an ideal in its intent to be "more" of "everything," to be more accessible, effective, flexible, and "realistic" through interactivity. [19] It is an ethical practice when it exposes the constructedness of knowledge as well as the very "fallenness" and impurity it also uses so well. Geraldo sees himself as "doing good" when he probes deceptive signs and appearances; such exposure even extends to his excessive public *self*-exposure in his explicit 1991 autobiography (a book that he, as guest, promoted on *other* talk-shows). Donahue claims that his best shows create a community through the "ultimate colloquium of today's video-oriented, high-tech world." Frank Rizzo promised that "we'll have our day" and with it, a better Philadelphia. And Ross Perot wanted to invite greater involvement and run the country by electronic "town meeting."

Using such language, the talkshow becomes a utopian fusion of the human, the social, and the technological in a rhetorical mastery—and a democratic scaling-down—of technology that puts even political "out-siders" inside. At the same time, it is a dystopian place where problems come to light and one can hear America snarling. For Donahue, the inter-active talkshow—the high-tech world's "town crier" and "lamplighter" (antiquarian metaphors)—provides "*you* with the best opportunity to make *your* point" (my emphasis), especially if you have "no other vehicle" to communicate your views. [20] But in the same breath he admits his show's impurity. It "frustrates" the participant because it only "scratches the sur-face" of issues. It is also only a "game": if the participant understands the rules, he or she has nothing to fear. An idealized institution, the talk-show is at the same time "fallen" in that as popular commodity it must "sandwich the Persian Gulf in between the male strippers" to generate an audience. [21] And, with a rare honesty, it acknowledges its "fallenness" and can use its "impurity" for the public good through its communicative action.

Now that the talkshow in its various forms has become integral to our culture, politics, and image economy, those in the talkshow business must recognize that in the expanded field of such a contingent medium, the boundary between "inside" and "outside" has indeed collapsed. Talk radio's "governors on the airwaves" are no longer outsiders, as much as they often define themselves that way; they must renounce deniability and face up to the responsibility of their very performative and powerful speech. By the same token, the old distinctions between public and private have, in the talkshow, given way to a new public sphere which we are all "inside" and thus responsible for—one of the new, cyberspatial neighborhoods we now live in.

Notes

Introduction: The Sense of the Talkshow

1. Steve Post, *Playing in the FM Band: A Personal Account of Free Radio* (New York: Viking Press, 1974), p. 101.

2. Stated by Williams at the June 9, 1989, meeting of the National Association of Radio Talk Show Hosts, "Talk Radio and the American Dream," Faneuil Hall, Boston (broadcast live on WRKO-AM Boston).

3. *Boston Globe*, June 16, 1992, p. 21.

4. See Sharon D. Moshavi, "Is Campaign '92 Bypassing Network News?" *Broadcasting*, June 15, 1992, pp. 4, 14. In that same issue, see "Talkradio a Player in Presidential Campaign," p. 14. Also Charles Krauthammer, "The Pornography of Self-Revelation," *Time*, Aug. 10, 1992, p. 72; and Ellen Goodman, "A Real-Life Family Portrait," *Boston Globe*, July 19, 1992, p. 63. For other comments on presidential campaign "confessionals," see Michael K. Frisby, "Soul-Baring on the Campaign Trail," *Boston Globe*, Aug. 6, 1992, p. 81. Regarding the candidates' specific talkshow appearances, see "Clinton Maps Investment Plan in 2-Hour TV Appearance," *Boston Globe*, June 16, 1992, p. 21. On the Oct. 15, 1992, talkshowlike debate, see for example, James Carroll, "The Process Succeeds," *Boston Globe*, Oct. 19, 1992, p. 15, and David S. Broder, "President's Last Hope," *Boston Globe*, Oct. 17, 1992, p. 11. Also see "2nd Debate Draws Larger TV Audience," *Boston Globe*, Oct. 17. 1992, p. 8. On Larry King, see "Larry King: Kingmaker to the Pols," *New York Times*, June 28, 1992, pp. 2–27.

5. Neil Postman, *Amusing Ourselves to Death: Public Discourse in the Age of Show Business* (New York: Viking Press, 1985).

6. See Jane Gaines, "From Elephants to Lux Soap: The Programming and 'Flow' of Early Motion Picture Exploitation," *Velvet Light Trap* 25 (Spring 1990): 29–43.

7. Pitching a book through authors' appearances on *The Oprah Winfrey Show*, *Donahue*, *Geraldo*, *Today*, and *Good Morning America* is considered publishing's most effective advertising (especially because it is free), capable of

producing instant best sellers. *Oprah* has been highly prized by publishers ever since it featured Harville Hendrix, author of *Getting the Love You Want*: his first appearance, in August 1988, put the languishing book on the *New York Times* best-seller list for a week; his second appearance, in February 1989, returned the book to the list for another seven weeks—the result of what publishers call "the Oprah factor." A Macmillan study of its ten best sellers revealed that each had been featured on national television programs, most notably talkshows. See Roger Cohen, "What Publishers Will Do for a Place on the Right List," *New York Times*, Aug. 12, 1990, p. E6.

8. Peter Viies, "Talk Radio Riding High," *Broadcasting*, June 15, 1992, p. 24. In that same issue, Mike Freeman, "Talk Shows Flourish during May Sweeps," p. 11, deals with television talkshows, as does Bill Carter's "Talk Is Cheap, but Profitable, on TV," *New York Times*, June 22, 1992, pp. D1, D8. The profitability of a successful television talkshow is ever so clear in the figures: against costs of only $10 million to $20 million a year to produce, 1991 revenues were $157 million for *The Oprah Winfrey Show*, about $90 million for *Donahue*, and $60 million for *Sally Jesse Raphael*. Bill Carter was the critic who declared the audience appetite for such shows "bottomless."

9. See, e.g., "Quota Issue Sizzles, Touches Nerve," *Boston Globe*, June 9, 1991, p. 1. A public opinion piece about a proposed civil rights bill accused of establishing racial quotas in the workplace, the article begins by describing Atlanta's talk radio "sport of the day" as "quota bill bashing."

10. Kirk Johnson, "To Sell Tax, Weicker Takes It on the Chin," *New York Times*, March 14, 1991, p. B1.

11. The date of the swap was June 17. Interestingly, Imus's on-air interview with Bill Clinton while he was campaigning earlier that spring—an interview that revealed his sense of humor as well as his tough hide—helped win the presidential candidate enough New Yorkers to clinch the state.

12. S. Robert Lichter, *Racial and Ethnic Images on Talk Radio*, Report to the American Jewish Committee, July 3, 1990 (Washington, D.C.: Center for Media and Public Affairs, 1990), p. 10.

13. *Nightline*, Sept. 20, 1989; "Rep. Frank Won't Quit; Wants Probe Finished," *Trenton Times*, Sept. 2, 1989.

14. Donahue made this comment on "The Other Side of the News: Entertainment News or Entertainment?" WNET-TV New York, April 12, 1989; moderator: Fred W. Friendly. This roundtable seminar was taped at the Columbia University School of Journalism during the annual meeting of the American Society of Newspaper Editors (see Chapter 3).

15. Interview with Paul Noble, former producer of *The Alan Burke Show*, in

New York at WNYW-TV, Jan. 1991. The show originated on WNEW-TV New York and was syndicated nationally during 1967. Like Joe Pyne, Burke specialized in "fringe" guests whom he confronted or ridiculed.

16. Andrew Pollack, "New Interactive TV Threatens the Bliss of Couch Potatoes," *New York Times*, June 18, 1990, p. 1. Developments made possible by computer networking also include interactive sports networks, available in bars, which allow participants to guess a quarterback's next play during a televised football game.

17. Richard Maltby, *Harmless Entertainment: Hollywood and the Ideology of Consensus* (Metuchen, N.J.: Scarecrow Press, 1983), p. 25.

18. James W. Carey, *Communication as Culture: Essays on Media and Society* (Boston: Unwin Hyman, 1989), pp. 204, 9.

19. Hal Foster, *Recodings: Art, Spectacle, Cultural Politics* (Seattle: Bay Press, 1985), p. 130.

20. One critic has described media postmodernism as "the David Letterman syndrome" because *Latenight with David Letterman* has come to typify postmodernist form in its *being* a talkshow and *mocking* talkshows at the same time. For a particular talkshow to epitomize postmodernity obscures the genre's general, additional, and often less obvious postmodern qualities. See Caryn James, "Postmodernism Edges into the Film Mainstream," *New York Times*, July 23, 1990, p. B1.

21. Bruce W. Marr, "Talk Radio Programming," in *Broadcast/Cable Programming: Strategies and Practices*, ed. Susan Tyler Eastman, Sydney W. Head, and Lewis Klein (Belmont, Calif.: Wadsworth, 1989), p. 444.

22. "More Voices Join Satellite-Delivered Talk Format," *Broadcasting*, Feb. 20, 1989, pp. 46–47.

23. Lawrence Grossberg, "Putting the Pop Back into Postmodernism," in *Universal Abandon? The Politics of Postmodernism*, ed. Andrew Ross (Minneapolis: University of Minnesota Press, 1988), pp. 178–79.

24. John Fiske, *Understanding Popular Culture* (Boston: Unwin Hyman, 1989), pp. 26–127. Fiske often cites M. de Certeau, *The Practice of Everyday Life* (Berkeley: University of California Press, 1984).

25. See Fredric Jameson, "Postmodernism, or the Cultural Logic of Late Capitalism," *New Left Review* 146 (July–August 1984): 53–92.

26. Carey, *Communication as Culture*, pp. 201–330.

27. Richard J. Bernstein, *The New Constellation: The Ethical-Political Horizons of Modernity/Postmodernity* (Cambridge: MIT Press, 1992), pp. 8–9, 225–26.

28. Lewis A. Erenberg, *Steppin' Out: New York Nightlife and the Transfor-*

mation of American Culture, 1890–1930 (Westport, Conn.: Greenwood Press, 1981), pp. 258–59. Also see Kathy Peiss, *Cheap Amusements: Working Women and Leisure in Turn-of-the-Century New York* (Philadelphia: Temple University Press, 1986), pp. 3–10.

29. Timothy Reiss, *The Discourse of Modernism* (Ithaca, N.Y.: Cornell University Press, 1982), pp. 21, 30, 41.

30. Ibid., p. 31.

31. Ibid., pp. 33, 41.

32. Barry Glassner, "Fitness and the Postmodern Self," *Journal of Health and Social Behavior* 30 (June 1989): 182.

33. Jürgen Habermas, "Modernity versus Postmodernity," *New German Critique* 22 (Winter 1981): 9.

34. See Andreas Huyssen, "Mapping the Postmodern," *New German Critique* 33 (Fall 1984): 48–49. Huyssen here locates the political manifestations of the postmodern critique of the teleology of modernization in the women's and ecology movements.

35. Matei Calinescu, *The Five Faces of Modernity: Modernism, Avant-Garde, Decadence, Kitsch, Postmodernism* (Durham, N.C.: Duke University Press, 1987), p. 265.

36. Jean-François Lyotard, *The Postmodern Condition: A Report on Knowledge*, trans. Geoff Bennington and Brian Massumi (Minneapolis: University of Minnesota Press, 1984), pp. 42–47.

37. Dana Polan, "Brief Encounters: Mass Culture and the Evacuation of Sense," in *Studies in Entertainment: Critical Approaches to Mass Culture*, ed. Tania Modleski (Bloomington: Indiana University Press, 1986), pp. 181–85.

38. Lawrence Grossberg, *It's a Sin: Essays on Postmodern Politics and Culture* (Sydney: Power Publications, 1988), pp. 40, 59–69.

39. Terry Eagleton, *Against the Grain: Essays, 1975–1985* (London: Verso, 1986), p. 146.

40. Ian Angus and Sut Jhally, eds., introduction to *Cultural Politics in Contemporary America* (New York: Routledge, 1989), p. 5.

41. Arthur Kroker and David Cook, *The Postmodern Scene: Excremental Culture and Hyper-Aesthetics* (New York: St. Martin's Press, 1986), p. 210.

42. Andrew Ross, *No Respect: Intellectuals and Popular Culture* (New York: Routledge, 1989), p. 9.

43. Jürgen Habermas, *The Structural Transformation of the Public Sphere: An Inquiry into a Category of Bourgeois Society*, trans. Thomas Burger with Frederick Lawrence (Cambridge, Mass.: MIT Press, 1989), pp. 51, 142–43, 160.

44. Paolo Carpignano, Robin Anderson, Stanley Aronowitz, and William

DiFazio, "Chatter in the Age of Electronic Reproduction: Talk Television and the 'Public Mind,' " *Social Text* 25–26 (1990): 50, 52, 54.

45. Horton and Wohl's essay first appeared in *Psychiatry* 19 (1956): 215–29; it is discussed in detail in Chapter 3.

46. Alan Hirsch, *Talking Heads: Political Talk Shows and Their Star Pundits* (New York: St. Martin's Press, 1991), pp. 66, 218.

47. Murray Burton Levin, *Talk Radio and the American Dream* (Lexington, Mass.: Lexington Books, 1987), pp. 19–23.

48. Donal Carbaugh, *Talking American: Cultural Discourses on "Donahue"* (Norwood, N.J.: Ablex, 1988), p. 19.

49. Gaye Tuchman, "Assembling a Network Talk-Show," in *The* TV *Establishment: Programming for Power and Profit*, ed. Gaye Tuchman (Englewood Cliffs, N.J.: Prentice-Hall, 1974), pp. 119–35.

50. See Andreas Huyssen, "Mass Culture as Woman: Modernism's Other," in Modleski, *Studies in Entertainment*, pp. 188–207.

51. See Ross, "Uses of Camp," in *No Respect*, pp. 135–70. Ross regards camp as a "disempowered" mode of production that parodically recycles and reworks historical mass/pop cultural products (e.g., old stars or genres); "a rediscovery of history's waste" by the disaffiliated (gays, intellectuals, members of the 1960s counterculture) in their negotiated and survivalist recognition of that mass/pop culture; an "unclean" break through the subcultural reclamation of spent cultural capital. The talkshow also recycles and reworks cultural products, but more current ones, in a process that expends or exhausts them and their "straight" meanings. The talkshow becomes part of the diachronic and paratextual process by which cultural topics are reduced to the "waste" whose surplus value may later be reused. It is almost as if talkshow practices had learned a lesson from Andy Warhol's reproductive reworking of cultural "leftovers."

52. ABC Talk Radio Vice-President Maurice Tunick, for example, is eminently aware of how his medium thrives on change: "What works best is if you can change from day to day, staying on top of whatever the people are talking about" (quoted in "Talk Networks Pursue Role of AM 'White Knight,' " *Broadcasting*, Aug. 27, 1990, p. 41).

53. See Robert Venturi, *Complexity and Contradiction in Architecture* (New York: Museum of Modern Art and Graham Foundation, in association with Doubleday, 1966), pp. 30–31: "Cleanth Brooks refers to Donne's art as 'having it both ways' but, he says, 'most of us in this latter day cannot. We are disciplined in the tradition either-or, and lack the mental agility—to say nothing of the maturity of attitude—which would allow us to indulge in the finer distinctions and more subtle reservations permitted by the tradition of both-and.' The tradition

'either-or' has characterized orthodox modern architecture. . . . An architecture of complexity and contradiction . . . tends to include 'both-and' rather than exclude 'either-or.' " Venturi established an opposition between what would later be called postmodern architecture—one of "complexity and contradiction"—and the modernist "either-or" aesthetic, which he says is simplistic and immature. But modernism's "either-or" may still be encompassed in postmodernism's "both-and"—a practice characteristic, as we shall see, of the talkshow's inclusiveness.

54. Joshua Meyrowitz, *No Sense of Place: The Impact of Electronic Media on Social Behavior* (New York: Oxford University Press, 1985), pp. 127, 319. For Erving Goffman's discussion of "back regions," see his *Presentation of the Self in Everyday Life* (New York: Anchor/Doubleday, 1959), pp. 106–40.

1. Turning to Talk: The Talkshow's Development

1. Todd Gitlin, *Inside Prime Time* (New York: Pantheon Books, 1983), p. 77.

2. Shelly Schwab, MCA-TV's president of domestic syndication, in reference to that company's daytime "talkstrip"—since canceled—hosted by Kitty Kelley (author of a scathing biography of Nancy Reagan); see "MCA Signs Kitty Kelley," *Broadcasting*, June 3, 1991, p. 36.

3. For example, on Aug. 2, 1990, the day after Iraq invaded Kuwait, National Public Radio (NPR) put together an ad hoc midday, nationwide call-in program in response to a flurry of listener queries on the crisis. Hosted by commentator Daniel Schorr, the two-hour show (never formally titled) connected audience callers with Schorr and an array of Mideast experts. NPR currently offers a regular afternoon call-in show, *Talk of the Nation*.

4. James Playstead Wood, *Magazines in the United States*, 3d ed. (New York: Ronald Press, 1971), pp. 3–7.

5. Michel Foucault considers the autonomous and participatory "attitude" of the Enlightenment—and modernity—in his interpretation of a 1784 Kant essay of the same name in "What Is Enlightenment?" trans. Catherine Porter, in *The Foucault Reader*, ed. Paul Rabinow (New York: Pantheon Books, 1984), pp. 32–50.

6. Jürgen Habermas, *The Structural Transformation of the Public Sphere: An Inquiry into a Category of Bourgeois Society*, trans. Thomas Burger with Frederick Lawrence (Cambridge, Mass.: MIT Press, 1989), pp. 42–43.

7. Ibid., pp. 27–56. For Habermas, this rational-critical public sphere was short-lived, since private interests (through their need for public relations and advertising) and the state (through its eventual need for regulation) would penetrate and dissolve it by the mid-nineteenth century.

8. Today, the cracker-barrel tradition continues in water-cooler or coffee-break chat, as noted by Shelly Schwab who, with characteristic hyperbole, complimented Kitty Kelley for an interview "that I am sure dominated water-cooler conversations at most workplaces around the country" ("MCA Signs Kitty Kelley," p. 3).

9. Merle Curti, *American Paradox: The Conflict of Thought and Action* (New Brunswick, N.J.: Rutgers University Press, 1956), p. 54.

10. Ibid.

11. See Carl Bode, *The American Lyceum: Town Meeting of the Mind* (New York: Oxford University Press, 1956); and Richard A. Weaver II, "Josiah Holbrook: Feeding the Passion for Self-Help," *Communication Quarterly* 24 (Fall 1976): 10–18.

12. Weaver, "Josiah Holbrook," p. 15.

13. Bode, *American Lyceum*, p. 249. Also see Donald M. Scott, "The Popular Lecture and the Creation of a Public in Mid-Nineteenth Century America" *Journal of American History* 66 (March 1980): 791–809. Scott details the role of the midcentury "circuit lyceums" in reasserting the concept of professionalization, career, and expertise regarding knowledge (a reaction against the Jacksonian self-help passion originally motivating the lyceum, a passion Holbrook profitably fed) and in developing a sense of a national public or audience. Like today's talkshow, the lecture circuit was a promotional opportunity for professionals.

Similarly, the chautauqua, begun in 1874 in upstate New York as a Methodist summer camp for the instruction of Sunday School teachers, became so well known for its wholesome and educational mix of information, entertainment, cultural events, performances, and participatory activities that the lyceum bureaus created national circuits of "tent chautauquas" that went from town to town. Thus the chautauqua, like the lyceum, moved from more to less audience participation and toward greater product standardization and professionalization. See Joseph E. Gould, *The Chautauqua Movement: An Episode in the Continuing American Revolution* (New York: SUNY Press, 1961); and Theodore Morrison, *Chautauqua: A Center for Education, Religion, and the Arts in America* (Chicago: University of Chicago Press, 1974).

14. Wood, *Magazines in the United States*, pp. 100–125.

15. David E. Shi, *The Simple Life: Plain Living and High Thinking in American Culture* (New York: Oxford University Press, 1985), pp. 181–93.

16. Wood, *Magazines in the United States*, p. 117.

17. Stuart Ewen and Elizabeth Ewen, *Channels of Desire: Mass Images and the Shaping of American Consciousness* (New York: McGraw-Hill, 1982), p. 70.

18. Ibid., pp. 64–65: "Sears understood that the penetration of local, rural

markets depended upon the ability to present new, often unfamiliar goods in a vernacular of 'trust' and 'friendship,' " and Montgomery Ward in his highly successful catalogue juxtaposed "beguiling images" with text he himself wrote in an "amateurish, folksy vernacular." At a time of increasing standardization, the anonymous national consumer was still studiously addressed as "the woman next door."

19. See Richard Hofstadter, *Anti-Intellectualism in American Life* (New York: Knopf, 1970). Hofstadter associates strains of anti-intellectualism with several historical developments: the highly participatory revivalism that began in the colonies with the Great Awakening (a reaction against the "expert" Puritan clergy, regarded as elite and authoritarian); the Jacksonian "decline of the gentleman," which gave way to a faith in the full participation of "the people," regardless of their lack of education; what David Shi called "progressive simplicity" (*The Simple Life*, pp. 175–80)—the concept of the strenuous, simple life advocated by Teddy Roosevelt and associated with reformism (although a reaction against the intellectual life and, paradoxically, against the expert, who was central to Progressive-era reform); and the self-help movement of the 1920s and 1930s and its reaction against the "brain trust" politics of expertise in favor of "common sense" and its participatory implications.

20. Kathy Peiss, *Cheap Amusements: Working Women and Leisure in Turn-of-the-Century New York* (Philadelphia: Temple University Press, 1986), p. 138.

21. Ibid., p. 69.

22. Ibid., p. 8.

23. Lewis Erenberg, *Steppin' Out: New York Nightlife and the Transformation of American Culture, 1890–1930* (Westport, Conn.: Greenwood Press, 1981), pp. 246–49. Erenberg notes two particular cabaret acts—Clayton, Jackson, and Durante; and "The Mad Waiter"—for their semi-improvisational interaction with audiences, such as seating couples as they came in or dancing with the women. The spectator who played along was a "good sport," socially malleable and expressive—modern—as opposed to the too respectable, overly serious "stuffed shirt" frequently ridiculed by those acts.

24. Ibid., pp. 113, 115.

25. Ibid., pp. 130, 176–205. Erenberg sees Sophie Tucker as typifying the cabaret personality who could "breach the barriers to the audience" (p. 178).

26. Ibid., pp. 133, 177. "Institutionalized spontaneity" was Robert and Helen Merrill Lynd's description of the cabaret; see Helen Merrill Lynd, *Middletown Revisited* (New York: Harvest Books, 1965), pp. 276–77. "Vicarious action" is from Erving Goffman, "Where the Action Is," in *Interaction Ritual* (Garden City, N.Y.: Doubleday, 1967), pp. 149–270. Erenberg (p. 133) recasts Goffman's term as

"vicarious bohemianism"; the cafe offered a "fancy milling," a "commercial form of action . . . in which direct participation occur[ed] in a commercial setting," permitting contact with the "nonrespectable" and a sense of "living-on-the-edge" danger. The patron's ostensible mastery of both and the opportunity to indulge in expressiveness in an unconstrained setting conferred a feeling of success and renewal in his or her triumph over danger.

27. Erenberg, *Steppin' Out*, p. 134.

28. Ibid., pp. 140–41.

29. William Stott, *Documentary Expression and Thirties America* (New York: Oxford University Press, 1973), pp. 85–86.

30. For example, of the 371 network shows listed for the 1939–40 radio broadcast season, 62 (17 percent) were considered various forms of talkshow (human interest, daytime homemaking, religion)—and this number does not include news programs, many of which involved interviews. See Harrison B. Summers, ed., *A Thirty-Year History of Programs Carried on National Radio Networks in the United States, 1926–1956* (Salem, N.H.: Ayer, 1958), pp. 83–90.

31. John Dunning, *Tune In Yesterday: The Ultimate Encyclopedia of Old-Time Radio, 1925–1956* (Englewood Cliffs, N.J.: Prentice-Hall, 1976), p. 633.

32. The difficulty of defining the talkshow as a discrete generic form has been observed before. Brian Rose, in his historically informative essay "The Talk Show" (in *TV Genres: A Handbook and Reference Guide*, ed. Brian G. Rose [Westport, Conn.: Greenwood Press, 1985], pp. 329–52), admits that the genre "is difficult to place" because the shows "don't depend on dramatic actions, the imaginary interplay of characters, or the foreseeable working out of formulaic themes." Yet they contain excitement, interest, conflict, efficient crafting, "the pleasures of a clearly defined structure, a variety of character collisions, and a feeling of affirmative resolution." Along with "the emotional intimacy of melodrama [and] the sprightliness of comedy," they offer "a compelling immediacy no work of TV fiction can provide."

33. Dunning, *Tune In Yesterday*, p. 41.

34. Ibid., pp. 37–47, 303, 339.

35. Ibid., p. 477.

36. Frank Buxton and Bill Owen, *The Big Broadcast, 1920–1950* (New York: Viking Press, 1972), p. 19.

37. Dunning, *Tune In Yesterday*, pp. 387–89.

38. Ibid., pp. 614–15.

39. Ibid., p. 50. Also see Buxton and Owen, *Big Broadcast*, p. 185.

40. Erik Barnouw, *The Golden Web: A History of Broadcasting in the United States*, vol. 2, *1933–1953* (New York: Oxford University Press, 1968), p. 156.

41. Dunning, *Tune In Yesterday*, pp. 634–35.

42. Warren I. Susman, *Culture as History: The Transformation of American Society in the Twentieth Century* (New York: Pantheon Books, 1984), pp. 217–28.

43. Ibid., p. xx.

44. Habermas, *Structural Transformation*, pp. 243–44.

45. The infamous term "illusion of intimacy" comes from Donald Horton and R. Richard Wohl's seminal (and repeatedly anthologized) essay on the talkshow, "Mass Communication and Para-Social Interaction: Observations on Intimacy at a Distance," *Psychiatry* 19 (1956): 215–29; see Chapter 3 for further discussion.

46. Marshall W. Fishwick, "Father Coughlin Time: The Radio and Redemption," *Journal of Popular Culture* 2 (Fall 1988): 33–47. Also see Barnouw, *The Golden Web*, pp. 44–51.

47. Stott, *Documentary Expression*, pp. 85–91.

48. Raymond Williams explores the implications of this broadcast structural model in his *Television: Technology and Cultural Form* (New York: Schocken Books, 1974).

49. See Peter Fornatale and Joshua E. Mills, *Radio in the Television Age* (Woodstock, N.Y.: Overlook Press, 1980).

50. Jane H. Bick, "The Development of Two-Way Talk Radio in America" (Ph.D. diss., University of Massachusetts, 1987), p. 29.

51. Ibid., p. 32.

52. Fornatale and Mills, *Radio in the Television Age*, pp. 82–83.

53. "Talk Radio Today," seminar at the Museum of Broadcasting, New York City, Aug. 6, 1985; moderator: Rick Sklar; panel: WABC morning host Alan Coombs, WMCA talkshow hosts Barry Gray and Barry Farber, and nationally syndicated advice talk host Bruce Williams. Sklar, who is widely considered the radio industry's pre-eminent "program doctor" and is probably more aware of the history and the individuals behind format radio than anyone else, called Barry Gray "the pioneer of talk radio."

54. Barry Gray, "Talk Radio Today."

55. Fornatale and Mills, *Television in the Radio Age*, p. 83.

56. Bick, "Two-Way Talk Radio," pp. 36–38. Bick also mentions that the taping and airing of phone calls was permitted in 1947, encouraging another participatory station practice: the "man-in-the-street" interview done via telephone.

57. "Talk Radio 1966," *Broadcasting*, June 27, 1966, p. 75.

58. Bick, "Two-Way Talk Radio," pp. 39–40.

59. "All-News Format Is Winning Friends," *Broadcasting*, June 27, 1966, pp. 100–106. Also see Fornatale and Mills, *Radio in the Television Age*, pp. 95–116.

60. "The Sound of Radio: News/Talk," *Broadcasting*, June 12, 1989, p. 43.

61. See Edd Routt, James B. McGrath, and Fredric A. Weiss, *The Radio Format Conundrum* (New York: Hastings House, 1978), pp. 168–207, as well as Fornatale and Mills, *Radio in the Television Age*.

62. "Want to Be Different? Turn to Talk," from "Talk Radio: A Special Report," *Broadcasting*, June 27, 1966, pp. 75–82.

63. Ibid., p. 78.

64. Ibid., pp. 78–79; and Fornatale and Mills, *Radio in the Television Age*, pp. 83–84.

65. "Phone Calls Galore," *Broadcasting*, July 4, 1966, p. 38.

66. "Here's How the All-Talk Stations Do It," *Broadcasting*, June 27, 1966, pp. 82–100.

67. Bruce W. Marr, "Talk Radio Programming," in *Broadcast/Cable Programming: Strategies and Practices*, ed. Susan Tyler Eastman, Sydney W. Head, and Lewis Klein (Belmont, Calif.: Wadsworth, 1989), p. 459; Fornatale and Mills, *Radio in the Television Age*, pp. 95–116.

68. Marr, "Talk Radio Programming," p. 459.

69. Bick, "Two-Way Talk Radio," p. 41.

70. "Here's How the All-Talk Stations Do It," p. 97.

71. Bick, "Two-Way Talk Radio," p. 41.

72. Ibid., pp. 72–74, 46.

73. Steve Post, *Playing in the* FM *Band: A Personal Account of Free Radio* (New York: Viking Press, 1974), pp. 101–25.

74. "Here's How the All-Talk Stations Do It," pp. 82–100.

75. Andrew Ross, *No Respect: Intellectuals and Popular Culture* (New York: Routledge, 1989), pp. 106–7.

76. Ibid., p. 124.

77. Morris Dickstein, *Gates of Eden: American Culture in the Sixties* (1977; New York: Penguin, 1989), p. 103.

78. Ibid., pp. 81, 107, 59, 272.

79. Ibid., p. 110.

80. Ibid., p. 272.

81. Fredric Jameson, "Periodizing the 60s," in *The 60s without Apology*, ed. Sohnya Sayres, Anders Stephanson, Stanley Aronowitz, and Fredric Jameson (Minneapolis: University of Minnesota Press, in cooperation with *Social Text*, 1984), p. 195.

82. Jürgen Habermas called postmodernity a negation of the "culture of expertise" in the wake of the breakdown of the Enlightenment project of "objective science, universal morality and law, and autonomous arts"—specializations that would enrich and rationalize everyday life; see Habermas, "Modernism: An In-

complete Project," in *The Anti-Aesthetic: Essays on Postmodern Culture*, ed. Hal Foster (Port Townsend, Wash.: Bay Press, 1983), pp. 9–10.

83. Even Morton Downey, Jr., whose style seemed similar, called Pyne "a raving lunatic" in an interview on *The Jerry Williams Show*, WFXT-TV Boston, Feb. 13, 1989. Downey said that advertiser refusals of his controversial and often nasty program were "hypocritical," given that Pyne's show was sponsored by Proctor and Gamble. For more on *Pyne* and *Burke*, see Alan Hirsch, *Talking Heads: Political Talk Shows and Their Star Pundits* (New York: St. Martin's Press, 1991), pp. 11–13.

84. "Talk Keeps Syndicators Busy," *Broadcasting*, June 27, 1966, pp. 104–6.

85. Rick Sklar's description of a successful call-in host (referring to one of the most enduring and successful, Barry Farber of ABC) is quoted from the "Talk Radio Today" seminar.

86. I have found only one industry assessment of this contradiction: "The problem is that, without controversy, mass audiences won't listen, and station ratings will remain low. *With* controversy, ratings will build, but many advertisers are reluctant to be associated with controversy. Sheer personality can build a talk show audience, but such personalities are rare" (Routt, McGrath, and Weiss, *The Radio Format Conundrum*, p. 197).

87. WRKO Boston talk host Gene Burns, speaking to a Framingham, Massachusetts, State College class in communication arts, Nov. 14, 1990. Burns has been a talk host since 1967, when he worked at a Metromedia station in Baltimore.

88. Bick, "Two-Way Talk Radio," p. 61.

89. "Repeat callers," still regarded as a problem particularly for late-night shows, were apparently responsible for the 1980s decline of that once-thriving subgenre. Drive-time, its number of call-ins recently enhanced by the increase in car phones, has become the prized talk day part. Like other drive-time formats, including music, it is made more highly charged and faster paced—more callers, a higher turnover per hour—as typified by Jerry Williams's WRKO Boston drive-time program (discussed in Williams's talk to a Framingham State College class in communication arts, Nov. 14, 1990).

90. Quoted in Bick, "Two-Way Talk Radio," pp. 80–81, 90. One wonders if the recent fact that the over-sixty-five cohort is now the wealthiest segment of the population has accounted for any changes in talk radio's handling of elderly callers; there seems to be no evidence to suggest such changes.

91. "Here's How the All-Talk Stations Do It," pp. 82–100. The station in question is KLAC Los Angeles.

92. Marr, "Talk Radio Programming," pp. 454–57.

93. Ibid. Apparently, some talk stations did not acquire delay systems until

after a close call. Barry Gray ("Talk Radio Today") has told the story of how WMCA balked at the expense of a delay system until, frustrated by the lack of it, he staged an obscene call during his program.

94. Maurice Tunick, director of talk programming for ABC, moderating the seminar "Talk Radio: What Is It Telling Us?" at the Center for Communication, New York City, Nov. 7, 1989; panel: talk hosts Barry Farber, Bob Law, and Lynn Samuels.

95. Marr, "Talk Radio Programming," p. 454. A constant theme throughout this management-oriented essay is the problem of control and the need to assert it through personnel, technology, and program as well as format design.

96. The association of the "hot" talk host with rock-and-roll and the DJ survives in such pronouncements as that of Jerry Williams to the Framingham State College class: "I'm like a rock-and-roll DJ—I like it loud, I like to be challenged." Morton Downey, Jr., has made similar comparisons.

97. Ward L. Quaal and James A. Brown, *Broadcast Management: Radio-Television*, 2d ed. (New York: Hastings House, 1976), p. 187.

98. "Talk Radio: In the Middle of America's Conversational Mainstream," *Broadcasting*, May 28, 1973, pp. 35–48.

99. "The FCC Hangs Up Talkshow Proposals," *Broadcasting*, Aug. 9, 1971, p. 32.

100. "Touchiest Topic on Radio Now: Talk about Sex," *Broadcasting*, March 19, 1973, pp. 118–19.

101. Ibid.

102. Maurice Tunick, in "Talk Radio: What Is It Telling Us?"

103. "FCC Turns Up Heat on Indecency," *Broadcasting*, Aug. 28, 1989, pp. 27–28; and "Where Things Stand: Indecency," *Broadcasting*, Sept. 4, 1989, p. 18. The FCC's intensified action came after the 1988 passage of a tougher law permitting the agency to prohibit indecent broadcasts twenty-four hours a day, rather than "channeling" such material into a midnight to 6:00 A.M. "safe harbor," as had been the policy. The 1988 law, however, was overturned in June 1992 on First Amendment grounds; the after-midnight "safe harbor" was reaffirmed.

104. Berkeley Rice, "Call-in Therapy: Reach Out and Shrink Someone," *Psychology Today*, Dec. 1981, p. 44.

105. Bick, "Two-Way Talk Radio," pp. 59–102.

106. Paul Noble, former producer of *The Alan Burke Show*, noted in our interview (WNYW–TV New York, Jan. 1991) that the "loud talk" of the 1960s subsided after the 1968 election of Richard Nixon to the presidency and his administration's law-and-order push, which included a stiffer enforcement of broadcast regulations such as the Fairness Doctrine.

107. Thomas A. Whiteside, "Profiles: The Communicator," *New Yorker*, Oct. 16 and 23, 1954.

108. *Letterman* producer Barry Sand, quoted in Bill Barol, "A Fine Madness at the Midnight Hour," *Newsweek*, Feb. 3, 1986, p. 48. This article, about the success of David Letterman's *Latenight* (a descendant of *Tonight*) indicates the degree to which the Steve Allen persona has been a calculated influence on Letterman.

109. Another occasional interactive Carson skit was "You Be the Author": prior to the show's taping, audience members wrote brief scenes from an imaginary romance novel using clichés typical of that genre. Carson read them aloud in no particular order, giving a chance-determined "exquisite corpse" effect that furthered the ingenuous humor of the audience participation.

110. This episode, the only one available at the Museum of Broadcasting, survives as a fifteen-minute fragment of what was then a thirty-minute show.

111. NBC made an attempt to revive the concept in the winter of 1990 with *House Party*, featuring a young male host, but the show was canceled after several weeks. Another 1950s "house" program was NBC's *The Home Show* (1954–57), brainchild of Pat Weaver and hosted by Arlene Francis; it ran weekday afternoons and emphasized advice.

112. This segment is missing from the Museum of Broadcasting's copy of the program.

113. CBS's *Person to Person* (1953–60), Murrow's "soft" news/interview show, overlapped through most of the 1950s with his "hard" *See It Now*, which William Paley canceled in 1958 because of its expense and the controversy it aroused. (Press conference–style shows such as *Face the Nation* cost less and became newsmakers in and of themselves.) *Person to Person*—less controversial, more cost-effective, and more acceptable to advertisers—exemplified the industry's early recognition of the "safety" and profitability of productively linking celebrity with the televisual codes of intimacy. Ad-libbed, seemingly casual, personalized live interviews were conducted by an already well-known host. The more recent Barbara Walters interviews use a similar approach. In each case, the interviewer becomes a spectatorial surrogate, a guest in the interviewee's house or space—even though Murrow remained in his self-referential studio "home" (into which the spectator was also invited). Both of his programs used the televisual apparatus to display a modernist faith in television's exciting capacities: Murrow can remain in the studio while he speaks, live, with a celebrity in his or her home, producing a feeling of interpersonal, nonmediated intimacy. By contrast, Walters's interviews make a point of her being spatiotemporally "there," in the immediate physical presence of the celebrity. Although her interviews are taped rather than

aired live, Walters usually anchors them through her live studio presence when they are broadcast (as on ABC's news/magazine program 20/20). The Walters format abandons Murrow's modernist inscription and celebration of the apparatus for a more seamless simulation of the interpersonal. See Erik Barnouw, *The Image Empire: A History of Broadcasting in the United States*, vol. 3, *From 1953* (New York: Oxford University Press, 1970), pp. 50–54, 116. *Person to Person* also pioneered the use of wireless microphones (see Erik Barnouw, *Tube of Plenty: The Evolution of American Television* ([New York: Oxford University Press, 1975], pp. 288–89), which have become crucial for such talkshows as *Donahue*, *Oprah*, and *Geraldo* by facilitating the host's mobility, auditory interaction, and sense of intimacy with the audience.

114. *Queen for a Day* was a daytime program in which women competed, by telling stories of personal hardship, to become the audience-designated "queen." Narratives of quietly suffered, painful, personal experience typified this program, *Stand Up and Be Counted!* and, of course, the soap operas. Such game shows positioned themselves therapeutically, seeming to offer "cures" while rewarding a woman's unresolved suffering with commodity prizes.

115. Considered chiefly an "advice show," *Stand Up and Be Counted!* aired on weekday afternoons from May 28, 1956, through Sept. 6, 1957. In its selection of a troubled female audience member through which to build a restorative narrative, the show resembled *Queen for a Day*, in which host Jack Bailey used an audience applause meter to decide who would be the "queen." As on the game shows, some of the air time was spent describing the prizes. *Queen* and *Stand Up* substituted difficult personal experience for the usual skill or knowledge of male game show participants, as if to imply that what women know best is experience and feeling rather than the objectified "knowledge" associated with modernity. These and many game shows, an extreme example being *Strike It Rich* (in which destitute men were the contestants), promoted a sense of the beneficence of both medium and consumer economy through their reward structures and the subject's willing, participatory affiliation with them.

116. Hal Erickson, *Syndicated Television: The First Forty Years* (Jefferson, N.C.: McFarland, 1989), p. 158.

117. David Marc, *Demographic Vistas: Television and American Culture* (Philadelphia: University of Pennsylvania Press, 1984), pp. 144–45.

118. Erickson, *Syndicated Television*, pp. 86–87.

119. Ibid., pp. 160–61.

120. For a thorough and appreciative discussion of *Firing Line* see Hirsch, *Talking Heads*, pp. 13–24, who generally accuses other political pundit shows of impoverishing political debate (and democracy along with it) by substituting

"spats" for genuine, in-depth debate. Hirsch lauds the post-1960s *Firing Line* for presenting "deeper, more enlightening (and entertaining) political discussion than television had offered before or has since" (p. 13). Long a one-hour examination of a single issue from two opposed perspectives, each questioned by an "examiner" (who replaced the earlier version's panel), the show was reduced to thirty minutes in 1988 as a response to the "aggressive, bite-size" political discussion of shows like *The McLaughlin Group*. In Buckley's words, it was "an acknowledgment of the hectic metabolic schedule of almost all television geared to public policy" (quoted in Hirsch, p. 23, from William F. Buckley, *On the Firing Line* [New York: Random House, 1989], p. xxxii).

121. Hirsch, *Talking Heads*, ibid., pp. 25–49.

122. Erickson, *Syndicated Television*, p. 163. Also see Hirsch, *Talking Heads*, p. 12.

123. Jerry Williams to Framingham class, Nov. 14, 1990. Williams added that today the talkshow can "literally say almost anything" thanks to the "conditioning process" of years of issue—and talkshow—exposure.

124. "The Talk of Television," *Newsweek*, Oct. 29, 1979, p. 76.

125. Rod Townley, "Talk Shows Seek the Fountain of Youth," *TV Guide*, July 5, 1980, pp. 2–5. In 1991 prominent independent writer and producer William Link (*Columbo*; *Murder, She Wrote*) predicted that by the mid-1990s one of the three broadcast television networks would go out of business and another would go all-news (speech at Fitchburg, Massachusetts, State College, Oct. 16, 1991).

126. "Is the Talkshow an Endangered Species?" *TV Guide*, July 30, 1977, pp. 2–6. For a discussion of late 1970s–early 1980s "reality" programming, see Sally Bedell, *Up the Tube: Prime-time TV and the Silverman Years* (New York: Viking Press, 1981), pp. 278–95.

127. Ian Angus, "Circumscribing Postmodern Culture" and "Media beyond Representation," in Ian Angus and Sut Jhally, *Cultural Politics in Contemporary America* (New York: Routledge, 1989), pp. 102, 344.

2. Constellations of Voices: How Talkshows Work

1. Robert Pittman's comments at the seminar "The Other Side of the News: Entertainment News or Entertainment?" WNET-TV New York, April 12, 1989; moderator: Fred W. Friendly.

2. Geraldo Rivera and Phil Donahue, ibid. In an interview, "Pushing the Limits of Talk-Show TV," in *Channels* 8 (May 1988): 94–95, Geraldo explained his multi-accentual role more fully, using an analogy that even taps his "more legitimate" journalistic intertexts: "People have to recognize that I don't sing

one song. I'm like the Sunday newspaper: There's a hard-news section, there's a human interest section, there are sports and style sections. I get very passionate about some things; I get very angry. I'll defend myself with violence if I have to. On the other hand, I get real sappy and schmaltzy, and I cry when things hurt me. And if there are [critics] who think that I have forfeited my right to be a newsman, I say bullshit."

3. Geraldo, quoted in Albert Scardino, "A Debate Heats Up: Is It News or Entertainment?" *New York Times*, Jan. 15, 1989, p. H29.

4. Geneva Overholser on "The Other Side of the News." Other print journalists who took part in the roundtable were Jack Nelson, Washington correspondent for the *Los Angeles Times*, media critic Tom Shales, and F. Gilman Spencer of the *New York Daily News*.

5. "The Other Side of the News."

6. From an interview with Downey on *The Jerry Williams Show*, WFXT-TV Boston, Feb. 13, 1989.

7. "The Other Side of the News."

8. Quoted in "Broadcasters, Others Talk Trash," *Broadcasting*, May 8, 1989, pp. 69–70.

9. Quoted in J. Max Robins, "Here Come the News Punks," *Channels* 8 (Sept. 1988): 39.

10. Quoted in Scardino, "Debate Heats Up," p. H29.

11. Fred W. Friendly ("On Television: News, Lies, and Videotape," *New York Times*, Aug. 6, 1989, p. H1) sees such forms and techniques as "contaminating" the major network's "hard" newscasts and inspiring softer, prime-time news magazine and intimate interview shows. Friendly's allegiance to Walter Lippmann's definition of news as "a picture of reality on which the citizen can act," while an admirable one, hardly precludes new ways of constructing that picture, nor does it necessarily mean (as he asserts) that news simulations "endanger the entire principle of a free people and a free press."

12. "Hill Steamed over Radio's Tea Time," *Broadcasting*, Feb. 13, 1989, p. 29.

13. Evidence of this tension is examined in William Boddy, *Fifties Television: The Industry and Its Critics* (Urbana: University of Illinois Press, 1990).

14. See Bill Carter, "News Is a Hit on TV's Bottom Line," *New York Times*, Sept. 13, 1989, p. D1. An hour of slick network entertainment programming costs an average of $900,000 to $1,000,000. Also see Robins, "Here Come the News Punks," p. 40; and Dennis Kneale, "Titillating Channels: TV Is Going Tabloid as Shows Seek Sleaze and Find Profits, Too," *Wall Street Journal*, May 18, 1988, pp. 1, 25.

15. Jeffrey Cohen, "Oprah, It's for You," *Emmy*, Oct. 1988, pp. 14–18.

16. Jeffrey Zaslow, "Talkshow Crisis," *Wall Street Journal*, Jan. 8, 1987, p. 1; Joanne Kaufman, "Hello, Can You Be a Talkshow Guest?" *New York Times*, May 31, 1987, p. B25; Ron Givens, "Talking People into Talking," *Newsweek*, July 17, 1989, pp. 44–45; and David Blum, "Loudmouth," *New York*, Jan. 18, 1988, pp. 36–41. Worth noting here is *Donahue* executive producer Richard Mincer's observation that well over 4,000 talkshows nationwide book about 1.7 million guests in any twelve-month period; see Richard Mincer and Deanne Mincer, *The Talkshow Book: An Engaging Primer on How to Talk Your Way to Success* (New York: Facts on File Publications, 1982), pp. xi–xiv.

17. Margaret B. Carlson, "Powertots: The Media Kids Who Run Washington," *New Republic*, May 9, 1988, pp. 13–14. Carlson, a regular contributor to *Time*, overstates the bookers' power in a way that divorces them from their institutional constraints, but she validly points out that by the late 1980s bookers had become increasingly important to the more cost-conscious broadcast industry. She characterizes political talk as a "producer's dream" because it is "cheap and highminded at the same time." The demand for good political talkers is such that some shows now have regulars under contract.

18. Mincer and Mincer, *Talkshow Book*, pp. 15–21.

19. Ibid. Richard Mincer has been executive producer of *Donahue* since its beginning in 1967. The Mincers' book is a "how-to" for prospective guests who see talkshow appearances as critical to the success of their causes or careers. Part of the authors' agenda, however, is to meet the endless need for well-spoken guests who have the "ordinariness" crucial to the talkshow's populist, town-meeting dynamic of identification.

20. Ibid., pp. 23–37, 39–70.

21. For a look at the consolidation and diversification of the broadcast-involved media industries, see "Concentrating on Concentration," *Broadcasting*, June 5, 1989, pp. 50–52. For a critical overview of broadcast deregulation in the 1980s, see Victor Ferrall, "The Impact of Television Deregulation on Private and Public Interests," *Journal of Communication* 39 (Winter 1989): 8–38.

22. See Alfred J. Jaffee, "Major Market TV Erosion Analysis Shows Continuation," *Television/Radio Age*, Aug. 21, 1989, pp. 36–39. According to Arbitron's analyses of the top fifty ADIs during sweeps periods from May 1984 through May 1989, the share drop in household viewing of broadcast television overall was 5 percentage points, averaging a 1 percent drop per year. Breaking out the broadcast percentages by network affiliate versus independent stations, however, reveals a significant contrast: "indie" shares have risen slightly, while the erosion in the top fifty markets has been "confined basically to affiliates" (p. 36). The drop in commercial television station shares, caused by the network affiliates'

losses, was from 81.9 percent in May 1984 to 76.9 percent in May 1989. During the same period, indie shares increased from 14.6 to 15.76 percent. By November 1989, Fox had 128 affiliates (17 VHF, 111 UHF), giving the network a reach of 90 percent of U.S. television homes. National advertisers require 70 percent of national coverage from networks. See Alex Ben Block, "Twenty-first Century Fox," *Channels* 10 (Jan. 1990): 36–40. Also see "Three-Network Viewing Falls below 70%," *Broadcasting*, April 17, 1989, pp. 29–30.

23. "The Talk of Television," *Newsweek*, Oct. 29, 1979, p. 76.

24. Quoted in Robins, "Here Come the News Punks," p. 40.

25. J. Max Robins, "Network News Sings the Blues," *Channels* 8 (Nov. 1988): 88–91. According to the Nielsen ratings, this decline in network news audiences was almost 8 percent over five years (1983–88).

26. J. Max Robins, "News in the 90's: Stretched to the Limit," *Channels* 9 (Sept. 1989): 42–56; and "Journalists on Journalism," *Broadcasting*, June 18, 1989, p. 47. The latter article quotes the former president of CBS News, Van Gordon Sauter, who sees the erosion of network news audiences as resulting from an increase in news available, forcing audiences to limit viewing, and from "effective" counterprogramming by indie stations using popular syndications. Also see Merrill Brown, "The Business Side: Is Local TV News at Risk?" *Channels* 9 (July–Aug. 1989): 20.

27. "Editorializing Falling out of Favor?" *Broadcasting*, Feb. 6, 1989, p. 45.

28. Chuck Reece, "News in the 90s: The Home Town Report," *Channels* 9 (Sept. 1989): 57–62.

29. Bill Carter, "With America Well Wired, Cable Industry Is Changing," *New York Times*, July 9, 1989, p. 1; and Carter, "Cable May Get Its Wings Clipped," *New York Times*, July 10, 1989, p. D1. On Oct. 5, 1992, Congress overrode a presidential veto to reimpose regulation on cable television following complaints of soaring subscriber rates and declining service. The law allows the FCC to determine "reasonable" basic service rates for monopoly systems based on the rates charged in the few places where cable competition actually exists; such rates have been about 20 percent lower. Basic cable prices rose about 50 percent between 1987, when the 1984 bill deregulating cable went into effect, and 1992. Cable television went from a $2.5 billion industry in 1980 to $20 billion in 1992. The 1992 reregulation also requires greater competition for cable programming, gives local broadcasters more power in negotiating retransmission fees and demanding cable carriage (which critics say would actually *raise* rates), and requires "reasonable" prices for cable equipment and installation. See Edmund L. Andrews, "Cable TV Regulation Advances," *New York Times,* Sept. 18, 1992. p. D1; and Peter G. Gosselin, "Cable Bill Is Passed in 1st Override of Bush Veto," *Boston Globe*, p. 1.

30. See "Database," *Channels* 10 (Jan. 1990): 76. A King World ad in the same trade paper cites Nielsen and Arbitron as indicating that the company had four first-run syndications in the top ten: *Wheel of Fortune*, *Jeopardy* (numbers one and two), and *The Oprah Winfrey Show* as well as *Inside Edition*.

31. Robins, "Network News Sings the Blues," pp. 88–91. The NBC *Nightly News* was the first commercial network newscast to make a regular practice of live, crosstalk interviews with anchor Tom Brokaw and longer "Special Segments" (although public television's *MacNeil-Lehrer News Hour* may actually have been the first overall). By 1988 the two other major networks were doing similar features (Dan Rather's confrontational interview with presidential candidate George Bush in February 1988 was considered a turning point for Bush in overcoming his widely perceived "wimp" persona) and also going to global news "hot spots": covering the dismantling of the Berlin Wall in the fall of 1989; reporting *perestroika* developments live from the Kremlin in January 1990. News savants believe that, given greater competition and financial pressure, network news should concentrate on *in-depth* coverage. Local news shows, after all, can now afford satellite communications and ad hoc networking to cover anything almost anywhere in the country or the world, thus encroaching on what used to be exclusive network turf.

Also significant is the influence of *Nightline*, which originated in the unprecedented, intense, often emotionally charged nightly coverage of the 1979–81 Iran hostage crisis; the show's original name was *The Iran Crisis: America Held Hostage*. Reaching twelve million viewers and shifting its nightly topics on the basis of the day's particular events, the program brought live, dramatic talk to what had been a standard news format airing in the late fringe period. It may have provided a significant instance of the media's political intervention and power in that its intense coverage pressured and "bloodied" President Carter, spurring an ill-fated rescue attempt. See Walter Goodman, "Day 3,650: Looking Back at the Hostage Crisis," *New York Times*, Nov. 7, 1989, p. C22.

32. See note 11 of Fred Friendly's "On Television." Also see "ABC Is Sorry for Slip-up on News Simulation," *Broadcasting*, July 31, 1989, pp. 41–42.

33. Standard or "hard" news, the major type of programming produced by the networks, is perishable and thus of little future syndication value. For this reason, the networks are moving into the production of prime-time entertainment: made-for-television movies and specials, but also—and especially—infotainment forms utilizing the networks' already developed news production capacity.

34. Carter, "News Is a Hit on TV's Bottom Line," p. D4. J. Max Robins, "All the News That's Glitz," *Channels* 9 (Dec. 1989): 44, reveals that even some local broadcast news operations are "going tabloid" with additional programs in an attempt to cash in on the "soft" news trend.

35. Carter, "News Is a Hit on TV's Bottom Line," p. D4.

36. In the meantime, the Motion Picture Association of America continues to lobby on behalf of the producers to maintain the status quo. The producers claim that they still bear most of the risk, since they take a loss from the initial network license fees in a common practice known as deficit financing. Yet if their shows become network hits and run for a number of years, the producers can eliminate their deficits quickly, and most of the syndication revenues become pure profit. See Bill Carter, "Battling Studios on Profits, Networks Become Producers," *New York Times*, June 5, 1989, p. D4.

37. The research, commissioned by *Channels* and considered by its editors to be "perhaps the most thorough look ever at the ways people use their televisions," was based on 7,800 random telephone surveys and in-depth focus groups conducted in a variety of locations nationwide. The phone sample netted 650 "qualified respondents" (eighteen or older, with at least one working TV set at home, and not employed in the media industry) who were interviewed for an average of thirty-three minutes each. The articles summarizing the study—Merrill Brown's "How Americans Watch TV" and Peter Ainslie's "The New TV Viewer," *Channels* 8 (Sept. 1988): 52–62—also cite confirming studies by other market research firms: Bortz, J. Walter Thompson, Percy, CBS's marketing division, and the National Association of Broadcasters. The importance of this kind of research lies in its influence on the industry's perception of and intentionality in its programming strategies.

38. The study found that 95 percent of TV households (sixty-six million) had a remote control for either the TV or the VCR, 54 percent had cable, and 46 percent had both by 1988 (ibid., p. 54).

39. Ibid., p. 57. A 1983 NAB study cited in the *Channels* report found that "viewers were watching television more but enjoying it less"; two out of every three Americans thought it had become "dull and repetitive" (p. 59).

40. Ibid., p. 62. Media researcher and consultant Paul Bortz reflected that programmers would "have to do a lot better" than LOP. In a desperate attempt to find what works where, the networks have themselves destabilized the viewing environment by constantly shifting their schedules. "Quicksilver scheduling" is an effort to counteract the destabilizing force of the spectator's remote control, as well as the program shifts of the competition.

41. Andrew Marton, "Ad Makers Zap Back," *Channels* 9 (Sept. 1989): 30–31. Also see "How MTV Rocked Television Commercials," *New York Times*, Oct. 9, 1989, p. D6; E. Ann Kaplan, *Rock around the Clock: Music Television, Postmodernism, and Consumer Culture* (New York: Methuen, 1987); and Jon Pareles, "After Music Videos, All the World Has Become a Screen," *New York Times*, Dec. 10, 1989, p. E6. MTV has apparently taught advertisers how to

present information very quickly and without narrative closure through "atmospheric advertising" using music video techniques: "pushing" film stock to graininess, matting "human cartoons" by way of computer graphics and digital effects, other special effects, unusual camera angles and movements, and abrupt, elliptical editing techniques. Institutionally, the result has been a boom for special effects houses.

42. Joachim Blunck, producer of *A Current Affair*, and John Walsh, host of *America's Most Wanted*, quoted in Robins, "Here Come the News Punks," p. 43. They and other tabloid and talkshow producers stress their intentional production of difference, asserting that each has designed a show that "doesn't look like anything else on TV."

43. "Harnessing Radio's Strengths for Television," *Broadcasting*, Jan. 9, 1989, p. 60. Radio station groups have been moving toward the increased purchase of television properties, confident of being able to manage them in a destabilized, more radiolike environment, using radio's time-honored strategies of local programming and promotion. It was in local radio, of course, that the call-in show first appeared and where loyalty-producing promotional gimmicks grew: request lines, call-in and call-out games, prizes, remote broadcasts from prominent community sites. All of these involve audience participation.

44. John McLaughlin, quoted in "Circus of the Stars," Edwin Diamond's review of *The McLaughlin Report*, *New York*, Feb. 3, 1986, pp. 18–20.

45. Alan Hirsch, *Talking Heads: Political Talkshows and Their Star Pundits* (New York: St. Martin's Press, 1991), pp. 31–49. Though Hirsch never develops the McLaughlin techniques' links to radio, he makes the important point that although these "wrestling match," "politics of kicks," and "style" talkshows claim to be "harmless fun" and "just . . . television," many political insiders watch and are likely influenced by them, if only as an impression of what the public is getting by way of opinion journalism. In reducing serious issues to "multiple choice games and one-to-ten ratings" (p. 70), such shows become part of the vital circuit of political exchange that "has helped make us a less reflective people with shorter attention spans" (p. 69).

46. Vice-president and general manager Michael B. Alexander and news vice-president Tom Petner, quoted in Jeremy Gerard, "A Channel Innovates and Moves Up," *New York Times*, Sept. 6, 1989, p. 50. Significantly, 9 *Broadcast Plaza*, like most talkshows, was developed very efficiently (no investment was required of MCA), and the first program aired the Monday after the last *Downey* show. For more on WWOR's behind-the-scenes-style newscast, see "The New Look of News," *Broadcasting*, July 24, 1989, pp. 86–87.

47. Alexander, quoted in Gerard, "A Channel Innovates." In nearly the same

breath, he referred to the raging "infotainment debate" and *Downey's* position within it: "Let the journalists and academics debate the social consequences of such a program." The clear implication was that for him and his station the debate was irrelevant, next to the need to produce and exploit infotainment's instabilities to survive in a multichannel mediasphere where spectators are technologically and perceptually empowered to become grazers.

48. Quoted in Ainslie, "New TV Viewer," p. 61.

49. The replacement opener centers on Geraldo's broad range of affects through a rapid, pixillated, MTV-style montage of the host in different talkshow situations.

50. For more on postmodern politics, see Stanley Aronowitz, "Postmodernism and Politics"; and Lawrence Grossberg, "Putting the Pop Back into Postmodernism," in *Universal Abandon? The Politics of Postmodernism*, ed. Andrew Ross (Minneapolis: University of Minnesota Press, 1988), pp. 46–62, 167–90.

51. Quoted in "Pushing the Limits of Talk-show TV," p. 94.

52. Quoted in "Geraldo Rivera: Bloodied but Unbowed," *Broadcasting*, Dec. 19, 1988, pp. 43–48.

53. Quoted in "Pushing the Limits of Talk-show TV," p. 94.

54. In response to the scathing reviews his prime-time documentaries received despite their popularity (fifty million viewers, a record for documentaries), Geraldo remarked on his first-name basis with his audience: "Do you know that everyone calls me by my first name? Young people, old people, black people, it's always 'Geraldo.' They don't call Dan and Tom and Peter by their first names. There's a love and affection there. I'll take the people over the critics any day" ("Trash TV," *Newsweek*, Nov. 14, 1988, p. 78).

55. Quoted in "Geraldo Rivera: Bloodied but Unbowed," p. 44.

56. "Trash TV," pp. 72–78. The article was especially harsh toward *Geraldo* in the wake of the show's November 2 brawl between black activist Roy Innis, a rabbi, and skinheads; it called "confrontainment" a "virus."

57. Quoted in Robins, "Here Come the News Punks," p. 42.

58. Quoted in "Geraldo Rivera: Bloodied but Unbowed," p. 47.

59. Ibid., p. 48.

60. "The Other Side of the News." Even as the title of Friendly's show implies, infotainment represents "otherness" for the standard journalist.

61. Quoted in Robins, "Here Come the News Punks," p. 40.

62. This analysis is generally applicable to *Donahue* as well. Both hosts become the channel most acknowledged by the apparatus: their mikes are always on, a camera is always on them, and they cue most of the conversational turn-taking.

63. *The Oprah Winfrey Show* and *Donahue* tend to approach the occasional

celebrities they interview as having "hidden lives," however mundane, which are revealed in the course of questioning. At the same time, the *host* as celebrity reveals more of his or her own personality during the interaction, which thus becomes a conversation between celebrities as well as between celebrities and fans.

64. See Donal Carbaugh, *Talking American: Cultural Discourses on "Donahue"* (Norwood, N.J.: Ablex, 1988), pp. 19, 28–32.

65. Margaret Morse, "Talk, Talk, Talk: The Space of Discourse in Television News, Talkshows, and Advertising," *Screen* 26 (March–April 1985): 2. Morse calls the talkshow's discursive space a "new mode of fiction" or "fictional form of dialogue" in that the space alternates between reflexive, direct-address partner (the audience as imagined interlocutor) and spectacle (with the audience as spectator); it allows "contact . . . without responsibility." Her argument is seriously challenged by the *audience-interactive* talkshow, which she happens to neglect; she ultimately swerves toward the old, worn objections of the "illusion of intimacy" and the "para-social" (see Chapter 3).

66. The talkshow's duplicitous capacity for play with the distinction between "real" and "fictional" revealed itself during the Feb. 21, 1990, *Geraldo* program titled "Blood Money: When Family Greed Leads to Murder." Early in the show a crawl at the bottom of the screen alerted viewers to an audio clip being played, which apparently was a recording of a call one guest's wife made to a life insurance agent to increase her husband's death benefit before she attempted to murder him. The crawl used the clip as a kind of teaser, hinting at some important revelation to come. In the program's final minutes, with Geraldo and the guest alone in the studio, the host declared the clip a fake. The man argued ineffectually. Geraldo called him a liar, then turned to the camera and apologized to the audience for the unintended moment of deception. *Geraldo* decries this sort of deception yet uses it effectively. The show's central inquiring subject, Geraldo, becomes the guarantor of veracity, one who here inscribes a suspicion of the media and its "slickness" even as he uses it.

67. Lawrence Grossberg, "It's a Sin: Politics, Postmodernity, and the Popular," in *It's a Sin: Essays on Postmodernism, Politics, and Culture*, ed. Lawrence Grossberg, Ann Curthoys, Paul Patton, and Tony Fry (Sydney: Power Publications, 1989), p. 67.

68. Dick Hebdige, *Hiding in the Light: On Images and Things* (London: Routledge/Comedia, 1988), pp. 210–12.

69. See M. Budd, S. Craig, and C. Steinman, "Fantasy Island: Marketplace of Desire," in *Mass Communications Review Yearbook*, vol. 5, ed. M. Gurevitch and M. Levy (Beverly Hills, Calif.: Sage, 1985), pp. 27–40; and Nick Browne, "The Political Economy of the Television (Super)Text," in *Television: The Critical View*, 4th ed., ed. Horace Newcomb (New York: Oxford University Press, 1987),

pp. 585–99. In this view, American commercial television is an indisputable ideological practice wedding plenitude with capitalist consumption; any gaps such programming opens up are closed accordingly. The advertised product becomes, for Browne, the "ultimate referent." Disputing this totalizing view, John Fiske, in *Television Culture* (New York: Metheun, 1987), p. 101, sees the programs and practices of television as replete with fissures that offer a myriad possibilities for negotiated or oppositional readings and even resistant spectatorial practices, such as the gay and camp audiences' use of the *Dynasty* series.

Many of the commercials inserted in *Geraldo* and the other daytime talkshows echo the problems taken up in the shows, offering commodified solutions; e.g., obesity and insurance needs are "solved" by weight-loss programs and no-one-will-be-refused policies for senior citizens. But, to posit a direct relationship between program and product is simplistic.

70. See C. Shine, "Agony Uncle: Geraldo Makes a Bid for the Misery Market," *Vogue*, May 1988, pp. 101–2.

71. See, e.g., Pat Colander, "Oprah Winfrey's Odyssey: Talk-show Host to Mogul," *New York Times*, March 12, 1989, pp. B31, B36; and "Oprah: The Winner Who's Taking It All," *Broadcasting*, March 27, 1989, pp. 35–36.

72. Colander, "Oprah Winfrey's Odyssey," p. B37.

73. Oprah's "high culture" critics have also observed her hybrid significations—in order to disparage them. Barbara Grizzuti Harrison ("The Importance of Being Oprah," *New York Times Magazine*, June 11, 1989, p. 28) rightly notes Oprah's "mixed message" of promoting human assertion and control while also affirming a belief in an unchangeable cosmic "fate." Harrison admits that "her contradictions work for her" but finds "her comfortable truths . . . perfect for the age of the sound bite." Harrison faults Oprah for "easy answers, quick fixes," and for a "carefree caring": "exploring people's feelings" without really changing or helping those people. The spectator is, for Harrison, "coddled" in her passivity and made to think that she is *doing* something by watching *Oprah* (television in general is also implicated here). Harrison, a novelist, imposes a modernist, reality-and-effects-based burden on a cultural product and practice—television—that she would likely not demand of her own novels.

74. Some feminists have criticized postmodern theory as a white male conspiracy intent on decentering subjectivity just at the time when women and other disenfranchised groups are *defining* their very subjectivities. As stated earlier, my notion of postmodern subjectivity is not to annihilate subjectivity per se but to multiply it within what was once "a" given human subject. For examples of the feminist responses, see Nancy Hartsock, "Rethinking Modernism: Minority vs. Majority Theories," *Cultural Critique* 7 (1987): 187–206; and Lynn Joyrich, "Critical and Textual Hypermasculinity," in *Logics of Television: Essays in Cul-*

tural Criticism, ed. Patricia Mellancamp (Bloomington: Indiana University Press, 1990), pp. 156–72.

75. These ideas, originally applied to architecture, are from Robert Venturi's *Complexity and Contradiction in Architecture* (New York: Museum of Modern Art and Graham Foundation, in association with Doubleday, 1966), pp. 30–31.

76. "Downey and Out in Secaucus," *Broadcasting*, July 24, 1989, p. 34. *The Morton Downey, Jr., Show* premiered as a local, live program on WWOR Secaucus, New Jersey, on Oct. 19, 1987, and had become a forty-station national syndication by May 1988. By the time it was canceled on July 20, 1989, the show was airing nationally on about seventy affiliates.

77. In "The Other Side of the News," Pittman described *Downey* as "a show of very frank emotions" that met what he saw as a need to "break the polite TV etiquette" typical of *Donahue* and *Oprah*.

78. "Broadcasters, Others Talk Trash," *Broadcasting*, May 8, 1989, p. 70.

79. "Here Come the News Punks," p. 40, and "Trash TV," p. 75. In the former, *America's Most Wanted* host John Walsh tells his tip-giving, crime-solving viewers that "you can make a difference." In the latter, sociologist Todd Gitlin explains the appeal of the interactive talkshows, the tabloid news syndications, and the crimestopper shows in terms of their offering spectators a unique chance to get involved.

80. John Hartley, "Invisible Fictions: Television Audience, Paedocracy, Pleasure," in *Television Studies: Textual Analysis*, ed. Gary Burns and Robert J. Thompson (New York: Praeger, 1989), pp. 223–43.

81. Morton Downey, Jr., with William Hoffer, *Mort! Mort! Mort!* (New York: Dell, 1988), p. 1.

82. Andreas Huyssen, "Mass Culture as Woman: Modernism's Other," in *Studies in Entertainment: Critical Approaches to Mass Culture*, ed. Tania Modleski (Bloomington: Indiana University Press, 1986), pp. 188–207. Huyssen also discusses some of the characteristics of aesthetic modernism: the emphasis on production and the self-referential artwork's fostering an awareness of itself over and above consumption and pleasure in reception; irony; self-consciousness; autonomy (the separation from "everyday life," of which mass culture was considered a part); individuality; and adversarialism.

83. For more on the processes of textual and institutional struggles, see Christine Gledhill, "Pleasurable Negotiations," in *Female Spectators: Looking at Film and Television*, ed. E. Diedre Pribram (London: Verso, 1988), pp. 64–89.

84. *Newsweek*, in "Trash TV," called Downey "a power mouth" and related him to *A Current Affair*'s then host Maury Povich, the "power peeper," ostensibly because the show's prying reportage echoed Povich's knowing, can-you-believe-it glances. Interestingly, the same article paid scant attention to *Sally Jesse Raphael*

and *The Oprah Winfrey Show*. Its focus was entirely on male-hosted programs, implying that talk, tabloid, or "soft news" becomes genuine "trash" only when *men* lower themselves to become involved in it. By implication, those genres *Newsweek* calls "muddied" journalism are somehow acceptable when practiced by and for women in a daytime programming context. The article essentially positions the new "trash" phenomenon as a masculinized response to the "normal," acceptable, participatory daytime service shows that target women. Once again, critical discourse positions "low" media forms as feminine and acceptable as such, whereas "high" forms like "real" journalism are somehow properly "male" and should remain unmolested by info- and confrontainment.

For a reasonably thorough look at shock radio, see Leonard Zeidenberg, "Indecency: Radio's Sound, FCC's Fury," *Broadcasting*, June 27, 1987, pp. 46–49. Shock or "raunch" radio had emerged by 1986 in drive-time morning programs characterized by the scatological, sexual, insult, or assault humor of the "shock jock." Also see "Where Things Stand: Indecency," *Broadcasting*, Sept. 4, 1989, p. 18.

85. Downey, executive producer Bill Boggs, and Goldsmith were interviewed the morning of the announcement of *Downey*'s cancellation on what was then WWOR's local morning talkshow, *People Are Talking* (July 20, 1989), which was replaced by *9 Broadcast Plaza* in September 1989.

86. Blum, "Loudmouth," p. 40. Blum bases this assessment on his informal survey of the studio audience during a show taped in Secaucus. It is important to note that *Downey* was also taped in a number of cities across the United States during its twenty-one-month existence, lending a greater diversity at least to its studio audiences. The program Blum attended concerned child custody fights and was particularly critical of the women engaged in them; Downey's own painful experiences came out to reinforce its misogynistic tone. Host biography in talk performance and persona is a key and determining participatory talkshow paradigm.

87. See Downey, *Mort! Mort! Mort!* pp. 12–15. He calls Phil Donahue "the epitome" of the "liberal pabulum-puker" whose solutions are "simplistic and based upon psychoanalytical baby food" because they absolve the individual of his or her actions: "society is at fault." For Donahue, "there is no good and evil in the world; everything is liberally shaded with gray." Downey also accuses him of not listening to his participants and of failing to compose his audiences of "representatives from the normal world." Invoking the Peter Finch character from the film *Network*, Downey constructs his show not only as oppositional to *Donahue* but as an improvement in its more highly focused anger and better job of listening.

88. Senior producer Peter Goldsmith, in the *People Are Talking* interview

(see note 85), emphasized that the show was recorded live and that little editing was done before airing (he claimed that only 1 percent of the obscenities were deleted—a claim that seems exaggerated, given their apparent frequency).

89. Edwin Diamond, "Squawk Show: Diamond Does Downey," *New York*, June 20, 1988, pp. 10–13.

90. Downey told David Blum that because of his financially secure background he never did anything for money, including his show.

91. See Susan Viafora, "Downey Mouths Off in New London," *Norwich* (Connecticut) *Bulletin*, June 18, 1989, p. B1. The article included interviews with several Downey fans.

92. From a rerun aired on WWOR, Sept. 7, 1989.

93. Blum, "Loudmouth," p. 39.

94. Diamond, "Squawk Show," p. 13.

95. See Viafora, "Downey Mouths Off," p. B1.

96. See "Downey to Turn Down Volume," *Broadcasting*, April 3, 1989, p. 33; "Clock Ticking on 'Downey,' " July 17, 1989, pp. 32–33; and "Downey and Out in Secaucus," July 24, 1989, p. 34. *Downey*'s ratings had sunk from a nine share in July 1988 to an eight in November, a six in February 1989, and a five in the Nielsen report issued in July, the month of the show's cancellation.

97. See "Morton Downey, Jr., Alleges 'Skinhead' Attack; Officials Unable to Verify Report," *Broadcasting*, May 1, 1989, p. 110.

98. The debate aired Oct. 11, 1989, on WNET-TV New York.

99. The review appears in Ron Powers, *The Eunuch, the Beast, and the Glass-Eyed Child* (New York: Harcourt Brace Jovanovich, 1990), pp. 94–104.

100. "Feeding time at the Roman Coliseum" was the analogy offered by Michael Eisner, chairman and chief executive officer of Disney. See "Eisner's Hope for TV in the 90s: BAP or MAP, no LOP," *Broadcasting*, Jan. 30, 1989, p. 32.

101. Diamond appeared on a show titled, "The Media: Are We Getting the Whole Story?" It aired June 13, 1988.

102. Blum, "Loudmouth," p. 38.

103. See Diamond, "Squawk Show," and Blum, "Loudmouth," p. 41.

104. In *Mort! Mort! Mort!* Downey elaborates on his political positions. One example of his inconsistency: despite his purported conservatism, he favors a more progressive income tax and giving impoverished families loans toward home ownership instead of paying astronomical welfare hotel prices—an idea he took from Bobby Kennedy and George McGovern (pp. 97–113, 131–35).

105. Some 50 of America's estimated 225 issue-oriented radio talk hosts, with daily programs running three to four hours, attended.

106. A comment made by Mills Crenshaw, Salt Lake City talk host and organizer of a Utah tax protest that drew 7,000 people to the state capital.

107. Quoted in Bruce MacCabe, "Williams Goes a-Bashing at Talk Fest," *Boston Globe*, June 10, 1989, p. 18. See also "Medium Is Message at Talk Radio Conference," *Broadcasting*, June 19, 1989, pp. 54–55.

108. By the end of 1989, House members had voted a 25 percent increase in their pay—to $125,100—but banned all honoraria and capped other earnings (a nonpartisan commission earlier that year had recommended a 51 percent raise). Until the summer of 1991, a senator was paid $101,900 but could accept a maximum of $23,068 in speaking fees. On July 17 of that year the senators followed the House in banning honoraria and giving themselves a $23,200 raise—but political sensitivities were such that the Senate took the vote late at night and unannounced.

109. "Hill Steamed over Radio's Tea Time," *Broadcasting*, Feb. 13, 1989, pp. 29–30.

110. "Broadcasters Have Created Congressional Antipathy toward Radio," *Broadcasting*, May 8, 1989, p. 42. Quello also drove a wedge between radio managers and their controversial air personalities with his comments on Ralph Nader: to help their cause, he said, the talk hosts opposing the congressional pay raise had "resurrected from the dead . . . the greatest overzealous regulator of them all" (Congress at the time was considering "radio-only" legislation that would have simplified the license renewal process to only two steps).

111. The opening was broadcast live on Friday afternoon, June 9, during Jerry Williams's regular afternoon program hours in Boston on WRKO-AM; it was simulcast in New York on WOR-AM.

112. Jerry Williams, during his Sept. 5, 1990, program.

113. Jerry Williams, in his Nov. 14, 1990, talk to a Framingham State College communications class.

114. Geoff Edwards of KFI Los Angeles, in denouncing the tactics of fellow KFI talk host Tom Leykis: Leykis had publicly burned Cat Stevens's records after Stevens announced his support for the Ayatollah Khomeini's death sentence on novelist Salmun Rushdie. Edwards's disagreement led to his dismissal from the station. See Richard Zoglin, "Bugle Boys of the Airwaves," *Newsweek*, May 15, 1989, pp. 88–89.

115. Walt Pogan, KCR Kansas City, during the opening of the 1989 talk radio conference.

116. MacCabe, "Williams Goes a-Bashing," p. 18.

117. ABC/Capital Cities later denied that it had forbidden its hosts to attend.

118. Quoted in Zoglin, "Bugle Boys," p. 89.

119. Williams to a Framingham State College class.

120. See Wayne King, "Tax Protest, Fueled by Talk Shows, Is Getting Steamed Voters Organized," *New York Times*, Oct. 26, 1990, p. A22.

121. Ibid. The protest, in which the National Association of Talk Show Hosts had a hand, was, according to the *Times*, "a curious but possibly potent alliance of ratings-conscious and often shrill talkshow hosts and their plain-folks, silent-majority listeners as well as national figures Phyllis Schlafly, founder of the Eagle Forum, Peter Sepp of the National Taxpayer Union, and J. Peter Grace, industrialist and author of the Grace Commission report on government waste and a sponsor of the rally." The rally's principal sponsor was a coalition called the Council for Citizens against Government Waste, a Washington lobby claiming 400,000 members. It was headed by Dr. Alan Keyes, who called the talk hosts' association and its president, Seattle talk host Mike Siegel, for help. Keyes and Siegel kicked off the event at a news conference at the National Press Club in Washington on Sept. 20, 1990.

122. Frank Phillips and Renee Loth, "No-tax Budget Survives Day 1 of Debate," *Boston Globe*, March 7, 1989, p. 17; Robert L. Turner, "Talk Radio Blows Hot Air on the Budget Debate," *Boston Globe*, July 11, 1989, p. 15.

123. Scott Lehigh, " 'Governors' on the Airwaves Spread Cynicism," *Boston Globe*, Nov. 20, 1989, pp. 1, 12.

124. Chris Black, "Public Service Has Lost Its Allure, Weld Is Finding," *Boston Globe*, Dec. 6, 1990, p. A15.

125. Jerry Williams noted that some ad agencies have a "built-in prejudice" against talk radio and never buy time on talkshows for their clients, nor will the *Boston Globe* buy ads on *his* station because "we're the one medium that answers back to the *Globe*" (talk to Framingham State College class). But by 1992, at the fourth annual meeting of NARTSH (held in Washington, D.C., the week of June 15), Jerry Williams declared that "we're finally getting some respect." See "Talk Radio Riding High," *Broadcasting*, June 15, 1992, p. 24.

126. As a guest speaker at the 1989 conference, Ralph Nader called talk radio "the working people's medium," suggesting that it provides a form of representation to workers on the job (callers do sometimes phone in from their worksites).
Popular representations of the radio personality, including the DJ and the talk host, inscribe the instability and high mobility of their profession. For example, the opener of the original *WKRP in Cincinnati* series visually represented the city in terms of the highway network in, around, and through it. Viewers saw the cityscape and its landmarks from a moving car among other moving cars; the theme's lyrics, in top-40, pop-song style, made it a love song whose enunciator is an uprooted DJ telling his former lover that after much moving around the

country, he is now "on the air in Cincinnati." Radio's link with the car and highway is maintained. Similarly, the radio professional becomes an apotheosis of the mobile, contemporary service or information worker.

127. Burns, who also has a talk program on WRKO (he dislikes and avoids the word "show" because he feels it trivializes what he does), further contrasted the talk host with today's more common corporate work and worker by calling talk radio "the ultimate entrepreneurial communication phenomenon. . . . it's all up to you . . . *you* are the product." In a time when "people feel essentially alienated from their reality . . . talkradio provides the reconnect mechanism" (Nov. 14, 1990, talk to a Framingham State College communications class).

128. Gene Burns also noted, in the same talk, that the demand on and scarcity of successful talk hosts is making it more and more difficult to sustain a profitable talk radio station.

129. For example, on Sept. 5, 1990, Jerry Williams implied that he earned about $400,000 annually. The topic came up on his show when he was arguing in support of a tax-rollback ballot question with a guest, Professor William Keogh of Fitchburg State College, whom he called a "hack" state employee; Keogh's "high" salary of just under $50,000 was questioned by Williams, *Boston Herald* columnist Howie Carr (who himself earned around $100,000 a year), and anti-tax crusader Barbara Anderson.

130. Murray Burton Levin, *Talk Radio and the American Dream* (Lexington, Mass.: Lexington Books, 1987), pp. xi–xv. Levin is also aware of the contradictory "postures" achieved by the medium's varying topic, tone, and guest, "appealing to one part of its audience by affirming the value of positive thinking and the American Dream, and to another part by delegitimizing that dream. . . . Talk radio portrays a Hobbesian America of unmitigated self-interest and a Whitmanesque land of milk and honey" (pp. 24, 26). As perceptive as Levin is, his approach falls short of explaining talk radio's contradictions; he prefers to declare in favor of the negative—"the impression of widespread distress, . . . of a stalemate." He seems to suggest that talk radio lets in "the official image of how life is lived in America" simply as a contrast to the actual "sordidness of daily life" (p. 21).

131. Robert Strauss, "Ex-Mayor Rizzo Comes Back, but on Radio, Not at the Polls," *New York Times*, July 9, 1989, p. 18.

132. Quoted in ibid. See also "Names Make News in Radio," *Broadcasting*, March 20, 1989, pp. 64–65, which concerns the hiring of the "famous or infamous" as radio talk hosts in an intensified competitive quest for ratings through publicity; for example, Ronald Reagan and Jessica Hahn have been sought after. Even where these "big names" may bear negative connotations to many listeners, the general industry feeling is that "the positives outweigh the negatives" because

practically any "big name" acts as a "clutter buster" to give the station "instant attention."

133. Quoted in Wil Haygood, "On the Air with Frank Rizzo," *Boston Globe*, April 5, 1989, p. 38. Rizzo's success had apparently cut into the audience of Irv Homer, whose call-in show had long "had a grip on the white ethnic listener in Philadelphia."

134. Strauss, "Ex-Mayor Rizzo Comes Back," p. 18.

135. Haygood, "On the Air with Frank Rizzo," p. 38.

136. There were, to be sure, disturbances during this period, though on a smaller scale than in many other large cities such as Newark and Detroit.

137. Haygood, "On the Air with Frank Rizzo," p. 38.

138. The full extent of the accident became clear later: four were killed and 165 hospitalized.

139. This echoes what Christina Reynolds, in " 'Donahue': A Rhetorical Analysis of Contemporary Television Culture" (Ph.D. diss., University of Minnesota, 1986), pp. 32–47, has called the "rhetorical ritual of identification" or "drama of communion." While such rituals or dramas may be typical, as she claims, they are not the talkshow's totality.

140. Similarly, in another call-in subgenre, sports talk, hosts and callers turn sports news into their playthings, generating a spiraling fantasy and intensity of feeling rendered "safe" by caller anonymity. Like talk radio in general, sports talk promiscuously plays with rumor, making it an imaginary and sometimes fantastic "what if" that echoes the "if only" of Rizzo's show. See Geoffrey Norman, "Yak Attack," *Sports Illustrated*, Oct. 8, 1990, pp. 108–21.

141. Hebdige, *Hiding in the Light*, p. 211.

142. Quoted in Haygood, "On the air with Frank Rizzo," p. 38. Weisberg's comment echoes Morton Downey, Jr.'s, description of himself as unpredictable: "You could call me a six-pack of surprises. I walk to the edge of the cliff, but I don't jump off" (quoted in Blum, "Loudmouth," p. 39). Taking the unpredictable to its limits through the extremity of host persona affect seems another key characteristic of the interactive talk host.

143. Fredric Jameson, "Postmodernism and Consumer Society," in *Postmodernism and Its Discontents: Theories, Practices*, ed. E. Ann Kaplan (London: Verso, 1988), p. 22.

144. Murray Burton Levin, *Talk Radio and the American Dream* (Lexington, Mass.: Lexington Books, 1987), p. 25, referring to Jerry Williams's late 1970s Boston call-in program.

145. Ibid., pp. xi–xv, 13–26. Though never using the language of postmodern theory to shape his keen insights, Levin, in his own particular way, also notes talk

radio's strange yet productive inclusion of contradictions and historical voices for an "impression of widespread distress" and a "subversive" or "delegitimizing" effect: "These tensions are evident in political talk radio. Callers are divided between those with a commitment to the more traditional and morally infused ethos of the nineteenth century—an ethos that elevates the family, religion, piety, and work, and rewards sexual repression—and those with a modernist outlook that emphasizes liberalizing social and sexual relations and state aid to the underclass" (p. 21). Levin also notes that talk radio blurs distinctions by giving "the sublime and the ridiculous equal time," and that it elevates the trivial and trivializes the significant "by democratizing and emotionalizing all issues" (p. 23).

3. Making Sense and Nonsense: Talk about the Talkshow

1. See Gary Mullinax, "*Talk Radio* Flirts with Societal Scourge," *Norwich* (Connecticut) *Bulletin*, Jan. 27, 1989, p. 11; Frank Phillips and Renee Loth, "No-Tax Budget Survives Day 1 of Debate," *Boston Globe*, March 7, 1989, p. 17; and Walter Goodman, "If Talkshow Personalities See Journalists in the Mirror," *New York Times*, June 5, 1989, p. C10.

2. William A. Henry III, "From the Dawn of Gab: The Evolution of T.V.'s Most Indigenous Form," *Channels* 3 (May-June 1983): 43.

3. Michael Schudson, *Discovering the News: A Social History of the Newspapers* (New York: Basic Books, 1978), p. 66.

4. Daniel J. Boorstin, *The Image: A Guide to Pseudo-Events in America* (New York: Atheneum, 1961). For a sound critical perspective on the naivité of Boorstin's "pre-postmodern" concept of "pseudo-event" and "graphic revolution," see Andrew Ross, *No Respect: Intellectuals and Popular Culture* (New York: Routledge, 1989), pp. 109–12.

5. Quoted in Boorstin, *The Image*, p. 15, from *The Nation*, Jan. 28, 1869.

6. Schudson, *Discovering the News*, pp. 63–71.

7. Ibid., p. 71.

8. Lena Williams, "It Was a Year When Civility Really Took It on the Chin," *New York Times*, Dec. 18, 1988, p. 1.

9. Ibid. Also see Michael Oreskes, " 'Attack' Politics, Rife in '88 Election, Comes into Its Own for Lesser Stakes," *New York Times*, Oct. 24, 1988, p. 24.

10. Don Herold, "Alexander Woollcott," in *Selected Radio and Television Criticism*, ed. Anthony Slide (Metuchen, N.J.: Scarecrow Press, 1987), p. 99 (reprinted from *Judge*, April 1937).

11. "The Tonight Show," in Slide, *Selected Radio and Television Criticism*, pp. 163–72 (reprinted from *Time*, Aug. 18, 1958).

12. See Henry, "From the Dawn of Gab," pp. 42–43.

13. John Crosby, "Dave Garroway," in Slide, *Selected Radio and Television Criticism*, pp. 150–51 (reprinted from *New York Herald Tribune*, Jan. 6, 1950).

14. Ibid.

15. Herold, "Alexander Woollcott," p. 99.

16. Henry, "From the Dawn of Gab," p. 42.

17. Richard Corliss, "The Talk of Our Town," *Film Comment* 17 (Jan.–Feb. 1981): 74–75.

18. Robert Sklar, "The Liberal Education of Dick Cavett," *American Film* (Oct. 1978): 24–29.

19. Quoted in Nan Robertson, "Donahue vs. Winfrey: A Clash of Talk Titans," *New York Times*, Feb. 1, 1988, p. C30.

20. Henry, "From the Dawn of Gab," p. 43.

21. "Donahue: The Talk of Television," *Newsweek*, Oct. 29, 1979, p. 76.

22. See the literature on the lyceum movement, ladies' reading circles, and other cultural societies and activities: e.g., David E. Shi, *The Simple Life: Plain Living and High Thinking in American Culture* (New York: Oxford University Press, 1985).

23. See Robert C. Allen, *Speaking of Soap Operas* (Chapel Hill: University of North Carolina Press, 1985).

24. Donald Horton and R. Richard Wohl, "Mass Communication and Para-Social Interaction: Observations on Intimacy at a Distance," was originally published in *Psychiatry* 19 (1956): 215–29. Among the anthologies in which it appears are *Intermedia: Interpersonal Communication in a Media Age*, ed. Gary Gumpert and Robert Cathcart (New York: Oxford University Press, 1979), pp. 32–55; and *Drama in Life: The Uses of Communication in Society*, ed. James E. Combs and Michael W. Mansfield (New York, Hastings House, 1976), pp. 213–28. Page numbers in the notes that follow refer to the latter collection.

25. Horton and Wohl, "Mass Communication," p. 213.

26. Ibid. The authors see the persona as a unique byproduct of the personality program, "a new kind of performer . . . whose existence is a function of the media themselves" and whose performance "is an objectively perceptible action in which the viewer is implicated imaginatively, but which he does not imagine."

27. Ibid.

28. Ibid., p. 217.

29. Ibid.

30. Ibid., p. 216.

31. Ibid., pp. 216–17.

32. Ibid., p. 225.

33. Ibid. Horton and Wohl offer as an example (p. 227) a fan who masqueraded as Dave Garroway's wife, established charge and bank accounts in his name, and attempted to move into his hotel room. David Letterman had similar problems with a woman who claimed to be his wife and stayed in his Connecticut home when he was not there.

34. Ibid., p. 220.

35. Ibid., pp. 219–20.

36. Ibid., p. 212.

37. See Allen, *Speaking of Soap Operas*, pp. 8–44.

38. See Cameron R. Armstrong and Alan M. Rubin, "Talk Radio as Interpersonal Communication," *Journal of Communication* 39 (Spring 1989): 84–94; Robert K. Avery and Donald G. Ellis, "Talk Radio as an Interpersonal Phenomenon," in Gumpert and Cathcart, *Intermedia*, pp. 108–15; R. K. Avery, D. G. Ellis, and T. W. Glover, "Pattern of Communication on Talk Radio," *Journal of Broadcasting* 22 (Winter 1978): 5–17; Jane H. Bick, *Talk Radio: A Selective Analysis of Audience and Programming* and *Talk Radio Callers: A Systems Perspective* (Washington, D.C.: National Association of Broadcasters Library, 1975, 1980); John Crittenden, "Democratic Function of the Open Mike Forum," *Public Opinion Quarterly* 35 (Summer 1971): 200–210; Mark R. Levy, "Watching TV News as Para-Social Interaction," *Journal of Broadcasting* 23 (Winter 1979): 69–80; Caren Rubenstein, "Who Calls In?" *Psychology Today*, Dec. 1981, pp. 89–90; Harriet Tramer and Leo W. Jeffres, "Talk Radio—Forum and Companion," *Journal of Broadcasting* 27 (Summer 1983): 297–300; Joseph Turow, "Talk Show Radio as Interpersonal Communication," *Journal of Broadcasting* 18 (Spring 1974): 171–79.

39. For the focus on patterns of talk and interaction, see Crittenden, "Democratic Function"; and Avery, Ellis, and Glover, "Pattern of Communication." The latter found that the interaction of host and caller had primarily to do with positive reinforcement of beliefs. Crittenden found that despite the complaining nature of the calls coming in to a local issue program, those who called were most positive about the program and its political and educational efficacy. Interestingly, both studies take a narrow approach to the radio call-in program as text but do so within a framework of negative hypotheses about talkshows and their callers, only to restore them in their conclusions.

40. Jane H. Bick, "The Development of Two-Way Talk Radio in America' (Ph.D. diss., University of Massachusetts, 1987), p. 42. The Los Angeles station originating "topless radio" with the program *Feminine Forum* used a survey by the Peat-Marwick accounting firm to show that the program's female audience was "normal": that is, reasonably well educated, economically secure, stable,

mature, and family-oriented. Audiences "avidly" supported the show "for its entertainment value and as a release from monotony."

41. See Chapter 1.

42. In his final years on the air, Johnny Carson joked that 40 percent of American citizens would soon have their own talkshows. Likewise, David Letterman quips that he is one of "several hundred lucky Americans who have their own talkshows." Hosting or being a guest on the talkshow, especially the late-night subgenre, may connote success and ego, but Letterman's remark counterposes to success an ironic diminution deriving from a recognition of the channel proliferation and program clutter encouraged by cable and deregulation. The remark also expresses the difficulty of dealing with the talkshow as a specific form, since its instances are diachonically and synchronically so numerous.

43. Horton and Wohl, "Mass Communication," pp. 219–21. The "new role possibilities" Pupkin achieves in and through the talkshow echo Lewis A. Erenberg's description of the early twentieth-century urban cabaret as "helping develop personalities more capable of self-development, self-gratification, and self-adjustment" and helping subjects find "their true, more vital selves" (Steppin' Out: New York Nightlife and the Transformation of American Culture, 1890– 1930 [Westport, Conn.: Greenwood Press, 1981], pp. 258–59). In The King of Comedy's postmodern framing, however, Pupkin makes a mockery of such modernist self-fulfillment by calling into question the very notion of the "true" self.

44. Quoted in Robert Goldberg, "Morton Downey Goes National," Wall Street Journal, June 20, 1988, p. 13.

45. Talk Radio was first produced in 1982 as a performance piece at the Portland, Oregon, Center for the Visual Arts, through an NEA grant. Bogosian credits Tad Savinar with initiating the project and creating its design and projections. The 1987 New York Shakespeare Festival production, directed by Frederick Zollo, featured Bogosian as Barry Champlain. The film version was based both on the play and on Talked to Death: The Life and Murder of Alan Berg (New York: Berkley Books, 1989), Stephen Singular's account of the Denver talk host who was gunned down by neo-Nazis.

46. Eric Bogosian, Talk Radio (New York: Random House, 1988), pp. 72–73.

47. Bogosian, Introduction to Talk Radio, pp. xv–xiv.

48. Rosalind Krauss, "Sculpture in the Expanded Field," October 8 (Spring 1979): 31–44; reprinted in The Anti-Aesthetic: Essays on Postmodern Culture, ed. Hal Foster (Port Townsend, Wash.: Bay Press, 1983), pp. 31–42. The notion of "expanded field," a key concept in postmodernism and postmodernity, further applies to the talkshow because like postmodern sculpture it embodies contingency and impurity by defying the autonomy of the modernist "siteless object."

Postmodern sculpture and the talkshow are both "site specific." The talkshow's topics are spatiotemporally local, evanescent, and unabashedly dependent on their media contexts and intertexts.

49. See "New Year's Evolutions in TV Programming," *Broadcasting*, Jan. 2, 1989, p. 40. Mel Harris, president of the Paramount Television Group, said that in a multichannel environment in which the spectator becomes a grazer, the grazing is stopped only by programming that "is not canned in appearance."

50. There were actually three Joey Bishop shows in the 1960s. The May 2, 1962 episode discussed here is from the first, in which Bishop played Joey Barnes, a sad-sack public relations man living in Los Angeles with his mother; his foray into the talkshow developed later in the series. The second, on both NBC and CBS from 1962 to 1965, relocated his character to New York City as a nightclub comedian. The third was his own ABC late-night celebrity talkshow, which aired from 1967 to 1969. For a review of *The Larry Sanders Show*, see Susan Bickelhaupt, "Gary Shandling Joins Talk-Show Fray—on an HBO Sitcom," *Boston Globe*, Aug. 14, 1992, p. 50.

51. See Barry Glassner, "Fitness and the Postmodern Self," *Journal of Health and Social Behavior* 30 (June 1989): 180–91. This article examines the products, practice, and ideology of the fitness craze, which is constructed in terms of a postmodern sociocultural aesthetic in that it uses pastiche and restoratively redefines selfhood as a reintegration of once independent or even contradictory qualities. Killian's hybrid roles, his living his work, and his talk radio performance's commodification of the avant-garde goal of collapsing the boundary between art and everyday life all make him quintessentially postmodern. For a discussion of the avant-garde and its appropriation by the consumer/commodity economy, see Andreas Huyssen, *After the Great Divide: Modernism, Mass Culture, Postmodernism* (Bloomington: Indiana University Press, 1986), pp. 1–6.

52. For a discussion of the panopticon as an important design element in modernity's social engineering, see Stuart Ewen, *All-Consuming Images: The Politics of Style in Contemporary Culture* (New York: Basic Books, 1988), pp. 199–203.

53. Talk hosts—both real and fictional—have used variants of this tag line (e.g., Frank Rizzo; see Chapter 2), which may go back to Jimmy Durante's "Goodnight, Mrs. Calabash, wherever you are."

54. See Peter Fornatale and Joshua E. Mills, *Radio in the Television Age* (Woodstock, N.Y.: Overlook Press, 1983), pp. 82–85; and Bruce W. Marr, "Talk Radio Programming," in *Broadcast/Cable Programming: Strategies and Practices*, ed. Susan Tyler Eastman, Sydney W. Head, and Lewis Klein (Belmont, Calif.: Wadsworth, 1989), pp. 443–60.

55. Interestingly, two of television's lawyer series, *L.A. Law* and *Matlock*, featured episodes in the 1989–90 season that centered on Morton Downey-like talk hosts and the legal-ethical concerns they raised. Each addressed the talkshow's and talk hosts' amoral play with and between truth and fictional staging, their responsibility for and complicity in the consequences of their programs, and their journalistic, detached, even exploitative denial—kinds of play that came up hard against the law's search for clear distinctions. The *L.A. Law* story involved the firm's defense of a talk host charged as an accessory to the murder of a liberal guest who was beaten by the host's frenzied crowd of "Joe Lunchbucket" supporters. The *Matlock* dealt with the eponymous protagonist's defense of a shock-jock wrongly suspected of murdering a rival talk host whom he had brutally berated on his show.

56. See Christina Reynolds, " 'Donahue': A Rhetorical Analysis of Contemporary Television Culture" (Ph.D. diss., University of Minnesota, 1986).

57. Barbara Grizzuti Harrison, "The Importance of Being Oprah," *New York Times Magazine*, June 11, 1989, p. 28.

58. Russell Baker, "I Hear America Snarling," *New York Times*, Aug. 9, 1989.

59. "Talk Radio Today," seminar at the Museum of Broadcasting, New York City, Aug. 6, 1985; moderator: Rick Sklar; panel: WABC morning host Alan Coombs, WMCA talkhosts Barry Farber and Barry Gray, and nationally syndicated advice talk host Bruce Williams.

60. See Todd Gitlin, *Inside Prime Time* (New York: Pantheon Books, 1983), pp. 63–85. This is where Gitlin's useful concept of "recombinant culture" originates, a concept recognizing that the media create from within—copying, synthesizing, and recombining parts of themselves and their past—because of the industry's "headlong pursuit of the logic of safety"; the result is a "sense of cultural exhaustion" (pp. 84–85).

61. Underscoring the linkage of the tabloid news programs to the audience participation talkshows, a Philadelphia station that airs *A Current Affair* after *The Oprah Winfrey Show* promotes it as "life after Oprah."

62. "The Other Side of the News" was aired on WNET-TV New York on the day it was taped, April 12, 1989, and again on June 5, 1989.

63. In the *Geraldo* segment, from a show on sexual surrogacy, the host pressed his guest, a female surrogate, to talk about the "10 percent of the time" that she, in the course of her job, takes her clothes off. The *Downey* segment featured the host's shouting match with one of his studio audience "loudmouths," which culminated in Downey's telling him to "suck my armpit" and throwing him out of the studio. The *Donahue* clip showed the host's sweeps month appearance in a woman's dress. The *60 Minutes* bit was from a story about women who alleged that they had been raped by their gynecologists.

64. Schudson, *Discovering the News*, pp. 129, 121–34.

65. Ibid., pp. 120–34. This ideal developed only "after World War I, when the worth of the democratic market society was itself radically questioned and its internal logic laid bare" (p. 122). A skepticism developed out of the awareness that "utilitarian culture," propelled by the interested "facts" of public relations propaganda, could manage public opinion and regiment the public mind for war *or* consumerism.

66. Herbert Gans, *Deciding What's News: A Study of the* CBS *Evening News,* NBC *Nightly News, Newsweek, and Time* (New York: Pantheon Books, 1979), pp. 68–69.

67. Schudson, *Discovering the News*, p. 118.

68. Ibid., p. 119.

69. Ibid., pp. 118–20.

70. Goodman, "If Talkshow Personalities See Journalists in the Mirror," p. C16.

71. Ibid.

72. Ellen Goodman, "Television Brawl Shows," *Boston Globe*, April 18, 1989.

73. Harrison, "Importance of Being Oprah," p. 28.

74. Ibid.

75. See John Hartley, "Invisible Fictions: Television Audiences, Paedocracy, Pleasure," in *Television Studies: Textual Analysis*, ed. Gary Burns and Robert J. Thompson (New York: Praeger, 1989), pp. 223–43. Here Hartley shows how the media construct the spectator as childlike. At the same time, much of the empirical research on media effects, particularly violence, centers on children. See, e.g., Robert Baker and Sandra Ball, eds., *Violence and the Media* (Washington, D.C.: Government Printing Office, 1969), a product of task force studies arising out of President Johnson's response to 1960s urban unrest and his formation of the National Commission on the Causes and Prevention of Violence. Also see National Institute of Mental Health research such as the Surgeon General's Scientific Advisory Committee on Television and Social Behavior, *Television and Growing Up: The Impact of Televised Violence*, Report to the Surgeon General, U.S. Public Health Service (Washington, D.C.: Government Printing Office, 1971), and its update ten years later: David Pearl, Lorraine Bouthilet, and Joyce Lazar, eds., *Television and Behavior: Ten years of Progress and Implications for the Eighties* (Washington, D.C.: Government Printing Office, 1982).

76. Pamela Reynolds, "Are Talk Shows Bad for You?" *Boston Globe*, July 17, 1989, p. 24.

77. One wonders what the American Psychological Association may have thought of a summer 1990 television commercial for White Cloud bathroom tissue, which parodies the talkshow. The product's "spokesperson"—an animated,

gentle-voiced "white cloud" vaguely shaped like a rotund man—appears as a guest on a talkshow hosted by a woman who, with her red-framed glasses, resembles Sally Jesse Raphael. The white cloud, sitting as something of a sympathetic expert before an audience of questioning women, comes off as especially sincere and confidential in revealing White Cloud's benefits. An androgynous icon for an intimate hygiene product that also somehow wants to be regarded as credible and gentle, the cloud "comes clean" in the talkshow's candid confessional. The "real" talkshow, of course, is also promotional as well as uninhibited and confessional, a place of excretion, and sometimes catharsis.

78. "Donahue: The Talk of Television," p. 76.

79. Reuven Frank, "Geraldo (Wham! Biff!) Enlightens (Crash!) the Public," *Wall Street Journal*, Nov. 21, 1988, p. A16.

80. Morris Shepard, " 'Morton Downey, Jr.' Takes Tube to Speaker's Corner," *Wall Street Journal*, July 21, 1988, p. A16.

81. "Donahue: The Talk of Television," p. 76.

82. David Rensin, "The Prime Time of Ms. Oprah Winfrey," TV *Guide*, May 16, 1992, p. 15.

83. See Marcia Ann Gillespie, "Smart Money Profile: Winfrey Takes All," *Ms.*, Nov. 1988, pp. 50–55; Richard Zoglin, "Bugle Boys of the Airwaves," *Time*, May 15, 1989, pp. 88–89; "Feeling Unloved, Radio Talkshow Hosts Gather for Strength," *Norwich* (Connecticut) *Bulletin*, June 18, 1989, p. A4; "Medium Is Message at Talk Radio Conference," *Broadcasting*, June 19, 1989, p. 54; and "Williams Goes a-Bashing at Talkfest," *Boston Globe*, June 13, 1989, p. 14.

Postscript: A New Sense of Place

1. By spring 1990 a number of press stories and op-ed pieces were relating instances of the supposedly ingenuous, accidental home video pratfall that had actually been staged—in effect, it was a fraud—in the quest for the $10,000 grand prize. Commentators objected—particularly when children were put at physical risk—and criticized the show's very concept of rewarding, *Candid Camera*-like, the pain or embarrassment of the most vulnerable individuals. *New York Times* television critic John J. O'Connor found the "funniest" clips "decidedly sadistic" (an observation difficult to dispute; to my mind the show is punishing for the viewer as well, and to the point of embarrassment). Interestingly, at the beginning and end of his review ("A Prime-Time Ratings Runaway with Low Costs," *New York Times*, March 1, 1990), O'Connor compares the program with *The Morton Downey, Jr., Show* in their both being "reality" entertainment and both, he predicted, tumbling "as fast as [they] soared" (a particular liability of "reality" programming).

The issue of fraud also looms over the interactive talkshow. It was revealed in 1988 that two actors—apparently unbeknownst to the talkshow producers—got on the talkshow circuit (*Oprah, Sally Jesse Raphael,* and *Geraldo*) in the roles of sex surrogate, sex-hating wife, and impotent husband. Predictably, the print media made much of the revelation as further evidence of the dangers of their talkshow competitors. In *Newsweek*'s words: "Unwittingly, the tolerant talkshows had opened their arms to another kind of social deviant: the outrageous prankster" ("Untrue Confessions of a Devious Duo," *Newsweek,* Sept. 12, 1988, p. 80).

2. Like the Massachusetts talk hosts during that state's 1989–90 tax controversy, New Jersey's WKXW aided anti-tax sentiment and organizational efforts through its constant call-in focus against Governor Jim Florio's tax plans, climaxed by a July 1, 1990, anti-tax rally and march on Trenton that drew an estimated 6,000 people. Conservative talk host Bob Grant of WABC New York was a featured speaker at the rally. See Charles Stile, "FM's 'Tax Revolt Central,'" *Trenton Times,* July 1, 1990, p. 1; and Steven Fromm, "Thousands Skewer Florio at Tax Protest," *Trenton Times,* July 2, 1990, p. 1.

3. "The Bob Grant Show," WABC New York, Jan. 7, 1991.

4. Lewis Grossberger, "The Rush Hours," *New York Times Magazine,* Dec. 16, 1990, p. 99.

5. See, e.g., Elizabeth Neufter, "Taking the Punches," *Boston Globe,* May 5, 1991, p. 37. The article describes the abysmal morale of Massachusetts state employees in the wake of cuts that also gravely affected the public served by those employees.

6. M. E. Malone, "Mass. Tax Burden Ranks High—And Low," *Boston Globe,* March 23, 1991, p. 25. The state's taxation seems high when measured per capita (cost of government divided by number of residents), or when viewed in terms of the state's reliance on it as one source of revenue (Massachusetts fees and fines are relatively low). For more on "Taxachusetts," see M. E. Malone, "A Derisive Nickname Lives On," *Boston Globe,* Dec. 1, 1989, p. 23. On the two 1990 defeat of Massachusetts' anti-tax Question Three and the talkhost who promoted it, see Joseph P. Kahn, "Talk Radio's Power Questioned in Wake of CLT Defeat," *Boston Globe,* Nov. 8, 1990, p. 44. The CLT, Citizens for Limited Taxation, was the principal advocate for Question Three along with talk hosts such as Jerry Williams. CLT's leader and spokesperson, Barbara Anderson, often appeared on Williams's show. She and *Boston Herald* columnist Howie Carr were, along with the talk hosts, "governors of the airwaves."

7. For more on deregulation of the telecommunications industries, see Jeremy Tunstall, *Communications Deregulation: The Unleashing of America's Communications Industry* (Oxford: Basil Blackwell, 1986).

8. See Joshua Meyrowitz, *No Sense of Place: The Impact of Electronic Media on Social Behavior* (New York: Oxford University Press, 1985), pp. 124–25, for a summary of this idea.

9. Like Horton and Wohl before him, Meyrowitz privileges interpersonal communication and *its* situational time-space continuum over the media, describing how electronic media have a " 'disrespect' for place and occasion," putting us "everywhere" but "also no place in particular." Highly influenced by Neil Postman, Meyrowitz sees the emergence of a "strong common denominator" where once there were separate group identities bred by spatiotemporal, situational separation.

10. See, e.g., Max Horkheimer and Theodor W. Adorno, *Dialectic of Enlightenment*, trans. John Cumming (1944; New York: Continuum, 1988), p. 127: "The might of industrial society is lodged in men's minds. The entertainments' manufacturers know that their products will be consumed with alertness even when the customer is distraught, for each of them is a model of the huge economic machinery which has always sustained the masses, whether at work or at leisure—which is akin to work. From every sound film and every broadcast program the social effect can be inferred which is exclusive to none but is shared by all alike. The culture industry as a whole has molded men as a type unfailingly reproduced in every product." Clearly, the representatives of the Frankfurt school and those taking a cultural studies approach would have much to argue regarding talkshows.

11. Jürgen Habermas, *The Structural Transformation of the Public Sphere: An Inquiry into a Category of Bourgeois Society*, trans. Thomas Burger with Frederick Lawrence (Cambridge, Mass.: MIT Press, 1989); Richard Sennett, *The Fall of Public Man* (New York: Knopf, 1977). Sennett laments the decline of a civilized public sphere and the impersonal yet necessary conventions that make it possible. Such conventions, he maintains, have been replaced by a public narcissism or intimacy impeding a civilized public intercourse that can thrive only under the dominance of highly formalized and impersonal behavioral codes.

12. These themes have, of course, come out in any number of her interviews. See, e.g., Marcia Ann Gillespie, "Smart Money Profile: Winfrey Takes All," *Ms.*, Nov. 1988, pp. 50–55. Oprah is a "firm believer in the power of positive thinking," and, believing that control of one's life goes hand in hand with success, she even signs all of Harpo, Inc.'s checks herself.

13. Jerold M. Starr, "Cultural Politics in the 60s" and "Cultural Politics and the Prospects for Radical Change in the 80s," both in *Cultural Politics: Radical Movements in Modern History*, ed. Jerold M. Starr (New York: Praeger, 1985).

14. Linda Hutcheon, *The Poetics of Postmodernism: History, Theory, Fiction* (New York: Routledge, 1988), p. 3.

15. Robert Venturi, *Complexity and Contradiction in Architecture* (New York: Museum of Modern Art and Graham Foundation, in association with Doubleday, 1966), pp. 30–31.

16. Jean Baudrillard, "The Ecstasy of Communication," in *The Anti-Aesthetic: Essays on Postmodern Culture*, ed. Hal Foster (Port Townsend, Wash.: Bay Press, 1983), 126–128.

17. James W. Carey, *Culture as Communication: Essays on Media and Society* (Boston: Unwin Hyman, 1989), p. 3.

18. Ibid., pp. 4–9.

19. Examining postmodern literature, Linda Hutcheon goes so far as to observe that postmodern forms, in their promiscuous incorporation, become so provisional that they are "*not . . .* 'confidently' anything" (*The Poetics of Post-modernism*, p. 19). As my study demonstrates, however, some formal specificities remain with respect to the audience participation talkshow, as blurred and contingent as they may be.

20. From Phil Donahue's introduction to Richard and Deanne Mincer, *The Talkshow Book: An Engaging Primer on How to Talk Your Way to Success* (New York: Facts on File Publications, 1982), pp. ix–x; also see pp. 71–79. The book is intended to be a "user's manual" for common citizens who espouse positions on vital issues and need the talkshow to promote their views.

21. Phil Donahue on "The Other Side of the News: Entertainment News or Entertainment?" WNET-TV New York April 12, 1989; moderator: Fred W. Friendly.

Index